MW01119684

THE ROAD TO NOW

/

The Road to Now

A HISTORY OF BLACKS IN MONTREAL

Dorothy W. Williams

160201

Véhicule Press

DOSSIER QUÉBEC

Published with the generous assistance of the Canada Council.

Cover photograph: Union United Church, circa 1943. Courtesy of Henry J. Langdon.
Imaging by Simon Garamond.
Printing by Imprimerie d'Édition Marquis Ltée

CANADIAN CATALOGUING IN PUBLICATION DATA

Williams, Dorothy W.
        The road to now : a history of Blacks in Montreal

(Dossier Quebec)
Includes bibliographical references and index.
ISBN 1-55065-065-3

        1. Black Canadians—Quebec (Province)—Montreal—
History. I. Title. II. Series.

FC2947.9.B6W54 1966   971.4'2800496   C95-900747-4
F1054.5M89N3 1966

Published by Véhicule Press, P.O.B. 125, Place du Parc Station, Montreal, Quebec H2W 2M9

http://www.cam.org/~vpress

Distributed by General Distribution Services, Don Mills, Ontario.

Printed in Canada on alkaline paper.

Contents

Acknowledgements

The background for the bulk of the written material used in *The Road to Now* was found in Montreal's Concordia and McGill universities. In the Department of Rare Books and Special Collections McGill University I found several obscure manuscripts in the Roy States Collection. The late Roy States, a local historian, was well known for his dedication and zeal in collecting written material on the black community in Montreal. At Concordia University, the reference librarians, only a call away, were wonderful and indefatigable as they hunted down obscure citations. I would like to thank the librarians at both Concordia and McGill for their invaluable assistance. The librarians of the Quebec Human Rights Commission also deserve my gratitude—they saved the day and pointed me in the right direction. For that you remain special to me.

The inspiration for the title of this book is taken from the title of an interview published by Patti Vipond which originally appeared in *Spear Magazine* (April 1976).

Finally, I would like to thank the following people for their professional and personal support: To Bernice Cooper, Gwen Husband, Robert "Bud" Jones, who made their phone lines available at any time to verify a fact; without them it would have been more difficult. To Sandra Markland, Linda Cormier and Emily Drysdale, who volunteered their time and their eyes to read and reread chapters. To Henry J. Langdon, your generosity still warms me. To Yvonne Greer, for *UHURU* and the oral material you hunted down. How else could the sixties and seventies seem so real? To others who gave time and support on the spur of the moment—Freddy Gale, Maisie Dash, and Eleitha Haynes. To Meri Tremblay, thanks for the time out. To those who waited patiently over the years until I got it together enough to do this again—my mother Betty Williams, Patricia Nolan, Doris Cunningham, Julie Samuels, Simon Dardick, Vicki Marcok, Evangeline Godron, Joe Burke, Lyda Peters, Frank Humphrey, and Carol Roach. To the unnamed, countless others who supported me because I was one of them—whose encouragement and belief in the project kept me focussed. Thank you.

Preface

The Road to Now is the follow-up to my book, *Blacks in Montreal 1628-1986:An Urban Demography** which was published in 1989. The black presence in Greater Montreal has never been fully chronicled and *Blacks in Montreal* was an attempt to define Montreal's black community over the years using demographics.

The organization of chapters in this book is centred around pivotal events that shaped community history. This is particularly noticeable in the contemporary material where the focus is on key events and their aftermath and where I was able to interview people who were directly involved.

As I lectured and taught black history to children and adults over the last eight years, my first book was constantly referred to as a history. It is true that the demographic study contained much historial material, but it was not the complete story. I was forced to leave out many stories I had already collected—there were controversies, data, competing viewpoints, and people whose stories I could not include in the text.

The Road to Now is my effort to describe the many facets of the black presence in Montreal. It is a rich story of a people struggling to adapt and endure, and to make better lives in the midst of deprivation while defining what it was, and is, to be a black Montrealer. From the beginning of the twentieth century their aspirations matched those of every new group of immigrants arriving in the city, while the struggle against discrimination made their communities unique. It is this story that I hope to reveal in the following pages.

What is the black community of Montreal? Only by understanding how blacks have identified with each other, and learning what their aspirations are, will this be answered. The social history paradigm is useful because it encompasses an analysis of the grassroots, which does not mean that the tale of ordinary people means that there were no leaders, only followers. The black community of Montreal was not one homogeneous and faceless group but many communities, at once different and the same.

Much of the current documentation included here is built from the voices of black Montrealers themselves. They spoke about language, immigration, education, racism and discrimination.

My journey began in 1983 with a phone call. The Quebec Human Rights Commission was looking for someone to provide them with some background on the black community in Greater Montreal for a proposed anti-discrimination campaign in housing. I agreed to assemble a modest document for internal use focussing only on the demography of the community. As the research progressed, I found so much more than demography and incorporated as much additional material as I could within the established framework. So, I wrote a historical demography, determined to demonstrate how the roots of racism stretched back over centuries to the beginnings of our sojourn on this continent. I created the document knowing that blacks would also want to know about their history in Montreal—to add to the treasury of stories they already possess. The Commission was convinced that all Montrealers should know what it contained, and urged its publication.

The black community embraced the book as their own. They were proud that their story had been chronicled with proof that blacks could claim a part of the grandeur of Montreal. Blacks and whites were interested in Montreal's black past and *Blacks in Montreal* went out of print in 1993.

When Simon Dardick of Véhicule Press and I began to discuss about how to republish *Blacks in Montreal,* I was buoyant. Our first idea was to incorporate the footnotes into the original text, which would have produced a new revised work while satisfying my desire not to research new material. Who was I fooling? Stories were aching to be told. The moment I started reworking the manuscript I realized that *The Road to Now: A History of Blacks in Montreal* would be more than what had been produced before. To all Montrealers, interested and curious, you share this part of my life's journey with me. Hold fast with me as we discover and rediscover the road to now.

Note: The term 'black' will be used to denote black African ancestry. For the most part this will include blacks from the Caribbean basin, North and South America, Europe and Africa, who came to Canada either as slaves or as immigrants. 'Negro' and 'coloured'—terms used by earlier writers, will be used only occasionally as context requires. 'West Indian' is a cultural/ethnic term, and refers specifically to blacks from the Caribbean basin and from South America. 'African' identifies blacks born in Africa. The terms Afro-Canadian, African-Canadian, American, British, etc. are used to define black nationality according to birthplace and/or citizenship.

*Williams, Dorothy W. *Blacks in Montreal 1628-1986: An Urban Demography* (Cowansville: Les Éditions Yvon Blais Inc., 1989).

Introduction

The reach of black history is long—blacks have been a part of the Canadian experience since the sixteenth century. They have figured in the Canadian drama from the original European explorations and the period of enslavement, from the coming of the railroads to the present day. Montreal, a city so crucial in the making of Canada, has been particularly affected by the development of a distinct black community. Yet the historical record remains silent, causing Montreal's black population to be invisible even today.*

The reasons for this obfuscation are many. Perhaps it began when slavery, and the scars it inflicted on Quebec, was categorically denied and ignored. In addition, black migration patterns differed in Montreal. Tens of thousands of American blacks—Loyalists, Fugitives, and Refugees came to this country, swelling the ranks of Canada's own slave population. (The Loyalists were blacks who fled to British North America from the United States at the time of the War of Independence. The Refugees arrived around the War of 1812, and the Fugitives came between 1815 and 1861). Strangely though, except for the twentieth century, blacks already residing in Quebec did not benefit significantly from the migration of these African-Americans. As well, separate black towns in Quebec have never existed as they have in the Maritimes, Ontario and the Prairies. Or, if they did exist on their own, (St. Armand in Quebec's Eastern Townships may be the exception) their duration and influence on the white communities around them was not significant enough to warrant separate records. Moreover, the Montreal black community was smaller than the Ontario and Maritime communities. The small number of blacks who entered Montreal during the last years of the nineteenth century and the early years of the twentieth did not create the same intense backlash in Montreal that occurred in these regions. Racism in Ontario and in the Maritimes led to the institutional, and even the physical segregation of blacks into separate townships or farming communities. Thus, because Quebec did not create distinct communities for blacks within the province, and the fact that blacks were never included in Quebec's historical record, blacks remained an invisible population in Montreal, with few references to blacks in Quebec's historical documents.

Numerically, blacks have not made a large impact on Montreal except during the last thirty years. Inter-provincial and international migration of blacks into Quebec was not a significant phenomenon until the early 1960s. Before this period Canada's federal government discouraged black immigration.

Our history then is of a people whose history has been ignored, deliberately omitted, or distorted. By excluding black history, especially the story of slavery, Canadians have distorted their own history. The writing of Afro-Canadian history re-aligns Canadian history by re-establishing continuity with the past.

The Road to Now affirms the presence of blacks on Montreal's landscape. It also demonstrates that oppression has a Canadian face and that blacks did not flee exploitation (so often depicted as American) and come to freedom in Canada (depicted as the black person's land of opportunity and equality). To present history this way would be to deliberately misconstrue what really happened to blacks in Canada.

The struggle to achieve equality and dignity did not begin in the 1950s or the 1960s; it had its roots in Montreal's days of slavery. For black women it is a struggle against racism *and* sexism. Although they share gender, black women and white women do not share the same history—black women also suffered while enslaved, at the hands of white women. Since the Emancipation Act of 1834, throughout the British Empire the economic and social freedom of black women has been circumscribed by the needs of Canada's labour market.

Black women played significant roles in the building of Montreal's black community. The historical narrative must illuminate their history, their collective contributions, their ideas, and their aspirations. I wish to investigate the strategies they employed and the alliances these women developed which help them to survive. This book is not intended to place black women within the context of other women of their day, although at times it was necessary to demonstrate how connected all women are to the forces around them. Although women's strategies and their choices appeared similar, their actions sprang from very different needs. *The Road to Now* is a glimpse into the world these women made. They are creators, mothers, providers, volunteers, workers and the independent women they were and are. But, to understand black women and their history we cannot only compare them to other women—they must be placed in the context of their families, their black sisterhood and especially their communities.

My previous book, *Blacks in Montreal* focussed on the the role of discrimination in the housing market and its effect on the mobility patterns of blacks. *The Road to Now* demonstrates that racism and discrimination have had major roles in the area of black employment which has affected the socio-economic mobility of blacks. Housing and employment discrimination affected all sectors of the community to such an extent that it altered or even hindered movement and mobility amongst blacks. Thus population distribution and the ebb and flow of black movement reveal a great deal about the community and plays a large part in the creation of the organizational structures that grew out of unique cultural needs.

The historian also empowers through the recording of different voices—different narratives. With the available recording technology it would be remiss of any historian not to tap the living stories of the people who lived through periods being researched. Was Robin Winks' account of blacks in World War II different than what black Montrealers really experienced? This is the time to investigate, for soon their voices will be silenced and we will wonder and speculate. In other parts of the country blacks are telling their stories and chronicling their histories. Toronto is producing black literature based on oral histories that all black Torontonians share. Montreal must develop its own too.

Montreal blacks share their own 350 years of history. What sets them apart from Montrealers of European descent is their African heritage and experience of slavery. The institution of slavery stripped slaves of their connection to land, tribe, clan or village. With few exceptions, no vestige of this heritage remains—not our names, our language, or our customs. As a person of African descent, all of Africa, anywhere, could have been home among any of its sixty or more nations and 1,700 languages. As an Afro-Canadian I claim it all. It is what binds Africans in the diaspora together under all the trappings of skin color, hair styles, mother tongue, and social and occupational status. Therefore blacks who have arrived in the last twenty or thirty years share a 350 year history that is as much theirs as the Afro-Canadian family whose roots can be traced to New France. We know, as part of the African diaspora, that the history of blacks of Montreal is the history of all blacks in Montreal. There is no break in our continuity. We were here, we are here, and as long as one black citizen calls it home, Montreal will be our history.

*During Montreal's 350th anniversary celebrations, black history and the contribution of blacks was ignored. Clifton Ruggles, *black...and invisible*. Montreal *Gazette*, October 17, 1992.

CHAPTER ONE

Slavery, Freedom and Obscurity
[1628-1888]

The earliest history of the black presence in New France was one of enslavement. Introduced by the French in 1628, African slavery developed slowly in
New France.[1] Olivier Le Jeune, a child from the island of Madagascar, was the
first slave to be imported and sold in New France (circa 1632).[2] Although this
was the beginning of black slavery in New France, it was not until 1685, with
the introduction of the Code Noir, that black slavery attained quasi-legal status.
The Code Noir protected owners from slave violence and escape,[3] and the
status of slaves in New France was regulated by this code, which, though never
officially proclaimed, was a customary law.

May 1, 1689 is considered the official birthdate of African slavery in Canada.
King Louis XIV of France, reluctantly gave permission to his subjects in New
France to import African slaves. After this date the practice of owning panis,
or Amerindian slaves, by the French merchant class and the clergy also became
common.

Historian Marcel Trudel's study of slave populations in French Canada, the
Dictionnaire des esclaves et de leurs propriétaires au Canada français,[4] disclosed many
fascinating statistics. Local records revealed that there was a total of 4,092
slaves during the French Regime; of these 1,400 were Negroes.[5] Most African
slaves arrived with the British following the Conquest of New France in 1760.
Women comprised 52 percent of the total Amerindian slave population in
French Canada. In the black slave population, men were more numerous,
totaling 57 percent.[6]

Most of the African slaves worked as domestic servants in or near Montreal,
where 52 percent lived. Unlike the American colonies, 87 percent of slaves in
Quebec, black and Amerindian, lived in towns.[7] The slave owners' social and
religious attitudes in New France differed greatly from those of the British
colonies to the south. The rare mention of slavery by Canadian historians often

described a romantic, idealized, slave regime in New France—an Eden for slaves.

Historians have had their own agendas when writing about Canada's slave history. The most blatant example was that of F.X. Garneau's *Histoire du Canada Français depuis sa découverte* (1846).[8] Garneau's objective was "to compare a slaveless French to the disadvantage of the British,"[9] claiming that slavery had never been known in Canada.[9] Though Garneau changed this deliberate obfuscation in his fourth edition, many accepted his original falsehood as fact, despite critics who attacked him for his lack of historical honesty. In 1855 the Quebec historian, François-Marie-Maximillien Bibaud went so far as to charge Garneau with charlatanism and incompetence.[10] Garneau's legacy continues. The subject of slavery has suffered as prominent Canadian historians neglected this "sombre and unattractive chapter."[11] During the nineteenth century there was little awareness that Canada had ever had slavery, and there was little improvement in the next century. In the 1930s, for example, historians deliberately "buried the Negro under a sense of embarrassment over slavery and from an apparent conviction that black history was not worth telling in its own right."[12] Not much in Canadian historiography has changed since, and a sampling of contemporary college and university textbooks confirms that the neglect of slavery in Canadian history continues.[13] According to Marcel Trudel any published paper on slavery evoked the reaction: "What! Slavery in Canada?"[14]

Once past the question, historians then wrestled with the blame and shame of the institution of slavery. French Canadian historians placed the blame on the English and English Canadian historians blamed it squarely on the inadequacies of the French Regime itself. The tone of this debate led to the inevitable comparisons between slavery under the French Catholic regime and slavery under the English Protestant regime. Many historians of New France believed that the very nature of Roman Catholicism affected attitudes toward the slave. This, they contend, was due to the Catholic doctrine "which held that the spiritual nature of the slave transcended his temporary status and that to give a man his freedom was to please God."[15] This theoretically should have resulted in more humane laws in New France but it was only one of many competing viewpoints. Throughout the slave era the Catholic Church debated the justness of slavery and attempted to reconcile freedom with the demands of an expanding economy in Europe.[16]

Did the Church's doctrine shape slavery in New France? The long life of slavery in Quebec would suggest not. It is ironic that the beliefs expressed by the Pope and the Holy Councils centered on slavery's effects on aboriginal populations, rather than on the growing African slave trade. The Papal Briefs issued during North America's colonial period were silent about the treatment of African slaves. This ecclesiastical silence was broken only in the nineteenth century when the Church was called upon to support abolitionists' efforts.[17] Even though the Church in New France moderated the effects of black slavery, the Church's silence condoned the institution while slaves were tortured and killed.[18]

A Portuguese-born slave, Marie-Joseph Angelique, owned by Mme. de Francheville of St. Paul Street, was suspected to be in love with Claude Thibault, a white man. It was assumed that Angelique started a house fire on April 10, 1734 to hide her escape with Thibault. She was accused of destroying almost half of Montreal by fire—forty-six buildings including the convent, the church, and the hospital.

Despite this disaster, there is no mention of the event in the recent literature on the history of Montreal. Is this because historians believed that the destruction of half the city had no impact on its social and economic development? Or is this another example of ignoring slavery and the early black presence in Montreal? Could it be that the actions of a recalcitrant slave were not worth noting? Angelique's execution as an arsonist is a testament to the fact that Montreal's citizens felt otherwise.

The authorities eventually apprehended Angelique. After an inconclusive trial where she maintained her innocence and refused to reveal Thibault's whereabouts on June 21, 1734 she was repeatedly tortured until she confessed her crime, insisting to the end that she had no accomplice.[19] According to official accounts:

> She was driven through the streets in the scavenger's wagon…A burning torch had been placed in her hand. At the main door of the parish church in Place d'Armes she was made to kneel. Then her hand was cut off. Once again she was placed in the scavenger's waggon (sic) and taken to the place of public execution and hanged. After her body was burnt at the stake, her ashes were then scattered in the wind.[20]

The story of Marie-Joseph Angelique captures the imagination of all who write about slavery because it illustrates so much about slave society and early Quebec society. Her story affirms a black presence in New France and her actions are seen as an example of slave resistance and of the roots of oppression in Quebec. For some Angelique is a tragic love story and proof of female resistance.[21]

Slavery is savage and brutal even in its most benign form—"slavery is slavery in whatever form it takes."[22] This was underscored in eighteenth century New France when slaves tried to escape.[23] Whether these slaves were aided by freed black men and women or by colonists of conscience, their anti-slave actions threatened the accepted right of slave ownership.

Determined slave owners fought back to protect their right to own human property, although who exactly was a slave was questionable. They wanted to know where they stood and presented a petition of demands to the colony's chief administrator, Intendant Jacques Raudot. He responded by issuing an ordinance—a common official response to petitions from concerned citizens. The 1709 Ordinance was explicit in two areas: all panis and Negroes who had been purchased would be considered slaves, and anyone who encouraged or who helped a slave to escape was guilty of a crime. All Negroes who were free had to obtain notarial papers stating that they were free. From this point onward, by social and legal definition, a Negro in the colony of New France was a slave unless he could prove otherwise. With this legal framework in place, slave ownership increased almost immediately.[24]

Raudot's ordinance did not solve the issue of manumission—the freeing of slaves. One consequence was that over time the social lines between free and enslaved blurred. Until 1736 the number of freed slaves had increased substantially as the result of intermarriage with colonists, stipulations of wills, or the purchase of one's freedom.[25] With a growing body of African and panis freedmen in the colony the question of who was a slave and who was not a slave became more ambiguous. The precarious status of freedmen and ex-slaves in Montreal impelled them to act, and they presented their own petition in 1736.[26]

A new ordinance was issued by Intendant Gilles Hocquart which created a standardized process for manumitting slaves. The regulation's passage confirmed that after one hundred years of slavery there were now sufficient numbers of slaves to require regulation by the colony itself. It was also a response to the growing number of colonists who wished to free slaves. The ordinance indicates that in the early days of the colony, slaves—Africans and panis—were cooperating to achieve common goals.

The strongest deterrent against escape was the Code Noir, which had been created originally for the French West Indies. The Code was designed to protect slave owners, but it also defined humane interactions with one's slaves. It was not always enforced in the colony but the threat of it was used to conrol slave behaviour.

If a Negro escapes we will cut off his ears and brand him with a fleur de lys on his left shoulder. If he tries again we will cut off his leg below the knee. If he dares to escape a third time, it is death.[27]

The benevolence exhibited by slave owners in New France towards their African slaves was based on economic and social factors rather than any humanistic tendency. Amerindian slaves were a cheap source of agricultural and hard manual labour, while the African represented a superior type of slave labour in the towns and cities. In part, the social structure of eighteenth century French North American slave society determined their status. The domestic or house slave was traditionally considered superior to the field or land slave. Not only were the expensive African slaves used as domestic labour, they were also considered valuable property which functioned as status symbols for the elite.[28]

Considering their domestic work status, high price, and the degree of difficulty in obtaining them, it has been assumed that most African slaves in New France were treated benevolently because they were expensive and long years of service were required on the investment. Paradoxical statistics on African infant mortality would tend to negate this assumption. African slaves suffered from a higher infant mortality than that suffered by either the panis or the European colonists. But after that crucial first year of life, the survival rate of the babies of African slaves was better than that experienced by the panis slaves and an analysis of death records demonstrates that this survival advantage continued even during periods of epidemics. Death rates during plagues were the same for Europeans and African slaves, except that the panis were affected more seriously.[29] Barring the first year, this pattern made the African's hardiness a useful advantage—black slaves stood a better chance of living through their prime working years and offsetting their purchase price. Under the British regime male slaves were generally considered to be more valuable than females because they were more likely to be used in heavy or skilled work, yet during the French regime women cost more even though men were also used as domestics.[30]

African slaves were useful in other ways. The variety of non-domestic work done by blacks in Montreal's labour market was crucial—free blacks and slaves were sawyers, carpenters, blacksmiths, and candlemakers. In the early days of Montreal, blacks held meaningful roles in the city's economy. A rarity before 1760, African slaves could afterwards be found in the houses of government officials, or of wealthy merchants and seigneurs.[31] Their participation in economic activity was only one aspect of their usefulness, because slavery facilitated the manner in which New France's culture and society evolved because it

> permirent a une classe aisee de s'approprier les fruits du labeur des esclaves et de s'abonner librement aux jeux de politique et au plaisir de la culture. En d'autres termes, la source possible de connaissance sur les Noirs ne se limite pas aux "influences exterieures."[32]

Officially slavery survived in New France for seventy-one years, and only briefly during this time were conditions favourable for potential growth of slavery. This occurred when Jean-Baptiste Colbert served as Minister of the Marine (Minister of the Navy and Colonial Affairs). Colbert's policies were designed to encourage the growth of the compact and thriving colony in Montreal. His Frenchification policy, which was the Christianization of, and intermarriage with the Native population, was doomed from the start. The native people showed no desire whatsoever to adopt European ways. Thus, in order to relieve the labour shortage the use of African slaves were promoted. Between 1663 and 1704, in an expanding New France, slave labour might have been used to considerable advantage but slavery was not given full legal support until 1709, well after the colony had developed its mercantile base. After 1713, when New France fell into economic decline, black slavery declined with it.

The principal reason slavery was not firmly established in New France is that the economy was based almost exclusively on the fur trade. Unlike the mass production, gang labour economies in the American South, entre-preneurial labour was more advantageous for the fur trade in the North. As long as the colony was dependent on the fur trade, there was little demand for either domestic servants or manual labourers. The decline in slavery, like the treatment of slaves, was not due to a particularly humane French regime, rather it was based on circumstance of geography and political economy.

Slaves played a key role in New France's attempt to promote and diversify agriculture and commerce, particularly with tobacco and the cultivation of tropical crops.[33] The limited and paternalistic character of slavery in New France was likely due to climatic conditions and economic and historical circum-stances which prevented the creation of a manpower intensive plantation economy. Economic demands were often more important than religious values.[34] The economic reality was competition from the American colonies. New France was not the only society that thought of, or dreamed of, competing with American colonies. Even after the Conquest, British colonial officials sent instructions to promote the establishment of plantations in Canada, similar to those of the American South. But Canada did not have the year-long growing season or the political and economic structures that existed in the United States. While a full-scale plantation system was not instituted, such official edicts clarified and re-established the widespread rights of slave ownership in the colony. In 1759, just prior to the defeat of New France, 962 households had black and Amerindian slaves.[35]

As the French Regime came to an end, slave owning was socially acceptable, but not all blacks in the colony were slaves since the clergy encouraged the freeing of slaves. There were freed black men who were fur traders and fishermen, some engaged in the important and prestigious role of mediator between the Amerindians and the French.[36] Although the colony's economic structure placed relatively little importance on the acquisition of slaves, slavery had been part of the accepted social order in New France.

With the signing of the Treaty of Paris in 1763 came the introduction of British laws and institutions into Lower Canada. Slavery had greater legal status and grew in importance. African slavery, which had been a dying institution under the French, was revived for another seventy-four years, in three stages, under the British.

First, General Amherst, in September, 1760, officially agreed to requests by the conquered French that both African and Amerindian slaves would remain enslaved. This policy was supported by the British government, and was stipulated in Article 47 of the Articles of Capitulation. The Treaty of Paris introduced English criminal and civil law to Lower Canada and deprived slaves of the few protections they had had under the Code Noir. Under the Code slaves were personal property, which meant that the slave was attached to his owner who had the personal responsibility to ensure the maintenance of his slave. Under English civil law slaves became chattel, attached to the land like a serf, and legally a possession like a piece of furniture. A slave could be sold for payment of a debt. For the first time, the acts of the British parliament which had regulated commerce with the American colonies, also came into force in Lower Canada.

Later, during and after the American War of Independence, 1776-88, Loyalists, black and white, slave and free, streamed into Canada. Twelve percent of the forty-two thousand United Empire Loyalists who came to Canada and who were registered to receive land grants in British North America, were of

African descent; most of the free black Loyalists went to the Maritimes.[37] Seven thousand Loyalists settled in Lower Canada and many brought their valuable slaves with them when they fled the United States, and their numbers substantially increased the population of black slaves. French citizens continued to own more Amerindian slaves than the English in Lower Canada.[38] Many Loyalists who had entered Canada without slaves considered slavery a symbol of the republicanism that they had abandoned. Eventually many of these Loyalists became abolitionists.

Approximately three hundred new slaves were brought into Lower Canada by Loyalists.[39] Although it is not possible to establish the exact number of slaves brought to Montreal, the number of slaves living there increased substantially and African slaves virtually supplanted panis slaves in Montreal.[40]

The majority of blacks who entered Lower Canada with the Loyalists were slaves, but the situation was reversed in the Maritimes and Upper Canada where the majority of blacks were free. A probable cause was the unavailability of fertile land in southern Quebec. Other than the slaves of Loyalists, free blacks could not settle in Quebec as easily as in the under-populated regions of Canada, since most of the fertile land in Lower Canada had been granted under the seigneurial system and was distributed through family and kinship ties. Since Lower Canada was the centre of colonial economic power in Canada, the new colonial administrators favoured the expansion of slavery. A slave economy increased the chances of maximizing production while at the same time extending the concept of private property, which was essential to the development of capitalism in the British colony.

The correspondence of the military governor of both Canadas, General James Murray, confirms that the British administrators stationed in the Canadas were anxious to develop such a trend in Quebec. In 1763 he wrote to a colleague in New York: "Without servants nothing can be done and (French) Canadians will work for nobody but themselves...black slaves are certainly the only people to be depended upon."[41] Subsequent British laws attempted to confirm and strengthen the rights of white property owners. An Imperial Act in 1799 was passed to encourage immigration to all British North America. It contained an article that specifically permitted the importation of "Negroes, household furniture, utensils of husbandry, and clothing." The same law discouraged the immigration of free blacks."[42]

The entrenchment of this attitude led to more hardship for the slaves in the colonies; so much so in fact, that slaves in the Canadian provinces under British rule increased their efforts to escape. A southbound underground railroad was established, and between 1788 and 1792 some slaves in Canada fled to the slave-free northern American states.[43] Contrary to popular belief, the first underground railroad between the U.S. and Canada existed to free slaves held on Canadian territory.[44]

The fight to abolish slavery in Quebec began in 1789 when Chief Justice Sir James Monk of the Court of King's Bench freed two slaves on a technicality, and went on to say that therefore "slavery did not exist in the province."[45] This decision was upheld by the courts in subsequent years.

In 1798 a recaptured escaped slave was released by a Montreal judge. Blacks in the city responded in unison, threatening mass escape. This precipitated a crisis for Montreal's slave owners. In April 1799, Joseph Papineau and John Black championed their cause in the House of Assembly, requesting that the Assembly clarify once and for all the tenuous rights of slave owners. The request was tabled.[46] Then in Montreal in 1803, Chief Justice Osgood ruled that "slavery was incompatible with the laws of the country."[47] These decisions created a climate of fear among Montreal's slave owners who believed that without the support of the courts, slave values would fall, and slaves would become more dangerous and escape more frequently. The owners lost their legal right to purchase and to sell human property.

Around 1790 William Brown, and later his nephew John Neilson, both owner-editors of the *Quebec-Gazette* and *Le Canadien* spearheaded the attack on slavery in the province. The *Quebec Herald* followed suit with several anti-slavery articles, poems, and caricatures.[48] The owners of these newspapers did not hesitate to reveal the names of individuals and institutions which continued to support the practice of slavery. Even though the legal and social climate was deteriorating, Joseph Papineau, on behalf of the slave owning citizens of Montreal, presented a petition to provincial authorities requesting either protection their right to have slave property or its abolition. Though nothing was done immediately, in 1800, 1801, and 1803, three abolitionist bills were presented in the provincial legislature.[49] Each of these bills was defeated, but the act of tabling them kept the abolition issue alive in Lower Canada.

This combination of judicial and legislative manipulation and media influence created an anti-slavery attitude and an unstable slave-owning climate. By 1820 this attitude helped to end legal slavery in Quebec. Given the social and legal climate in the province this eradication appears to have occurred even earlier. Even the last slave transaction had the distinction of being overthrown by judicial interference.[50]

Over a period of 200 years, a total of 4,092 Amerindian and black people had been enslaved in the province—1,400 of them were of African descent.[51]

On August 1, 1834, when the Imperial Act freed nearly 800,000 slaves in the British colonies, there were "probably fewer than half a hundred" left in all of British North America.[52]

There is no record indicating how many blacks were in Montreal on Emancipation Day, August 1, 1834.[53] Early writers were frustrated by this gap and the lack of documentation on the black community which lasted until 1885. Wilfred Israel as early as 1928 noted that "the period from 1834...is obscure."[54] This obscurity remained in place until the 1880s when records document the emergence of a black presence. There were blacks in the city throughout this period; not enough, however, create a sense of community. Did the freed blacks and emancipated slaves create a community, or did they find themselves so isolated that they abandoned Montreal?

With little documentation available, researchers have speculated about what may have happened to Montreal's slaves.[55] One theory is that slaves were attracted to available fertile land in the Eastern Townships.[56] Though this may have happened to the slaves in Montreal, it is never explained why they chose not to remain in Montreal. Perhaps racial prejudice or better economic opportunities may have encouraged an exodus to black communities in Ontario or the Maritimes. Correspondence between blacks living in Canada East (Quebec) and Canada West (Ontario) indicate that either reason might have been the motivation for leaving Canada East.[57]

Conversely, integration and assimilation may have been the way of survival for the freed blacks and for the few black slaves. They could have "intermarried and lost, after a few generations, their distinctive physical characteristics."[58] Documents from some slaves and freed blacks attest that in Canada East this was the case. According to a local Montreal historian, R. W. Jones, many blacks did intermarry with the French in the Abitibi and Gaspé regions.[59]

Another possibility may have been that towards the end of slavery, the few remaining slaves and freed blacks scattered all over the island did not have the means or opportunity to congregate.[60] The conditions of emancipation in 1834 may have contributed to this—to ease the loss of slave property the Emancipation Act allowed that a slave could pass into a legal period of indentured labour and slave owners who still had slaves on August 1, 1834 could have exercised this option.[61] So slaves would have remained tied to a specific household even after emancipation, and would not have been at liberty to freely associate with other blacks.

What happened to Montreal's black slaves during this fifty-year period may never be completely understood. By the time of Emancipation more than Montreal's ex-slave population had to be considered because it was during this period Canada experienced an explosion of black immigration. Freed American blacks as well as Refugee and Fugitive slaves entered the country in successive waves.[62] Thousands of Refugee blacks had went to the Maritimes and Upper Canada after the War of Independence in the United States and the War of 1812. For decades Fugitive slaves had been escaping into Canadian territory via the Underground Railroad.

The Underground Railroad is often portrayed as an antebellum network composed of sympathetic free blacks, Quakers, and other abolitionists who assisted Fugitive slaves as they escaped to Canada. Abolitionist, southern, and Canadian propaganda frequently mythologized these networks as highly complex secret organizations, but they were often haphazard, localized, and semi-public in nature.[63] It is extremely difficult to establish the numbers of Fugitives who entered Canada via this system and to estimate the number of blacks in the country at any one time. E. Thornhill estimated that in 1838 over 100,000 blacks lived in Canada and that by the 1850s this figure had doubled to 200,000 as American fugitives continued to be attracted by Canada's reputation as a land of freedom and opportunity. By 1871, even as thousands of blacks reversed direction and returned to the United States, blacks were still the fifth largest ethnic group in the nation.[64]

The figures in Canada East are not nearly as impressive, the 1844 federal census listed only 266 blacks in the whole province. In 1861 that number had dropped to 190.[65] The difference between the two census figures was so significant that two city newspapers commented on its inaccuracy. The Montreal daily newspaper, *The Pilot*, called the census figures "scandalous and unbelievable" and, with the *Montreal Gazette*, asserted that in Montreal there were five to ten times more blacks than were counted in the census.[66]

Sociologist Daniel Gay's analysis of the 1861 census reveals some of the issues faced when determining who was of African descent. These early enumerators created an identity problem. Perhaps it was related to Canada's slave era when both Amerindians and Africans were slaves, and confusion existed between the categories *Indien* and *Noirs*, with biracial Indian and black *mulatres*. Children of unions between blacks and whites bedevilled enumerators because there was no uniform system of classification. Classifying the children as *nègre*, *mulatre*, or *blanche*, was left to the discretion of the census agent.[67]

Were there large numbers of black families in Montreal during this period? One eyewitness account suggests that the numbers were insignificant. The family records of one local historian reveal that when his first ancestor arrived in Montreal in the late 1840s, there were only four black families living in Montreal at that time.[68] This account is supported by historians who have tended to believe that not many blacks lived in Canada East or Montreal because there is little evidence that they exerted any socio-economic or political influence. The historians assume that if blacks had been in Montreal in significant numbers much more would have been written about them. Such has been the position of black historians, and to emphasize this point, the historian James Walker concluded that there "are no records of blacks entering Montreal between 1812 and 1850."[69]

This conclusion does not consider clandestine black immigration, particularly in the summer of 1831. It was estimated that 10,000 unregistered immigrants arrived in Montreal then, and one observer wrote that blacks from the United States, Scotland, Ireland, Australia and the West Indies were included in this group.[70] In addition, a sizable number of blacks lived, if not in Montreal, at least in other parts of the province, because historian Robin Winks writes that "a (black militia) company was raised in Canada East in 1846."[71]

Another indication of a black presence and a sign that Montreal's citizens were comfortable with the presence of blacks, was the appointment of Thomas Wily as chief of police in 1844. Wily, a former colonel of the British 83rd Regiment, had come to serve in Quebec in 1837, was black. Because he was perfectly bilingual he was made drillmaster of the Royal Quebec Volunteers, a position he held until 1842. He served as Montreal police chief until 1849.[72]

By 1857 there were enough blacks in Montreal to support the renowned Shadrach restaurant. Frederick 'Shadrach' Wilkins was an escaped Virginia slave who, in 1851 with the help of the Boston Vigilance Committee, was brought to Montreal via the Underground Railroad. Within a year he had opened a saloon, a restaurant, joined a church, married an Irish woman, and fathered a child.[73] This upward mobility was exceptional. It was also unusual that men like Wilkins ended up in Montreal. By most accounts Montreal was not the first choice of fugitives entering the Canadas. Few found their way to Montreal during the first seventy-five years of the nineteenth century. This can perhaps can best be explained by the fact that Canada East, and therefore Montreal by extension, had the reputation of being a cold, bleak, out-of-the-way part of the world. How that perception came to be is unclear. There was negative press in the United States about Canada and southern slave-owners created negative propaganda to undermine the idyllic myth of a Beulah land and Eden in Canada. Their misrepresentations did not specifically centre around Canada East, so this misperception was not solely of their making.

During the nineteenth century, abolitionists in the Canadas debated the merits of Canada West over Canada East. The correspondence of John Lewis, a black clergyman and anti-slavery lecturer, expounded on what he believed to be the reason Fugitives on the Underground Railroad stayed away from Montreal. Lewis attributed it to the "Americanized," "Yankeeized" Canadians living near the United States, particularly those close to Vermont, who did not, "manifest that noble spirit of philanthropy...that is seen and felt in the Western Townships [Canada West]." Conceding that all Fugitives became free, regardless which province they entered, Lewis lamented that the anti-Catholic fervour exhibited by the Americanized Canadians in Canada East was far more pronounced than their anti-slavery sentiment. This emphasis on religion rather than on race made "the work of reform drag along."[74]

Throughout the northern United States it was the custom that an underground railroad terminus would be in those areas where there were sufficient numbers of blacks to support resettlement activities.[75] In recognizing that the Eastern Townships region was a terminus, there is credence added to the assertion that there were significant numbers of black families in these communities. It is not surprising that there may be a connection between the underground railroad and the existence of the only black village that existed in the Eastern Townships. An underground railroad station is reputed to have been at St. Armand Station, a town on Missisquoi Bay situated at the northern tip of Lake Champlain across from New York State. This is the same Loyalist settlement Claude Marcil sugested that blacks founded in 1784.[76] Some members of the Quebec Black Historical Society have traced their ancestors' entry into the province back to the station at St. Armand.[77]

The village and vicinity of Coaticook, near the Vermont border, and home of the 'Yankeeized' Canadians was another depot on the underground railroad. John Lewis, attempting to refute myths about the Eastern Townships, extolled the virtues and breadth of "hospitable kindness" that passengers on the underground railroad could expect to find in Coaticook.[78] From this and other stops in the Eastern Townships the black Fugitive had two options—turn west into Montreal or continue into Canada West. Obviously the few who ventured into Montreal sojourned briefly.

During the mid-nineteenth century negrophobia was at its height in Canada and the high visibility of Africans produced a backlash of segregationist legislation in the Canadas. The white population in Upper Canada and Nova Scotia did not want to associate or compete with blacks. A system of separate schools and separate communities was set up in each province, and "separate but equal" legislation, was used to segregate Canadians of African origin.[79] In other provinces with pockets of blacks, local ordinances kept blacks out of the local and provincial mainstream.

In Quebec the absence of such legislation appears to indicate that the small number of resident blacks did not pose a threat. As late as 1871 the census recorded only 72 Africans in Montreal's seven wards.[80] This figure substantiates the belief that there was no black community, just isolated households in Montreal. Nevertheless there are several indicators pointing to a cohesiveness among the blacks living in the city. There was contact between the black anti-slavery elements in Canada West and the anti-slavery elements in Canada East. D. S. Janes, a black citizen of Montreal who was one of fourteen vice-presidents of the nation-wide Anti-Slavery Society of Canada during the 1850s, is the most prominent example.[81] Between 1840 and 1900 Quebec, particularly Montreal, was one of North American's major anti-slavery centres. Black American leaders joined with Quebecers of all stripes—Protestant, Catholic, and Jew—to fight slavery. Abolitionist Frederick Douglass used Montreal as a base in 1846, and then again in 1859-60.[82] This suggests that significant support existed among Montreal blacks to morally and financially champion the anti-slavery cause.[83]

The correspondence of black abolitionists indicates that Montreal's black population maintained contact with blacks outside the province.[84] The image of Montreal with small pockets of isolated blacks is questionable. It was this same population that declined dramatically when the majority of blacks in Canada East returned to the United States during the period immediately following the American Civil War.[85]

Unlike the free black Loyalist elements in Canada West or Nova Scotia, few blacks in Canada East became economically independent. Loyalist, Refugee, and Fugitive blacks in Canada West and in the Maritimes were able to build new communities of their own.[86] The children and grandchildren of the Loyalists and of the Refugees and Fugitives became professionals and skilled tradesmen. The period following the end of the Civil War marked a decline in the black communities of the Canadas when many skilled and educated blacks returned home to the United States. These capable men and women went on to create and to rebuild black America after the Civil War. The zenith of black actvity and contribution in Canada was over.

By 1834 in Quebec there were few old line blacks or even Refugees, and therefore no middle class economic base for slaves or for other blacks to integrate into once they entered the province. After 1834 blacks in Montreal were part of a growing labour pool, vying for jobs with the Irish, Scots, and the French. Blacks held the lowest positions on the occupational scale, those of barber, shoe shiner, domestic,[87] elevator boy, busboy, water boy, and porter.[88] Those blacks with professions or marketable skills went to the larger and wealthier black communities in Ontario where they could more easily obtain or create jobs better suited to their education and skills.

Montreal was unique among the growing number of black communities even before the advent of the railroad. It was a major city but it did not attract significant numbers of Refugee and Fugitive blacks. The city was a temporary stop. "Montreal was just a stop-over on the way to *Somewhere Else...*"[89]

CHAPTER TWO

The St. Antoine District
[1856-1897]

By 1856 the Grand Trunk Railway (GTR) was operating between Montreal and Toronto. Three years later a link was established between Montreal and Chicago and sleeping cars were put into service. There were already several small American rail companies operating out of Montreal. About 1886 the American-owned Pullman Palace Car Company hired blacks in the United States to work as sleeping car porters on the four rail lines connecting with Montreal, and the Grand Trunk Railway hired black cooks and waiters.[1] These American blacks became more numerous in Montreal just as the city was becoming a major North American rail terminal.

Although there is no evidence that there had ever been a group of blacks working in one specific occupational sector in the city prior to the 1880s, the development of the railways changed all that. It was the beginning of the era in Montreal when the word porter was synonymous with black man. The reasons are at the heart of the racism which framed society's relations in the nineteenth and twentieth centuries. They go beyond the fact that the Pullman Palace Car Company deliberately instituted an ethnic and racially-segregated hiring policy. In her study of the sleeping car porters, sociologist Agnes Calliste suggests that there were three reasons why labour stratification became so rigid.[2] An obvious incentive for the Company was the cheap wage rate black labour commanded which went hand in hand with their lack of collective power.

The second reason had to do with a legacy of slavery—the social distance created by race. Black men were invisible to the clientele they served, which was perfect should there be any indiscretions during overnight travel. The company counted on social conventions and social mores to control the porters.

The third reason was a throwback to the slave/master relationship. The traditional service roles that blacks performed conveyed status to the white person being ministered to. This status played a large role in the satisfaction of the clientele and enhanced the romance of long distance train travel. [3]

Thus, when the Canadian West opened up, both Canadian-owned rail companies followed the lead of the American Pullman Palace Car Company. Beginning around 1897, they began to hire black men to work on their sleeping cars. Canadian Pacific Railway (CPR) employed blacks directly from its Montreal offices, rather than from American cities. American blacks were able to obtain employment in Montreal without having to compete for jobs in the United States.

The porters were a group of young temporary residents, constantly on the road and ending or changing runs in Montreal. The rail companies were hired strong men in their twenties and thirties. "The post of porter is one which can be filled by only those in the prime of life. In rare cases young men at nineteen have been employed."[4] Initially, to accommodate this transient population, the railroads established "quarters" or "layovers" for them throughout the city. These quarters were small, isolated boarding houses operated by the railroad companies.[5] American porters prior to 1897 viewed Montreal simply as a layover place between arrival and departure.

The first American porters on the island were "citizens of Montreal between the trains."[6] This attitude, which lingered for decades, has its roots in the early years of the railroad. Putting down roots in Montreal was not simply a matter of finding work. The Canadian government actively discouraged the wives and families of migrant American porters from entering the country, even for a visit. Fear and racism was behind the decision of the federal immigration department to control black communities across the country. One immigration official wrote:

For obvious reasons I do not think we would want to add to our coloured population and I do not believe that the arrangement with the Canadian Pacific Railway for the admission of these coloured porters contemplated the entry of their families. We have been discouraging their admission as visitors or otherwise, by every means possible here on this assumption.[7]

As many black Americans coming to Montreal discovered, it would not be an easy feat to make a home here as their loyalties would be divided. Maintaining two homes in two countries would make the task even harder. Not until World War II were these men allowed to bring in their families, but only if they were sponsored by the CPR [8]

The Red Caps, one of the first groups of resident black railroad workers in Montreal, worked only in the train stations where they handled luggage and the boarding and disembarking of passengers. There were not as many Red Caps as there were porters. Only fifty Red Caps were employed by the CPR on the island at any one time. Their salary scale differed greatly from that of the porters. Red Caps were hired by number. Those numbered from 1 to 10 received wages plus tips. Numbers 11 to 50 were hired on a tip basis only. Generally, those who became Red Caps were men who had a viable skill or profession but who were unable to find jobs in their chosen area. These men were usually willing to accept the decreased hours and substantial loss of pay to give themselves the opportunity to pursue other employment. Unlike the migrant porters, the Red Caps were able to make Montreal their permanent home because they did not have to travel.

In many North American cities an interdependent relationship was evolving between the railways and black men. For over eighty years Montreal was no exception. As early as the 1880s private rail companies recruited men directly from the United States. Later their reach extended to the Caribbean. First the Americans, then black Canadians, and later the West Indians, were recruited, hired, and shipped out from the island of Montreal.

The Canadian railway companies did not have to look far for American labour since many had been farm labour Refugees who had entered the country between 1812 and 1850. Over 2,500 eventually found diverse employment with the railroads.[9] These men stayed in the quarters along with the porters.

Unlike Americans, the Canadian and West Indian blacks were resident workers who made Montreal their home, and in this way Montreal's Negro community emerged. Within a set geographical area—mostly in the area of St. Antoine—blacks lived almost exclusively within the lodgers' section—the blocks between the Windsor Depot (CPR tracks) and the Bonaventure Station (GTR tracks). The migrant porters' and the permanent porters' families lived together. This was typical of residential patterns in mid-nineteenth century cities where groups tended "to congregate...in order to minimize transport costs and time lost in going to and from work."[10]

The close proximity of the lodgers' section benefitted black women as well. St. Antoine 'above the hill' was well served by the domestics who lived below. Alongside the Irish and British women of St. Antoine, black women worked in the homes of the wealthy who lived on the upper sections of St. Antoine.[11] This was a daily phenomenon they shared with other women of the neighbourhood as domestic service, "continued to be the single most important paid employment for women..."[12] It would be several decades before black women replaced the first and second generation Irish and Scots women who had flooded the domestic field during the last two decades of the nineteenth century.

The snapshot that demographer Herbert Ames presents in *The City Below the Hill* provides a comprehensive demographic view of the St. Antoine neighbourhood where blacks lived at the turn of the century.[13] Despite the fact that they canvassed door-to-door, Ames' surveyors found only twenty-four black families in the area.[14] The number of black households translates to about 120 people, if the average family size throughout the neighbourhood was five persons. It would increase after accounting for lodgers, although Ames took great pains to eliminate lodgers from many of the calculations.

In any case, Ames' breakdown underestimated the total number of blacks in the district. He did not consider the blacks residing in households not classified as Negro. The survey suffered from the same type of error that characterized the census—the misclassification of Negroes, due to the unclear and limiting definitions of the term Negro.

Wilfred Israel described the problems of data collecting in 1897:

When the census representative calls, in…cases of miscegenation, he meets (what may appear to be) a white woman. There are many women who are…as of white birth. Does she reveal the racial origin of (herself) or her husband?…is she classed (for purpose of the census) white or black? If she is considered white, sociologically it is misleading…(does the census-taker class the children as white or black?)…Again, many of the homes…have borders (sic) who also are Negroes. (If they are even mentioned) are they reported after the color of the white wife or that which is theirs? In many Negro families both the husband and the wife are working daily…these homes are omitted in the returns.[15]

Ida Greaves, in 1930, also underscored the lack of accuracy in the censuses of the early twentieth century. She noted that "according to the current 1930 classification, Haytians (sic), and Jamaicans (most West Indians are Jamaicans) are excluded from Negro division and listed among the Various races."[16] She commented that enumerators invariably classified the entire household, including the black spouse, according to the nationality of the white respondent.

Another reason for the chronic under-estimation, is that census takers were looking for Canadian citizens, or individuals with resident status. Most

Americans kept their status as Americans. They lived, socialized, and worked in Montreal, but they did not want to become Canadian citizens. Nor were they encouraged to integrate into the fabric of the city. Although they were American citizens, most of them did not register with the American consulate, despite the fact that many had families here—Montreal was only a temporary home.[17]

Contrary to the popular belief that blacks were a sizable majority in the St. Antoine area, blacks have historically always been a minority.[18] In 1897 Montreal had more than a quarter million residents and St. Antoine below the hill had over 37,500.[19] Yet Israel, using the estimates by blacks themselves, put the total number of blacks throughout the city in 1897 around 300, 90 percent of whom were Americans.[20] By 1897 the thriving and expanding Negro community in Montreal had grown to include those blacks who lived in the mostly French-speaking satellite municipalities of Ste. Cunégonde and St. Henri to the west of St. Antoine.

By 1897 the majority of quarters were located just west of the older quarters between Windsor, (now Peel) and Mountain streets.[21] This small area is where the first signs of an identifiable Negro community became evident. Facilities opened to cater to the social and recreational needs of the resident porters and Red Caps, as well as the international travelling public. They included barbershops, clubs, restaurants, tailors, and other establishments that served blacks without discrimination.[22] Blacks, travelling or resident, blended into the cosmopolitan milieu that was St. Antoine at the turn of the century.

All of this took place in a section of St. Antoine ward north of the Irish ward of St. Ann's, commonly called Griffintown. At the turn of the century St. Antoine ward was the largest political division in the city of Montreal, encompassing the entire western end of the city limits.[23] It ranged from Cedar avenue in the north to Nôtre-Dame in the south, and east from Durocher and St. Alexander streets to the municipal limits of Ste. Cunégonde and Westmount in the west. The southwestern and northern parts of the ward were almost exclusively residential, while the eastern areas bordering on Griffintown were commercial and manufacturing businesses. The escarpment, just below Dorchester street, ran along almost the entire length of the ward and split the ward into "those above" and "those below" the hill.[24]

Blacks who lived below the hill made the north central part of the district their home even though the railroads established porters' quarters in the heart of Irish Catholic Griffintown. Thus the St. Antoine district was synonymous with the growth of the black community in the southwest core of the city of Montreal. The current dimensions of section that was the St. Antoine district includes Little Burgundy and St. Henri. Little Burgundy runs from Atwater avenue east to Peel street, from the Lachine Canal north to the Ville Marie expressway. St. Henri extends along St. Antoine, from Atwater west to Glen Road.[25]

During the early and mid-nineteenth century the main thoroughfare of the St. Antoine ward was St. Antoine street which was lined with the stately residences of doctors, lawyers, and financiers. Over time, as new districts opened up, and as the working class encroached, professionals vacated the lower sections of the district for the Golden Mile—the upper sections of St. Antoine ward. Many, not so wealthy, move to other exclusive jurisdictions north and west of St. Antoine. As the elite moved out, real estate speculators and private holding companies bought up the mansions in St. Antoine, subdivided the homes, and began to rent out flats and rooms to immigrant and working-class families. Slowly, ownership by absentee landlords contributed to a deterioration of housing in lower St. Antoine, resulting in slum-like conditions. To minimize costs and maximize profits the owners did little to maintain the properties, while at the same time low rents encouraged high occupancy.

The area below the hill in the St. Antoine district was a homogeneous community without extreme wealth or extreme poverty.[27] Blacks shared the community with other groups of working poor. Residents lived in dilapidated and dangerous housing that was sub-standard even for its day. In many cases the buildings had been condemned, and outdoor privy pits were breeding grounds for disease and death.[28]

Nevertheless, as early as 1897 this area was the natural home for blacks on the island of Montreal because it had affordable and accessible housing, the rail companies were located nearby, and temporary residents—out-of-town porters—used company accommodation while in Montreal for brief stopover periods.[29] The needs of the transient and resident porters and their families could be met with relative ease and the concentration of blacks made it possible for a community to develop.[30]

CHAPTER THREE

The Negro Community
(1897-1930)

The period between 1897 and 1930 marked the beginning of a genuine black community in Montreal.[1] Major institutions such as the Union United Church (Union) in 1907, the Universal Negro Improvement Association (UNIA) in 1919, and the Negro Community Centre (NCC) in 1927 were established. Their creation marked a period of institutional activity which permeated the cultural and social fabric of the community.[2]

The daily lives of people and the evolution of their community cannot be understood without appreciating the role that organizations played. Blacks experimented with many types including mutual aid societies.[3] By pooling resources, mutual aid groups provided insurance to cover health and death benefits for members, occasionally they became meeting places for social activities. Branches of these mostly American fraternal organizations provided opportunities for interaction and mutual benefit.[4] There were also ethnic and cultural recreational organizations.[5] A plethora of groups and clubs emerged to meet the black community's cultural, political, and economic needs.[6] Special interest groups often grew out of programs offered by the parent organizations.[7]

The life span of these organizations varied wildly, some lasting only one season, others for decades. Each, though different in scope, had one basic aim—to help Montreal blacks survive the discrimination and isolation imposed by the surrounding white population. The institutions provided links between families and cultures, and in these early years, helped to establish the unique black Montreal identity.

After 1897 black Canadians from Nova Scotia, New Brunswick, and Ontario joined the influx of West Indians and Americans moving to Montreal. They were part of a community which grew from 300 to an estimated 5,000 blacks distributed throughout the city.[8] Those who were lucky worked on the rails.

The railways' hold on male employment gave life to the black community—the lure of jobs brought men and their families to Montreal. This control was so strong that by 1928, 90 percent of all working men were employed on the railways.[9] The situation was similar for black women who, regardless of their skills, worked as domestics.

For men and women surviving the employment situation in the Montreal during these years required an enormous amount of time and energy, and the struggle for suitable jobs which were commensurate with experience, expectation, and aptitude pushed the limits of endurance and obliged some to leave the city in search of work.[10] For others settling in in Montreal meant settling for its meagre opportunities—unfortunate fact because since the turn of the century, West Indians as a group upon entry into the country, had been Canada's most educated and skilled immigrants.[11]

During the first three decades of the twentieth century blacks in Montreal, like their brothers and sisters across the country, survived anti-black sentiment or negrophobia as it was manifested daily with social and economic barriers. Mr. Tucker, a resident of Montreal during the period remembers that:

> In restaurants you sat together, wherever you went. Otherwise, if a black person sat alone, he looked like a curio. You could not sit with a white man, and sitting with white women was worse. Some places would indicate outright that blacks were not allowed and you never went there. You went where you were welcome, otherwise you wouldn't be served. If you made a fuss, you could be arrested, but in those days there were so few of us you would try not to make a fuss. You'd go about your business quietly.[12]

In rare instances an individual would challenge the status quo. On March 12, 1898, a black man named Johnson bought two orchestra seats for a concert at the Montreal Academy of Music. He and his companion were prevented from sitting in the orchestra section and were offered 'alternate' seating. After protesting they were forcibly removed from the theare. Johnson sued, claiming damages for breach of contract. The Academy asserted that they had the right to refuse blacks seating in the orchestra section by a longstanding verbal agreement between the establishment and its black customers. The case, Johnson vs. Sparrow was heard by Justice J.S. Archibald of Quebec Superior Court who rendered his judgement on January 5, 1899.[13] He found that Johnson's claim was legitimate and that "the regulations [of the Academy] are without doubt a throwback of prejudice created from black slavery." Although he believed that slavery did not have much impact on Canada he stated that "all men are created equal before the law and everyone has equal rights in society."[14] Sparrow was ordered to pay Mr. Johnson fifty dollars in damages for breach of contract and humiliation.[15]

The victory was hollow because when Sparrow appealed to the Court of Queen's Bench, the thread of civil liberty in Archibald's reasonings were dismissed. The four justices who heard the case did not find that excluding blacks from a theatre was illegal, unreasonable, or undemocratic. Citing the legal precedence of segregation in the United States, they disassociated themselves from Justice Archibald's principles of equality. However, they upheld the damages for Johnson on the basis of breach of contract only.[16]

The American Civil War (1861-1865) and the anti-black backlash which followed also contributed to fear and intolerance among Canadians. Nor were Canadians immune to the prevailing scientific race theories of the late nineteenth and early twentieth centuries including class dialectics and social Darwinism theories. French and English Canadians worked toward defining their vision of this newborn nation, and the tenets of such race theories were openly expressed by progressive men and women of the time. In 1915 Agnes Laut, a respected populariser of Canadian history, expressed the best and worst of negrophobia when she stated: "Theoretically...the colored man should be as clean and upright and free-and-equal and dependable as the white man; but...practically he isn't." She expressed her fear that there were, "too many Little Brown Brothers" who could not be assimilated and that the Little Brown Brothers were part of the "dangers within" the nation."[17]

For blacks the first thirty years of the century brought rejection during wartime and a nascent union movement. Canada's attitude towards black enlistment during World War I demonstrated how unwelcome blacks were. The same was true on the labour front. As blacks rallied to assert control over their working conditions they found little support, especially from other workers. The situation for blacks in Montreal was hampered by racist immigration practices and the day-to-day struggle for a decent existence. For blacks who had assumed that Canada was a land of equal opportunity, the reality of racial inequality was to be very disappointing. The basic purpose of black community life was to ameliorate conditions and to encourage those who called Montreal home to stay.

Canadian immigration policy did not encourage blacks to remain in Montreal or Canada. The black population increased slowly between 1900 and 1930 while other ethnic communities were coping with massive waves of new immigrants. From 1897 to 1912, in the largest immigration Canada has ever experienced, 2.3 million Europeans and Americans came to Canada while less than 1,000 blacks were officially admitted into Canada.[18] From 1916 to 1928 official immigration figures indicate that 1,519 blacks had immigrated to Canada.[19] Like most official figures of this era it is low; the actual numbers were probably between 2,000 to 3,000. Immigration officers often registered people by their place of birth rather than by racial criteria, which misrepresented hundreds of immigrating blacks. This was particularly true for blacks who came from England, Europe or elsewhere overseas via American ports. The official records also do not consider illegal immigration. The low number of official black immigrants indicates clearly that there was little demand for blacks—Canada's pressing need for labour was being filled with white European and American immigrants.

Whites were strongly encouraged to immigrate by the Canadian government, while at the same time it was made clear that black immigration, particularly from the United States, was not desirable. American blacks still perceived Canada as the Land of Milk and Honey.[20] Had it not been the home of the Fugitive slave? Had it not been a land free from the scourge of slavery? Whatever fuelled this image, Canada was seen as a desirable place to settle.

The Canadian government wanted American immigrants but could not legally prevent undesirable black American citizens from crossing the border. Uncomfortable with this situation, immigration officers tried to resolve the problem by establishing their own methods to deter black immigration. The challenge was to be anti-black without seeming anti-black. In 1911 Canadian agents stationed in the United States informed Immigration Department officials in Canada that they believed they had made progress toward checking the movement of America's black population into Canada. They had persuaded scores of families that Canada was not the place for them.[21] Canadian immigration agents on the Canadian side of the border had the same goal. Individual blacks and groups attempting to enter the country were stopped at the border and sometimes forcibly returned to American soil. These aggressive efforts on the part of Canadian officials strained Canada-U.S. relations[22]

This policy of discrimination toward blacks spilled over into private industry. Pressure was put on railroad companies to reduce Canada's attractiveness to blacks in tourist, travel and homesteading advertisements. The most obliging company, the Great Northern Railway, told its employees that blacks would not be admitted into Canada and that they were to discourage ticket sales to blacks wanting to enter the country. The government did not stop there:

> Blacks were not given any of the assistance and incentives which were freely available to whites…propaganda material…was kept away from blacks. The Canadian government went even so far as to employ unprincipled Negroes to go among their own and discourage them from thinking of moving into Canada. Routine character and medical tests were conducted and interpreted in such a way at the Canadian border that very few blacks could pass them…The…government was so determined to keep people of African descent out of this country that Ottawa did not find it demeaning to correspond with local U.S. postmasters to determine the race of a prospective immigrant.[23]

To a certain extent such measures simply reflected the prevailing anti-black bias of white Canadians.[24] Canada was no longer a haven for oppressed blacks during this period. Petitions from concerned Canadians were sent to Ottawa demanding limits to black immigration. Discriminatory bills aimed specifically at black immigration were tabled and defeated in Parliament. However the Immigration Act of 1910, passed at the height of Canadian negrophobia, was an attempt by Canadian officials to prevent further immigration of non-whites.[25] Bureaucratic obstacles were put in place against visiting blacks, since it was assumed visitors might attempt to remain permanently in the country.[26] The Act also prevented migrant American workers from bringing wives and families with them to Canada to discourage any increase in the black population.

The repercussions of such a policy were felt in the black community until well into the 1930s. One of the immediate consequences was the increase in inter-racial relationships. In 1928 40% of black men in the Montreal area were married to, or in committed relationships with white women. The incidence of inter-racial relationships in Montreal was six times the national average.

Another result of the 1910 Immigration Act was its legal provision to prevent undesirables from entering the country. This was also the first time that the Canadian climate was used as a criterion to refuse prospective immigrants! Despite the fact that generations of blacks had lived through three centuries of Canadian and American winters, officials claimed that blacks and other non-whites would not integrate well because they could not survive the cold, inhospitable Canadian climate. For a period of one year—1911—black immigration was halted on the basis of climate unsuitability! The Minister of the Interior, Frank Oliver obtained the approval of Governor-General Grey to prohibit "any immigrant belonging to the Negro race, which race is deemed unsuitable to the climate and requirements of Canada."[27] Plans were underway to extend this ban, but after the defeat of the Liberals, the crisis of black immigration was forgotten.

As unbelievable these actions may seem today, the official and unofficial strategies which discouraged black immigration were successful. From 1897 to 1930, less than one percent of the immigrants allowed into Canada were of African descent. Although so much effort was expended by government and citizens to exclude blacks, for many Canadians even this paltry level was still too much, and demonstrations and petitions resulted.[28] From its beginning, the composition of Montreal's black community was shaped by racist policies of the government and its bureaucrats, with the apparent approval of the Canadian population.

From 1897 to 1930 Montreal's black community was composed of three distinct cultures: American, West Indian, and Canadian. Most members of Montreal's white community perceived the Americans as the most important group in the black community. They were the largest, originating in New York, Philadelphia, Washington, and Chicago. This dominant group created the reputation, lifestyle, and economic life of the St. Antoine district.

There were three waves of black American immigration into the district.[29] The first wave was the migrant porters who used Montreal as a three or four day stopover. Although not permanent residents, they had been a part of Montreal's black population since 1886.

The second wave of 802 people arrived just before and during the World War I.[30] Between 1916 and 1928 only 98 blacks came to Montreal to work.[31] These migrant workers were employed in the war industries situated in the Montreal region which needed cheap, abundant labour. After the war they were squeezed out of these jobs by a white labour force and some managed to obtain jobs on the railroads and eventually became part of the permanent community.

The summer Americans were the third wave. About 150 black American students arrived annually for summer employment on the railroads. Each spring railroad company representatives scoured black colleges and universities in the United States to recruit students for summer work in Montreal.[32] The fact that they were educated young men did not in any way present better choices for them—despite their education they had dead-end summer jobs. Some stayed for just the season; others were employed by the CPR on six month contracts.

The more notorious Americans were the approximately 300 blacks from Harlem who dominated Montreal during the summer months. The ones who stayed longer opened Montreal's famous downtown nightclubs, and ran the infamous gambling joints and prostitution rings on St. Antoine street.[33] They catered to the white population that travelled to Montreal for the horse racing season, and to avoid Prohibition. The tourists who flocked north in unprecedented numbers kept the sporting district alive and humming and also patronized the great variety of vaudeville theatres, cabarets, dance halls, and even amusement parks located in other areas of the city.

By the 1920s jazz reigned supreme in Montreal's night life. The city was a the ideal North American location for a developing black identity focussed on jazz. Jam sessions went on into the early hours of the morning—Montreal was the jazz capital north of the border. In the midst of Prohibition many musicians from across North America had their start in Montreal, and some stayed to live and work in the city. As the result of Prohibition, Montreal was *the* place to be.[34]

American blacks, mostly men, lived mainly between Windsor (now Peel) and Mountain streets, from St. Antoine to St. James (now St-Jacques) in Montreal's famous sporting district.' Until the 1940s this area continued to have the largest number of black residents in the city.

As early as 1914 the Afro-American percentage of Montreal's black population began to decrease. A large number of black Americans left Montreal during the recession in Canada between 1921 and 1923,[35] and by1930, black Americans were less than 50 percent of the black population. The arrival of other black groups also contributed to the decline.

Officially 700 black West Indians immigrated to Canada between 1916 and 1928.[36] Each summer new ships would bring them to Montreal directly from the Caribbean.[37] Those who arrived by ship at Halifax or other Atlantic ports would winter over there and then, the next summer, lured by exaggerated tales of fortunes to be made working for the railroad, move on to Montreal. West Indians had been arriving in Montreal steadily since the turn of the century and their numbers increased during the following decade. However, the period of mass West Indian immigration coincided with the First World War.

This influx began in 1914 when British subjects from the West Indies tried to enlist in His Majesty's Armed Forces in Canada and discovered that they were not wanted. Some West Indians who had been employed in wartime factories were without work at the end of the war. For most West Indian men the alternative to the army and employment in the factories was menial labour—waiting tables, bussing, shoeshining—or the railway. Discrimination in other areas of employment was not the only factor which propelled men towards the railways. Over time, the chaos and uncertainty of the rails was mitigated by other factors—it was a time when jobs were not valued solely for their wages but also by the public respect and the fraternity they garnered. With the uncertain state of the economy, the rails' stability and image was a lure for men working in menial jobs. Railroad men wore clean suits and were recipients of the public's friendly attitude.[38]

In the black community the railroad workers had status, prestige, and later, an image of professionalism. St. Antoine district resident Sylvia Warner remembered that as a child "there was certain type of glamour associated with it"—an aura of prosperity, education and class.[39] The men also fostered the image. Though employment in a stratified, racist labour force never compensated for the abuse, lost opportunities, and discrimination, working in a respectable job was attractive to educated, skilled West Indian men. These men eventually became what has been called the porter's aristocracy.[40]

Many West Indian men were craftsmen or had technical or clerical backgrounds and tried to find employment suited to their training. Leo Bertley's 1982 doctoral thesis on the Universal Negro Improvement sheds some light on the varied occupations of men in the community. Of the twenty-five members Bertley sampled, only nine worked for the railways, although only one was a porter. The remaining sixteen worked as carpenters, welders, bakers, shippers, blacksmiths, electricians, brassmoulders, oilers, compositors, shoemakers, and in other trades.[41] This diversity of skills is one reason that West Indian men did not enter the railroad in large numbers until vacancies opened during the Depression.

There were other reasons to explain this anomaly. There was the obvious fact that the West Indian islands did not have railroads and there was no rail tradition in their culture. Also, in their countries of origin, where blacks were the majority, trades and skills were easier to acquire than for the average black Canadian. When West Indians immigrated to Montreal they assumed that they would be able to use their training. It "would take many disappointments and setbacks in order for them to understand the type of job classification based on ethnic factors…"[42]

Montreal in the early part of the century had another small group of West Indians who were so affected by these conditions that they never really made the city their home. These were the few West Indians who studied at McGill University. They studied in various departments although most were registered in medicine and agriculture. During their studies they lived in St. Antoine district and returned home when their studies concluded.

One exception was Dr. Melville Duporte, who came to McGill University from Nevis in 1910 with an interest in zoology. He completed a four year program in only three years, and he became the first-ever Macdonald College zoology graduate to obtain his M.Sc in 1913 and his Ph.D. in 1921 at McGill. He had the distinction of being the first black in Canada to receive his Ph.D. in zoology in 1921. In 1915 he was the first black to teach at McGill University. His major contribution to entomology was his research on plant and insect morphology and animal parasites which helped shape the federal government's policy on agricultural parasitology. He developed McGill University's Faculty of Agriculture and Department of Entomology, established the Institute of Parasitology at Macdonald College, and became chairman of his department. He has been called the father of Canadian entomology—his legacy is an outstanding and enduring one. [43]

Dr. Duporte's was the exception rather than the rule. The social and cultural climate was different for other graduates who experienced overwhelming discrimination, and as a result, few of these students remained in Montreal. It was not unusual to find that some of the most highly educated men accepted employment on the railroads only because white employers would not hire them. The first black lawyer to graduate from Queen's University in Kingston, Ontario was not able to practice his profession because of the discriminatory policies of the Canadian Bar. He became a waiter on the trains and worked for several decades as a union activist and legal counsel for rail employees. [44]

In 1928 three West Indian doctors worked as porters to earn enough money to open private practices because, as blacks, they were not considered acceptable for hospital or team medicine. [45] The railway companies in Canada benefited from racism and discrimination in the labour market because they were able to hire the most educated and able men to work as porters. This refutes the stereotype of the ignorant, happy, black porter—a useful image for the railway companies to foster to justify ongoing low wages and poor working conditions.

Not everyone accepted this situation—some blacks tried other options. There were more West Indian men in industry than any other sector. [46] Two areas that favoured blacks were shipbuilding and railroad bridge construction. Ships were dry-docked in St. Antoine near Atwater avenue and around 1911 West Indians with shipbuilding experience began working for private companies. The railroad bridges were part of the CPR industry and an alternative to portering. Determined to break away from the railways' hold, these men attempted to work for themselves where and when they could. The West Indians who settled in Montreal, while not alone the struggle, attempted to create a black economic base.[47] From 1897 to 1930 several black businesses were inaugurated: a bread factory, a community newspaper, a doll repair store, a mineral water company, a truck cartage business, cafés, clubs, several restaurants, barber shops, and rooming houses. Often enterprising efforts went unrewarded—when the banks refused them capital many failed.[48]

Israel estimated that by 1928 West Indians made up forty percent of the total black population in Montreal, with the women outnumbering the men. Being well educated they had little in common with the Americans who had arrived before them. Unlike the Americans, West Indians, who claimed a British heritage, intended to stay in Montreal. The single most important area of employment for men and the whole community was the railroad, but the majority of West Indian women were in domestic service.

Roughly ten percent of the total population of the black community were Canadian blacks—the small core of black families who had settled in Montreal following the American Civil War. This group also included poorer black Canadians who had migrated from rural parts of the Maritimes and Ontario specifically to work on the railroad.

Blacks from the Maritimes were "slowly being driven off the land with the introduction of labor saving machinery by…white farmers."[49] Whole families were uprooted and they came to Montreal in search of railway employment. West Indians and American blacks thought they were uneducated and crude; Canadian blacks had the lowest status in Montreal's Negro community. Some West Indians had originally settled in Halifax or in other Maritime centres, and their decision to settle in the Maritimes prior to coming to Montreal also placed them at a social disadvantage because they were called "Canadians" a negative term used to describe the low status blacks from the Martimes.

The railroad provided a way out, but it was not easy to get hired. West Indian and Canadian men resented the dominance of the Americans on the rails and up to the time of the Depression, ethnic tensions existed between these groups.[50] This division was fostered by, and played into the hands of the railways by keeping the men divided. The importation of temporary migrant workers from the United States helped create and maintain a labour market divided between black Canadians and black Americans in Canada's railway industry.[51]

Of all the companies, the CPR hired the most black American labour. They were persistent about this policy. Even during periods of recession the CPR hired and imported transient Americans on short-term contract. The CPR always claimed that Canada did not have enough black men of experience and character available to meet its needs.[52] As the CNR and other companies knew, the ever-present pool of black men available for portering in Montreal or Winnipeg belied this statement. The CPR manipulated the labour market in this way to control their permanent staff. In a racist labour market black men were assigned portering, which was increasingly defined as menial. This categorization, coupled with ethnic divisions and depressed wages prevented any collective action against employers.

The wealthy of "upper" St. Antoine recruited their "high class" domestic servants—butlers, cooks, nannies, and governesses—from the United Kingdom. The major employment for most black women of St. Antoine and St. Ann wards, was as domestic day labour[53]—housekeeping, washing windows, laundry, and assisting in the kitchen. Black women in the lowest occupations found themselves at the mercy of their employer when sexual harrassment and physical intimidation were part of the job.

At the turn of the century domestic work was a nation-wide industry. Private domestic agencies employed 41 percent of all working women in 1891 and most of the domestic business in Canada, except for Quebec, was handled by private domestic agencies. In 1911 there was a short lived scheme initiated by the federal government to provide French-speaking black women from Guadeloupe for the French-speaking elite of Montreal.[54] The women were expected to be between twenty-one and thirty-five years old, single and childless. Under this plan 100 women from Guadeloupe came to Quebec as domestics. Initially it was a success because in the eyes of their Quebec mistresses, these domestics were fond of children, knew their place, and were acceptable as long as they remained in the country as servants.[55] Employing Guadeloupan women had a number of attractive features. Firstly, the women were on two-year, instead of the usual one-year contract. Secondly, they were paid only $5 monthly compared to the $12-15 monthly paid to white Canadian and European domestics.[56] The scheme was terminated after some of the unmarried women gave birth to children while in service. All the women were eventually deported back to Guadeloupe—even those with children born in Canada.[57]

This treatment of black female labour was not unique. The deportation of Guadeloupeans coincided with the deportation of other black women. As a result of the recession Canada experienced between 1913 and 1915, there was pressure to open jobs for Canadian women. Based on stories of scores of unemployed Canadian women in cities and towns willing to do domestic work, and worried that black women might become public charges, immigration officials deported other black Caribbean women as well. For decades, these deportations were used to justify the restricted entry of Caribbean women.[58]

By 1921 only 18 percent of the working women in Canada were domestic workers.[59] In black communities across the country and in Montreal's English speaking black community the figure was closer to 25 percent. Bertley pushed this percentage to 80 percent based upon the findings of Montreal sociologist Harold Potter,[60] who maintained that 80 percent of black working women in the 1940s were domestics. In Bertley's opinion, Potter's percentage could also be applied to the 1920s.[61]

The majority of West Indian immigration directly from the Caribbean was female.[62] From 1916 to 1928, only 238 West Indian males came directly into Canada from the islands. Of the 411 West Indian women who entered Canada during the same period, 329 or 80 percent came to work as domestics.[63] This was their stated area of employment on entry, but their work background revealed something quite different.

West Indian women had trained as teachers, secretaries or nurses and they entered Canada believing that these skills were wanted and would be welcomed.[64] To their surprise and dismay, once in Montreal, they found that they had to deal with the day-to-day constraints of the ethnically-defined job market. The skills that they could use were domestic related. The roots of this labour pattern rest in a shared slave past where domestic work was perceived as an appropriate occupation for black labour—it was menial, low paying, lacking job security, and with no opportunity for advancement. It is little wonder that black woman was synonymous with domestic work.

Domestic work was work that women did only when they had to, as was the case with the wives of the fifty Red Caps of the CPR. Forty of these men did not earn salaries—they had to live on the tips they received, ranging from $4 per day in the summer to $1.50 per day in the winter.[65] The seasonal variations made their income so uncertain that their wives, and sometimes their daughters, were almost always forced to work outside of the home—usually domestic work. Lucille Cuevas, reminiscing about her mother and other black mothers in that era, recalled that it was not unusual for women to hold two domestic jobs, and still run their own households!.[66] Payment of five to eight dollars a month per job made the difference between marginal and satisfactory living conditions.

Domestic service was performed in an institutional setting as well. Hotels used women as housekeeping staff and during the 1920s the YMCA's head housekeeper and several other members of the housekeeping and kitchen staff were black women.[67]

There were women in the community with rooms to spare who converted their homes, or parts of their homes, into rooming houses. These rooms were rented to transient porters, visitors to the city, and, in rare instances, to permanent bachelor residents. These rooming houses were a conduit for information and social conventions and news was exchanged about other parts of the black diaspora; as well, the resident gained the benefit of being introduced to St. Antoine life through the family's connections. For women who lived in a world circumscribed by racism, opening up their homes to roomers was a creative way to make money.

Women who did not work outside the home were more flexible with their time and were able to involve themselves with activities that improved their community, such as running youth programes and creating social clubs and other institutions.

The first outward sign of black community identity was the founding of the Coloured Women's Club of Montreal (CWCM) in 1902 in the St. Antoine district. It was the first formal attempt by members of the community to assist themselves, since it was the aim of the Club was to aid black people in Montreal in every way possible.[68]

The CWCM emerged during the era of suffragettes and organized women—a time when women's auxiliaries and clubs proliferated across the country, when the collective activities of women were becoming the mainstay of churches, schools, and other social and culturel organizations. The Coloured Women's Club was also a reaction to the many mainstream white, Anglo-Saxon womens' groups which excluded women of other races, religions and ethnic groups.[69]

In its earliest years of serving the black community, the CWCM was also an exclusive club of only fifteen women—all wives of American porters. These women were housewives who had the time for charitable activities because of their husbands' length of railway service and incomes that were among the highest in the community. The Club remained ethnically and culturally exclusive until 1928 when they admitted the first West Indian woman.[70]

The establishment of black institutions provided public and fulfilling outlets. Women involved in social clubs led a very active life. Clubs such as the Benevolent Club, and the CWCM met on a monthly basis and meetings were usually held in homes of members. These formal gatherings were supplemented by group outings, and social and charitable activities in other venues. Meeting social and spiritual needs was just a part of their many activities; their charitable work improved the material well-being of their communities.

The Coloured Women's Club of Montreal responded to the pressing problems of housing, food, and clothing. In 1908 they started a clothing depot for immigrants facing their first Montreal winters. At the same time as it was a social club, the members of the CWCM also attempted to provide moral leadership and much-needed psychological and emotional support for members of the black community. This mission was very necessary in 1902 because Montreal experienced four epidemics. In 1901 and 1902 thousands were stricken by typhoid, scarlet fever, diphtheria, or smallpox.[71] Although there is no record of the effect of these epidemics in the community, the fact that the CWCM evolved from a social club to a self-help society suggests that it stemmed from the lack of resources available to blacks during these emergencies.

Years later, during the Depression, the women of the black community dedicated themselves to another challenge. Montreal, well into the Depression, had one of the highest child mortality rates of any city in the world.[72] Living conditions in Montreal were poor for all but the wealthy, and the city lagged far behind the rest of North American cities in improving health, sanitation, and housing conditions for its citizens.[73] Open sewers, outside toilets, and filthy, crowded tenements were the norm in the poorer sections of Montreal, where it was not at all unusual for ten to twelve people or two families to live in a single room, and outdoor toilets frequently served more than one family.[74]

Conditions were so bad that Montreal earned the dubious distinction as "the most dangerous city in the civilised world to be born in."[75] Although thousands of babies died each year, health and social welfare were not high priorities for the city or the province,[76] such issues were generally the concern of churches, private agencies or benevolent individuals.[77] It is not surprising that community activism was so high in the black community. Unsanitary living conditions in the St. Antoine area and the lack of a health services network for blacks prompted action, especially after an excessive death rate from pneumonia that occurred among West Indian porters.[78]

The black community was not alone in how it coped. Each ethnic and religious group in the city was responsible for its own community's health and welfare.[79] In addition, as the country emerged from the Boer War, civic-minded citizens like the members of the Coloured Women's Club came together to assist in the relief efforts. Soldiers returning from the War were provided with temporary homes and the Coloured Women's Club took care of the injured, organized soup kitchens, and rolled bandages.[80]

Women created and sustained the institutional life in the community through groups and auxiliaries run solely by women. Their organizations aimed to bring blacks together and encouraged and supported family life. Some women were involved in the organization of more than one institution. In the major institutions the volunteers were mainly women, and when direct executive control was assumed by men, women continued to participate as volunteers and occasionally as staff members. This was the usual pattern that emerged in the formation of organizations that served the entire community. The Union Congregational Church (UCC) founded in 1907, and the Negro Community Centre (NCC) launched in 1927, are two institutions which owe their existence to the energies of black women in Montreal.

It is widely acknowledged in the black community and beyond that the church is an institution which embodies black identity and collective kinship. It represented, in the words of Montrealer Betty Riley, "the coming together of a people to share in fellowship, social interaction, relevance and historical significance."[81] Another Montrealer, Henry J. Langdon, described the church as a "beacon to the people because it provided guidance, unity, and a sense of pride."[82] Creating a black church in Montreal was clearly seen as another step toward spiritual and cultural unification.

The religious face of Montreal's coloured community at the turn of the century was a patchwork of basement churches and gospel halls—many led by itinerant American preachers. In response to this liturgical hodgepodge and "because of the hostility encountered in attempting to worship at white churches," there was an urgency to establish a community church for all, regardless of denomination.[83] The barriers blacks sometimes encountered when they tried to reach outside of their community is underlined by Mr. Tucker's well-known story of his experience of visiting an Anglican church. Appreciating the humour and the irony of the story he remembered that:

The stewards...in a most Christian-like manner, directed him to a position under the stairs and behind a hefty pillar. Mr Tucker, unsuspectingly and gratefully accepted this seat. After the service he was hastily guided towards the door. On reaching outside, some of the Christian-minded teenagers, just fresh from spiritual devotions grabbed stones and shouted 'let's stone the nigger.' Mr. Tucker took to his heels and did not stop until he reached his rooming house. At this point the Jewish landlord stepped outside and proceeded to lustily berate the teenagers.[84]

The need for a people's church, a black church, was evident even as blacks continued to attend Anglican, Catholic, Methodist, and Baptist services. A number of the American porters attended the Erskine and American Church. Others found a home at St. George's Anglican, or the Salvation Army, or even the Bethel African Methodist Episcopal Churches. A core of worshippers who desired a unique environment remained committed to a community church. Black women once again collaborated to create an enduring institution which would offer an alternative to the rum shops and gambling halls of the day. The push for a community church was spearheaded by the wives of American porters.[85] Official UCC documents indicate that the church was founded by a group of American CPR porters *and* by their wives. The participation and recognition of these women has not been diminished or lost, even though their husbands' signatures were required to be legally binding.

The Union Congregational Church opened in the Welsh Dance Hall on Inspector street on September 1, 1910 with opening ceremonies presided over by the invited minister, Samuel Brown of Boston. A special covenant was added to the church constitution to promote ecumenical openness for all blacks in the city.

Spiritual needs were not the only items that these women had on their agenda; they recognized that one of the most pressing needs in their working-class community was day care. Clara de Shield, along with other women of the church, created the first day care for children in the black community.[86]

The Union Congregational Church was truly a community church because it brought together the different religious denominations of the black community. Still there was something more radical in its stance than just an ecumenical posture:

> This congregational structure de-emphasized denomination and stressed black brotherhood. An adherent may very well be a baptized anglican, methodist, presbyterian, or catholic... Niceties about

doctrine, liturgy, and other factors...were irrelevant..[87]

Race took precedence over doctrine in the church, unlike the discrimination across the country which created social and geographical barriers difficult to overcome. Simply being black ensured that one would receive help or be accepted into the congregation. In 1928 the UCC had approximately twenty-two official members, although weekly church and Sunday school attendance was close to one hundred.[88]

Through the efforts of the first minister, Reverend Samuel Bowser and Mr. Johnson, a parishoner, for the first years the congregation held services in the CPR's own Olivet Baptist Church on the corner of Mountain and Osborne (now Lagauchetière). In 1910, with Reverend Gantt, a new minister, the American Presbyterian Mission on Inspector street became home until 1917. Later that year, under the leadership of Reverend Arnold Gregory of Oberlin, the congregation established the church in its present location, on the corner of Atwater and Delisle streets in St. Henri. "The Coloured Church" had arrived![89]

There have been several pastors of Union Church, but there is little doubt that the legend and legacy of Reverend Charles Este has become synonymous with the church itself. Charles Este, the son of a Pentecostal minister on Antigua, West Indies, came to Montreal in the spring of 1923 as a divinity student to study at Congregational College of Canada which was affiliated with McGill University. He was appointed to the church as minister in June, 1925.[90] Unable to get a job on the rails, he worked at the Carona Hotel as a bellhop and boot black. Throughout his university years at McGill he kept in touch with the Church and the national body.

Este was instrumental in the formation of the United Church of Canada in 1925, and as a result, the Union Congregational Church became the Union United Church.[91] Este also shaped the open ministerial style which exists in the Union United Church to this day.

As the minister of the church, Reverend Este was more than a leader in name only. He is still fondly remembered by many families as a bulwark of strength and support for everyone in the community. Often described as "steady, steadfast, and determined," Este helped to unify a diverse community. He was a problem solver; not afraid to act when necessary. For these qualities, Reverend Este was an outstanding leader during the early days of the black community's institutional life. To many he was the only leader. Mrs. Anne Packwood, an elder, said Reverend Este "succeeded where others who also tried, failed, and not because they wanted to. It was because of his outstanding qualities that he succeeded."[92]

One of those qualities was the sharing of ministry. From the beginning Union Church encouraged the congregational nature of its mission: it is reflected in the ministerial roles of women members. When Charles Este became minister lay groups already had a visible role in the liturgy and women's groups, including the Household of Ruth, were invited to conduct church services.[93] At first they substituted in the event of sickness or vacation; but gradually women's groups in the congregation occasionally led regular services, or they took responsibility for certain parts of the regular weekly services. There was an open and accepting attitude to their participation in the religious life of the church.

For almost two decades Union Church was the only institution serving the Negro population in Montreal. Until the founding of the UNIA in 1919, the church, with its volunteers and pastoral staff, was the focus of the Negro community and viewed the community as its responsibility. Union Church was also a great social and class leveller. When social divisions based on gradations of skin color, place of birth, level of education, or job status threatened to divide the community, congregants were reminded on Sundays from the pulpit that everyone was all the same in church.[94] Union Church was the voice of conciliation, empowerment and mediation. The church's mission was to meet the needs of the community on a spiritual and emotional level through its choir, Sunday school, and ministries. In a six-day work week, these activities provided structure and rhythm to community life. This rhythm was constant until the outbreak of the World War I in 1914.

At the beginning of the war black men discovered that many white officers, their units, and senior staff, did not want them in Canadian uniforms.[95] Initially Colonel Sam Hughes, Canada's Minister of Militia and Defence, was not against the enlistment of black men. After realizing that his recruiting officers refused blacks on the mistaken assumption that an all-black battalion was forming, he issued a terse letter informing them that no such plan was in the works and that blacks could be inducted into the army. Resistance to the enlistment of blacks continued which forced the department to send a memorandum to every adjutant general in 1915: "The fiat has gone forth: There is to be no colored line; colored Battalions are not to be raised; Colored men are to be allowed to enlist in any battalion of the C.E.F."[96]

This memorandum then contradicted Hugh's earlier stance. Empathizing with blacks in awkward positions, the previous memorandum had stated that it would be humiliating to the coloured men themselves to serve in a battalion where they were not wanted. To reluctant commanding officers this first memorandum provided the justification they needed; indecision and confusion among the army's top brass emboldened those who stood against integration of units.

Voicing the sentiment of a significant number of senior military officers, W. G. Gwatkin, Major General and Chief of the General Staff in Ottawa, issued a memorandum in April, 1916 which stated:

> Nothing is to be gained in blinking facts, the civilised negro is vain and imitative; In Canada he is not impelled to enlist by a high sense of duty. In the trenches he is not likely to make a good fighter; and the average white man will not associate with him on terms of equality. Further...there is no place for a black Battalion, it would be eyed askance;...it would be difficult to re-inforce (sic). No white officer would accept an all-black Platoon.[97]

It is not surprising that many black men were repeatedly rebuffed when they tried to enlist. This did not deter the most insistent—Canada was their country and they wanted the opportunity to serve. Blacks believed that enlisting in the war was an opportunity to serve in a manner that would be meaningful to the white population. According to Mr. Ashby, "there were black men who felt they would better their positions by being in the army."[98] They did not accept that this was just a white man's war as they had been told.

The memorandum of April, 1916 had repercussions. The most damaging effect was that blacks lost their chance to join combat units and this racist diatribe became the rationale to recruit black men for a construction battalion rather than for the expeditionary forces.

Though a few blacks eventually served in individual combat units their acceptance was at the discretion of the units' commanding officers. Responding to pressure from the black community the Department of Militia and Defense established a Negro battalion on July 5, 1916 called the Number Two Construction Battalion-C.E.F., for overseas service.[99] More than 500 black Canadians and about 150 Americans served in this unit. Their main task was building railroads in France for the transport of goods. These men saw combat twice—both times against civilians. The first altercation occurred in Liverpool, England. Anti-Negro tensions coupled with impatience over the slow pace of demobilization combined to produce a riot when whites blocked a line of parading blacks. Canada offered no better security, as Truro, Nova Scotia was the scene of the next incident when resentful whites, fuelled by the fear that a local Negro battalion would be established, attacked members of the construction battalion.[100]

This violent expression of negrophobia, was effective and within a year the Construction Battalion was disbanded—but the struggle was not over for these veterans. The white men who served in segregated forces were unwilling to change their views after the war—white veterans segregated the Canadian Legion Halls, Negro veterans were forced to open their own branch in Montreal.[101] The Construction Battalion was a reminder that even in a world war black labour was fit only to serve white needs. Many in the small Montreal community remember the forty veterans with pride, believing their service was a valued one. An Honour Roll was established at Union United Church in their memory.[102]

Montrealers also served the war effort in other ways. Black women participated in the war by redoubling their charitable activities. In 1914 The Colored Women's Club purchased a burial plot in Mount Royal cemetery so that black men in the navy who were killed would be buried with dignity.[103] The Hostesses, an auxiliary of Union United Church, in *The Hostesses Memory Book*, recounted that women formed a branch of the Red Cross and a large number of these volunteers were members of the Colored Women's Club. They did volunteer work for the Red Cross and met in various homes to make bandages and knitted garments. Although this branch disbanded after the war there was ongoing interest in community work. Since the Colored Women's Club would not admit new members, in 1918 several women established the Colored Women's Charitable and Benevolent Club.[104]

In contrast to these efforts supporting the war, some men reacted to conscription by fleeing or going underground.[105] A small group emerged called the Universal Loyal Negroes Association which challenged the appropriateness of black enlistment. West Indians who had been associated with the organization in Central America, brought it to Montreal. The members of the Association agreed to fight for Britain "on condition that the British government would undertake to intensify efforts to alleviate the circumstances under which her black citizens lived."[106] Whether this group was successful in deterring or fostering enlistment in Montreal is unclear, but they waged their battle for reparations even beyond the end of World War I.

Another group active during the war was the Colored Political and

Protective Association.[107]Organized in 1917, it was the first racial advancement association with the goal of affecting election results in black neighbourhoods through increased awareness and black voting in municipal and federal elections. Material from political parties was analyzed and members were advised to vote for certain councillors and members of Parliament.

By the end of World War I several community organizations had developed within the black community to promote the black race and racial pride. Racial pride was a way to propel blacks into industry or self-employment. But starting a business was hindered by lack of confidence and uncertainty which discouraged many gifted and talented people from leaving the security of a wage-earning job and striking out on their own. A sense of pride was the first requirement for blacks to counter the defeatism and negativity they faced in Canadian society. At the end of the war, Montreal's race-centered Universal Loyal Negroes Association decided to expand its mandate and applied to the Universal Negro Improvement Association (UNIA), centred in New York City, for membership. On June 9, 1919 in the porters' quarters on St. Antoine street, Division 5 of the Universal Negro Improvement Association was officially established.[108]

The UNIA advocated "self-help and self-reliance…in everything that contributes to human happiness and human well-being."[109] The UNIA of Montreal was part of a worldwide organization committed to the goals of Marcus Garvey. Garvey founded the UNIA in Jamaica in 1914 and introduced it to the United States in 1916. Garvey advocated black kinship and a segregationist stance which most urban American blacks did not agree with, and a Back-to-Africa call which most Canadian blacks found offensive.[110] From the inception of the UNIA these tenets were contentious.

Garveyites were unique because they promoted segregation in Montreal as a way to uplift the black community. They felt that segregation would allow blacks to pool resources and to care for their own society. Slavery had created many different black cultures in North America and the Garveyites believed that segregation could reverse that history by encourging the creation of one united, equal people.

Countering Garvey's segregationism was the integrationism of Asa Philip Randolph, a prominent black American union organizer and civil rights activist. His aim was to unite all workers regardless of race. He believed that blacks had helped to build North America and that now they had a right to claim what all workers at that time were fighting for—a decent wage and decent working conditions.

Garvey believed that race, rather than class, was the primary social conflict. His suspicions of trade unions and communists led him to claim that "99.5 percent of lynch mobs were made up of communists,"[111] and that white unionists were the enemy.

Both men expended considerable energy undermining each other. Randolph attacked Garvey and led a campaign to have him deported from the United States. Garvey's vitriolic responses in the UNIA newspaper, *The Negro Messenger*, became part of the black Montrealer's essential reading during the 1920s. At the same time Garvey's followers spread the message that blacks should avoid unions, since unionists would see themselves as white and not as a brotherhood of unionists including blacks. Perhaps this was true. The treatment of black porters by their fellow CPR workers supports Garvey's assertion. The black porters' acceptance into related unions was the result of great effort. Labour historians often wonder why the industrial unions did not welcome black membership. "Pervasive racism…counteracted this logical incentive so that blacks were either excluded or denied equal participation in most industrial unions."[112]

Black Montrealers were not convinced of Garvey's message. Randolph's viewpoint made more sense as they suffered the coercion, abuse, and deprivation in their non-unionized workplaces. Blacks in Montreal were not convinced that white workers were the enemy, despite the fact that their relations with the railway companies, especially the CPR, emphasized how unfriendly the white capitalist could be. The firings, and other divide and conquer tactics employed by the rail companies stalled unionization for almost two decades, and the rivalry between Garvey and Randolph supporters, dissipated the energy and focus of black workers. By the mid-thirties, Randolph was embraced and honoured by all but the staunchest Garveyites in Montreal.[113]

Back-to-Africa, the Garveyite slogan, however, had a more lasting consequence.[114] It was taken by most Garveyites to mean the actual return of blacks to Africa, but this tenet was taken too literally. What Garvey really meant was "the repatriation of the thoughtful and industrious of the race." Garvey's intention was to cull only the best black minds for his resettlement project, producing a brain drain or decapitation of black societies abroad.[115] Preaching Back-to-Africa at a time when Europe was negotiating post-war reparations, Garvey believed that the Europeans and the Americans had a moral obligation to repatriate peoples of African descent to an African homeland. Repatriation was an extremely controversial issue—Garvey saw America and Canada as the white man's country which should be abandoned. On the other hand, blacks who thought otherwise felt they had laboured to create Canada and would not even consider giving up their claim to it.

Whether or not the whole issue of Back-to-Africa was rhetorical, it had taken on definite proportions when Garvey began negotiating with Liberia for settlement of twenty to thirty thousand families from North America and the Caribbean. To further his plans for settlement Garvey collected $750,000 from UNIA members to finance his Black Star Line.[116] An ocean liner was purchased and plans were drawn up for African settlement. Garvey's fortunes plummeted following a series of mishaps and scandals. The Liberian government, fearing Garvey planned a coup, seized $50,000 of UNIA settlement materials. American government investigations revealed that the huge sum collected by Garvey had disappeared and the UNIA's Death Benefit Fund had been cleaned out. Garveyites in Montreal stopped or considerably reduced their financial support for the Liberian settlement project.[117] Still, Back-to-Africa remained an enduring dream more powerful than other aspects of the UNIA creed.

Despite the failure of classic Garveyism, the UNIA in its early years flourished in Montreal with great numbers of West Indian working class members.[118] Although the membership of the UNIA was decidedly working class the association also had college and university educated members—men and women. On paper, the UNIA constitution called for the sharing of gender power because "no race can rise higher than its women." From the beginning, as the backbone of the UNIA, women were to play crucial roles at the executive level. The UNIA constitution called for the establishment of a joint presidency where "lady" presidents were elected by the local membership.[119] Although her role was not quite equal partnership with her male counterpart, the female president was to coordinate and assist where necessary and to co-ordinate the women volunteers in the various UNIA programs. There was an awareness that women, who had been "instrumental in the formation of the UNIA" and, "who were always there first and foremost in activities" needed to be recognized. The major role of a "lady" president was to "give these women a voice that would be strong and clear."[120] In Montreal, with their tradition of leadership within the church and other organizations, women accepted this and for many years played a major role in maintaining the organization.[121]

Women were also responsible for the organization and running of the Black Cross Nurses (BCN) [122]—a UNIA unit which provided education, training, first-aid and other services to the sick. The BCN issued publications and actively worked to improve sanitation, to prevent accidents, and create a master plan in the event of disaster. The Black Cross auxillary in Montreal began on March 29, 1921. Unfortunately none of the members had the necessary skills or professional expertise to keep the BCN in operation. The demise of the BCN four years later was a blow to the community because black people in St. Antoine were living under terrible health conditions. They did not have access to a social service network which could be relied on for non-discriminatory assistance.[123] Nor did it have proper medical and nursing care. Early community-based organizations were the only forms of self-help that the community could rely on.

In the heyday of the UNIA in Montreal (1919-1928), people attended Union Church in the morning and UNIA social activities at Liberty Hall in the afternoon. The Sunday Mass meetings, as these gatherings were called, included propaganda about UNIA philosophy and news about the activities of blacks throughout the world. Concerts, dances, socials, or parties rounded out the offerings at Liberty Hall. One unique feature of the Sunday Mass meeting was its focus on Pan-Africanism[124] —the goal was to educate members about Negro peoples world-wide. Montreal blacks developed a cosmopolitan outlook as guest speakers from the United States and elsewhere came to Montreal to speak about the issues of the day. Support was strong for these meetings because they were seen as an educational component which was crucial for the development of black youth and for the continuing education of adults.

Montreal's school system did not provide adequate opportunities for black students.[125] There were no laws restricting blacks from attending schools, but prejudice discouraged them from continuing their education. The teachers, "in the best interests of the students," made it clear that an academic education was a waste of time for students who would inevitably become porters or domestics.[126]

These attitudes made racism much more difficult to overcome. Mothers nurtured and cared for their children knowing that individual and institutional racism in Montreal would be directed at them. Anne Packwood recalled that when she was a child growing up on Nôtre-Dame street around the turn of the century her sisters and brother were called nigger by other children in the neighbourhood.[127] Thelma Wallen, another resident of Montreal recalled that during the 1920s when she began attending classes, one of the nuns called her by the derogatory term "sunshine." ("This incident on the first day of school prepared me for life.") From year to year the racial attacks differed but never subsided."[128]These were not isolated incidents.

Bob White recounted similar events from the 1930s and 1940s. "The white people used to call me... 'pickaninny,' 'snowball,' 'Tomtom'... You beat them up and you kicked them and they still called you 'nigger, nigger.'"[129]This is why the community worked hard to empower their children to counter racism.

Small wonder that education and empowerment were two major priorities of the UNIA. The UNIA constitution allowed for classes ranging from preschool to adult education.[130]The adversity faced by the women and men of the UNIA in their daily lives moved them to set an example and challenge the status quo. This can be seen in the structure and program of the UNIA kindergarten which went far beyond being a baby-sitting service and became a vehicle for racial pride and Garveyism. The Constitution outlined the programme for five-year-old children:

a) Bible Class and Prayer
b) Doctrine of the UNIA and ACL[131]
c) Facts about the Black Star Line
d) The Negro Factories Corporation
e) History of Africa[132]

This program was built on the principle that every child, like every adult, was a member of the community and should be treated with respect. All adults had a responsibility and a part in the rearing of children and each adult acted as surrogate parent. Children were taught that respect for elders was important. The kindergarden was one illustration of the UNIA's moral and social role in the community. Other classes were held on Saturdays. The thrust of each class varied little. Activities were intermingled with Negro catechism where the history of blacks would be paramount. The general philosophy of the adult education classes was to encourage individuals or groups to develop business acumen and the ability to stand tall with dignity.[133]

Putting one's best foot forward with pride and dignity was the hallmark of a Garveyite. In 1922 the UNIA was in the midst of a move to Chatham street in the heart of the St. Antoine district. Almost immediately they were confronted with the racism of Ste. Cunégonde's alderman Hushion. He was strongly opposed to the UNIA and to their desire to hold dances in the Chatham Street building—dances were a major source of revenue for the UNIA and for other groups renting space in the UNIA premises. The UNIA fought to have the same basic right that other groups in St. Antoine enjoyed. They got nowhere at the city's permit office, representatives of UNIA finally secured an audience with Mederic Martin, Mayor of Montreal. Discovering that the UNIA's record was beyond reproach Martin ordered that a license be issued immediately with six months at no charge.[135]

The UNIA's concern for its community was intimately tied to its philosophy and its vision of itself as a resource for the community it served. An example of their resolve to work for the benefit of their people was in the consideration the UNIA gave when it came time for them to vacate the porter's quarters. Lack of space and inadequate facilities were the apparent reasons precipitating the move, although their presence in the porter's quarters was beginning to be seen as a political problem. Three concerns were voiced by the UNIA:

a) the Pan-African and black nationalist philosophy of the UNIA was not something that the Canadian Pacific Railway (CPR) was likely to view neutrally, thus endangering company jobs;

b) the incipient union movement might be confused with UNIA;

c) the close proximity to the CPR may retard UNIA membership since employees might have misgivings about being openly identified.[141]

With these concerns at the forefront their move was successfully planned and achieved. The UNIA continued to be supportive of black men at a time when labour issues on the railways were increasing. As the UNIA developed, blacks began to take steps toward unionization at CPR. This was the case even as World War I ended and the railroad companies reduced staff in all departments. The companies used this downsizing to control or stifle the movement towards unionization.

Without fanfare the Order of Sleeping Car Porters was set up at Canadian National Railway (CNR) in 1918. Since most of Montreal's porters worked for Canadian Pacific Railway, unionization attempts then centred around the porters at CPR. Previous attempts at unionization at the CPR had been met with immediate firings. The anti-union CPR did not want any collective body in place which they could not control. Between 1917 and 1919 CPR porters were divided over the type of union they wanted for themselves. Those who had witnessed or had experienced the retaliatory moves of the CPR wanted to create a closed unaffiliated organization which would include only immediate staff. These men set up the Porter's Mutual Benefit Association (PMBA) in 1917. The porters who wanted trade union affiliation, assuming there would be strength in numbers, organized themselves into the Order of Sleeping Car Porters after 1919. Then they affiliated with the Canadian Brotherhood of Railway Employees (CBRE) in 1921.

This divided black labour force worked to CPR's advantage when they dismissed thirty-six workers without cause in 1919.[142] At an arbitration board hearing the CPR defended itself, and claimed that it was exercising its rights according to the contract and refused to give any reason for the firings. Though the arbitration board decided in favour of the workers. CPR temporarily accepted defeat. Emphasizing that they would have final control, they rehired the men and then after due time, dismissed them once again. The setback CPR suffered as a result of the decision of the arbitration board forced the company to change tactics—CPR determined that they would have to treat black labour differently. Their strategy was to co-opt the union movement by ignoring the trade union affiliate, the Order of Sleeping Car Porters, and formally recognize the Porter's Mutual Benefit Association in 1920-21. One of their tactics was to invite representatives of the Association to a management grievance committee meeting to discuss matters of mutual interest.

Realizing the value of the Porter's Mutual Benefit Association, the CPR encouraged and helped consolidate the mutual aid organization. They donated CPR property for the offices of the PMBA, put in place measures to sign up men to join the PMBA, and then collected Association dues for the sickness and funeral benefits. Since Montreal was the CPR's hiring depot, the PMBA was administered by porters in the city for the mutual benefit of porters across the country. With that much economic control, coupled with the 22-room mansion placed at their disposal by the CPR, the PMBA became an institution in its own right in the city. The PMBA was able to offer meeting rooms, recreational facilities, and an additional twelve rooms for porters' layovers. Over time these services, the result of the layovers of the CPR, elevated the status of the porters in the eyes of the men and other members of the community.[137]

The short term benefits which accrued to the PMBA as a result of company collaboration were overshadowed by the long term negative effects: "As a Company union the [PMBA] was powerless to adequately represent its members' interests."[138] With no power to negotiate and without the recognition of labour union status, the situation of the majority of porters in this city continued to be dictated by their superiors. Overtime without pay, company-controlled grievances, firings without cause or appeal—all continued. Despite the mutual aid component the socio-economic marginality would continue for many men and their families for decades. The union was dormant and it would remain so for another twenty-two years.

It was different at CNR. In 1918 mutual aid among black porters at CNR was invested in the Order of Sleeping Car Porters. They wanted to join the Canadian Brotherhood of Railway Employees, but the CBRE constitution specified that it was a white-only union. Their first attempt for acceptance in the CBRE gained them auxiliary status. The Brotherhood—due to the lobbying of three black men from the CNR's Montreal division and St. Joseph district alderman William Hushion—relented, and at their convention in 1921 the racial clause was removed.[139] The CBRE became the first Canadian union to remove their constitutionally defined racial barriers when the Order of Sleeping Car Porters was accepted in 1921 with full status as First Local no. 128 of the CBRE.

Nonetheless, this did not end the CBRE's discriminatory policy. The method of discrimination merely changed. All sleeping and dining car locals now had to maintain their separate identities within their own locals. For purposes of promotion there was Group I (white) and Group II (black). The seniority of sleeping car porters in Group II was never considered for supervisory jobs in Group I. The CBRE had established a unionized labour caste system based on race. In other words, "the company collaborated with the union to exclude blacks from higher paying [Group I] jobs."[140]

For black men in Montreal the CBRE recognition was a coup, signalling the beginning of the trade union fight between the rail companies and the porters. Despite the fact that the PMBA was not a union, the Charter of Local 128 bears evidence that there was a class awareness among these men. Their charter reads:

> While realizing that the workers can never obtain the full value of their labour in return for the work done under the present economic system, in which the natural resources and the means of production are privately owned, this organization shall aim, nevertheless, to obtain the highest wages and the best working conditions possible at all times; and furthermore, it shall endeavour to promote a thorough understanding of economics among the workers, in preparation for the emancipation.[141]

Local 128 of the CBRE in Montreal was already in place seven years before Randolph's Brotherhood of Sleeping Car Porters was formed in 1925 in New York. For the remainder of the decade, conflict between the Order and the CNR focussed on the formal racial categorizing of the porters, which began in

1926. The few men working in jobs other than portering were shifted into porter positions. Some were even kept on the payroll until porter openings occurred. The CNR was determined to maintain low wages for blacks on the pretext that blacks were qualified only for porter positions. Thus, more and more blacks turned to mutual benefit groups for support.

Two fraternal organizations emerged during the 1920s. The first in 1920 was an affiliation with the male-only sect called the Grand United Order of the Odd Fellows. Two years later the success of the Odd Fellows was a springboard for the Household of Ruth, the Odd Fellows women's auxiliary. The other fraternal organization introduced was the International Benevolent and Protective Order of Elks (IBPOE), better known as the Elks. They established the Pride of Montreal 678, as the Montreal affiliate was called, in 1926. Three years later the women's auxiliary, Beaver Temple 578, was set up. The membership of the Elks was mostly West Indian.

The mutual aid component of these fraternities was a very important reason for their success and longevity. Members were cared for when sick, visits were made to shut-ins, and sickness and death benefits were paid out to members. Their charitable work was directed towards the membership by offering scholarships to the children of members, as well as aid for special needs. The incentives for membership were high—mutual responsibility involved members' participation in charity and fundraising events. The monthly or bimonthly meetings were also strong attractions. Besides the business component, these meetings were major social activities. The fraternities held dances, teas, and other events to raise money for charity—special or emergency programs needs of the UNIA, Union Church, or the Negro Community Centre.

As the 1920s ended the UNIA was reeling under the scandal of Garvey's mail fraud and the embezzlement of corporate funds.[142] Interest in the UNIA waned, many units folded, and the community needed a new organization to replace it. Reverend Este, along with several American and West Indian members of Union Church, both women and men, began to investigate the possibility of establishing a community centre. Their commitment to social action was very strong and contacts were made with like-minded philanthropic whites.[143] Together they established the Negro Community Association in 1927 for the benefit of the whole community. Its stated aims were to alleviate social and economic conditions among Negroes in Montreal and to promote racial advancement. The Negro Community Association eventually became the Negro Community Centre and focussed on legal, social, housing, employment issues, and immigration problems.[144] This mandate complemented the religious/social offerings of the church. Activities were social, recreational, and eventually educational in nature.

Like the church, the only requirement for participation in the NCC was need, desire, and the annual membership fee. Although official membership for non-blacks was accepted only after World War II, in the early years anyone, black or white, who went to the NCC received help. The NCC was unlike any other group in the community. In its earliest days the founders of the Negro Community Association comprised its Board. The NCC soon applied to join the Council of Social Agencies and the Financial Federation of Montreal. One of the conditions for membership was an inter-racial board of directors. White and black members worked together. The NCC saw their mission as the improvement "of the conditions under which all people work, live and spend their leisure time," while seeking "a community morale which would bind all together, and give sustaining power to each individual and the community as a whole."[145]

One advantage of this broad vision was that it enabled blacks to raise funds in the greater Montreal community. Using board contacts, businesses were solicited, and the railroad companies became their major benefactors. After the NCC joined the Council of Social Agencies and the Financial Federation of Montreal in 1929, fundraising was regularized through the structure of this umbrella group of charities.

Several noted women of Union United Church—Clara de Shield, Hattie Olley, and Mamie Morris—were intimately involved in the establishment of the NCC. One of the first functions of the NCC was to bring women together to sew, knit, plan entertainment, or prepare meals for large community activities. Originally located in the basement of the church, the Centre comprised a school, play area and a common room. People contributed what they could, whether a nickel, some food, or clothing. Community support and gifts kept the Centre going. What was volunteered was given back twofold to meet community needs as the NCC strove to assist families and the youth in its immediate area.

The initial reaction to the NCC ran the gamut from indifference among Canadian blacks, support from American blacks, and opposition from West Indian blacks. The Americans who started the NCC already had some experience with similar organizations in the United States. They saw the Centre as a means of breaking down discrimination and allowing blacks to participate more fully in the life of the city. Canadian blacks seemed ignorant of the potential of the NCC. The opposition to the NCC from the West Indians reflected the same condition. They believed that the creation of such a Centre was:

> a frank admission of the inferiority of the Negro people in the competitive struggle. The words 'Community centre'…mean[s] only charity and 'the colored man…wants a job not charity'… 'the Commuity centre tends towards segregation and the Negro does not want segregation.'[146]

There was a fear that the Centre's presence would further isolate blacks from the white community and help and maintain prejudice and discrimination. It was not just opposition to the existence of the Centre. The active support of the railway companies was perceived as a threat to career aspirations and to their struggle as a race. Many felt that the companies supported the Centre because it would "prevent the Negro from getting into industry and if the Negro gets into industry the railroad will be at a loss to get porters."[147] The misconception of those who were against the Centre was that the railroad companies' endorsement was proof that the NCC supported the status quo. Others supported the NCC's concerns such as unemployment, which was seen as the cause of poverty, the breakdown of the family, and the social ills that plague a poverty-stricken and marginalized community. The NCC functioned as a representative for black Montreal, as a protector of human rights, and as a facilitator for black participation in all areas of society.

The mobility of blacks throughout the period they lived in the St. Antoine district paralleled the westward movement of the white population, although this was a slow process because of white resistance. The success of one black family eventually made it easier for others to follow. Today many elders of the black community still remember the name of the first black family to move onto a white segregated street or neighborhood.[148] Most blacks, particularly West Indians, were not content to stay in the deteriorating houses of the eastern section of St. Antoine. Even poor West Indians had had their own homes in the Caribbean and they did not readily accept the poor housing conditions of St. Antoine—they wanted their families to live in the better housing available west of Guy street. They were willing to endure snubs and insults in order to secure better housing.

This was not a struggle that blacks experienced alone. Abject poverty affected the poor—black and white alike—except that the climb out of cesspool conditions was quicker and easier for whites. As working class and poor whites moved westward during the 1920s, the flats and rooms they left became home for blacks who moved in to take their place.

By 1928 more blacks lived between Peel street and Richmond Square than in any other section of the St. Antoine district. Numerous black families who were attracted by the presence of the Eureka Association Inc. lived around Richmond Square.[149] The Eureka Association—a black real estate company incorporated by blacks—was one of many black business enterprises that flourished during the 1920s. Blacks purchased company shares and the money was pooled in order to buy tenement housing for rental to blacks. Constant and overt discrimination made apartment hunting a difficult and painful experience. A pamphlet entitled *Outlook*, published in 1917 by the Eureka Association is an indictment of the widespread discrimination that existed in Montreal:

> The housing situation among Negroes in Montreal gives no hope of improvement in the future. We are still forced to live in unsanitary houses, to pay high rentals and suffer humiliation from landlords whilst endeavouring to procure suitable residences. This condition will continue indefinitely unless offset by the development of the Eureka Association which is already for the task.[150]

In addition to Richmond Square, the Eureka Association purchased property on Plymouth Grove street in Ville Émard and land on the South Shore.[151] Despite a healthy bank balance of $20,000 in 1928, the Eureka Association was crippled during the Depression because it could not obtain financial backing from the banks. For the short period of its existence, the Eureka Association was one means for blacks to humanize the process of locating suitable living quarters.

Blacks lived in St. Henri as well as St. Antoine. There were black establishments such as a barber shop, a tailor, and the European Club between St. Marguerite street and the Glen Road. The presence of blacks in the extreme western section of St. Henri was due to its proximity to the CN and CP yards. The porters' school and the personnel offices were also located in St. Henri, and it was here, rather than Peel or Bonaventure, where porters checked in and out of Montreal on their runs.

Although a majority of blacks lived in the St. Antoine/St. Henri area, they also lived in many other districts around the island of Montreal such as Maisonneuve, Park Extension, Nôtre-Dame-de-Grace, Ville Émard, and Côte St. Paul.

Outside of St. Antoine the largest concentration blacks lived in the North End districts of Amherst, Delormier, and Christophe-Colombe—over 1,000 blacks in 1930.[152]However, in 1928 the only form of black social clubs outside the limits of St. Antoine was in Verdun.[153] A local newspaper article stated that the black population of Verdun in 1928 was already large enough to support the practice of a black doctor, Dr. Gaspar Phillips.[154] By the mid-twenties, due to the availability of reasonably priced, decent housing, blacks began to move into Verdun in increasing numbers—mostly renting in the centre of the city, although a few purchased homes.

Verdun was not the only area where blacks were buying property. The opening up of new areas on the South Shore permitted blacks to buy land in an area once called Mackayville, now part of St. Hubert. For those who wanted to own land, property on the South Shore was cheaper than on the island of Montreal. For fifty dollars an individual could buy a 100-square-foot lot, but for most, after the land was purchased it was a long process to build their home. Permanent dwellings were constructed during free weekends and holidays, so they took years to complete. In the meantime, tarpaper shacks were built and some families saved money by living in them during the summer and by growing food on their property.[155]

Renting homes outside the district was sometimes just as difficult. Westmount, immediately to the west of St. Antoine, was basically restricted. The few blacks who could live in Westmount usually were either light-skinned blacks who could 'pass,' or those with white spouses. Living in Westmount was considered a privilege because of its better schools and superior municipal services. Blacks ringed the city of Westmount and while living on the south side of St. Antoine street, they hoped to be able to eventually moveacross the street into Westmount. In one case, a black family paid $300 to obtain the key to an apartment on the north side of St. Antoine street, the Westmount side of the street. The family did not live there but they were allowed to use the address so their children were able to go to school in Westmount.[156]

The City of Montreal did not define black districts, nor was there any formal segregation of blacks in residential areas in the first quarter of the century. Still the majority of blacks lived in groups or clusters. This may be attributed to racial or cultural affinity, but economics was the fundamental reason in certain districts.[157]

There had always been a greater number of whites than blacks in St. Antoine. Yet the Montreal Negro district was so named because successive waves of white immigrants passed through St. Antoine, while blacks remained for generations. It was a stepping stone for many whites who stayed until they bettered themselves, then left for newer areas. Labour stratification and underemployment caused blacks to remain poor— they remained in St. Antoine and in other low-rent areas.

One of the exceptions was Pointe St. Charles. In spite of its proximity to the St Antoine district few blacks lived there. This was unusual considering that housing and employment patterns were similar. Even the fact that Pointe St. Charles was a predominantly English-speaking area was not a sufficient attraction. Elders in the black community have explained that racism was pronounced in the large Irish community. Even today, Pointe St. Charles has only a handful of black families.[158]

Those blacks who could afford to move from the St. Antoine district were hampered by the attitude of whites in Montreal. Landlords were reluctant to rent because they were "afraid that the psychological effect on other tenants would lower rental values."[159] Once a landlord was willing to rent, racist neighbours were the next obstacle to deal with. Fighting these attitudes was time-consuming, and not everyone was willing to endure them.[160] Blacks who could move were doubly penalized, since they were not able to enjoy the benefits they hoped their higher incomes could provide, and they could not always move where they wanted. Many were forced to settle for their second or third choice. Even remaining within the district was a risk. Often blacks accepted sub-standard accommodation because they were determined to do the renovation themselves. This sometimes led to their eviction when the landlord would rent the newly-renovated lodging at a higher rate to whites. This is a major reason for those who could afford to own property. The initial economic struggle would be offset by the security of being in their own home.

These factors contributed to the high mobility rate of blacks. It was not unusual for a family to move two or three times a year. The residential mobility of blacks in the early twentieth century, due to family resources, was strongly influenced by the attitudes and discriminatory practices of whites.

Thirty years of shared social experiences had created a new community. Three diverse groups were bound together by their common need for mutual support. The social fabric of the black community developed with the establishment of major institutions. This was a small and intimate community where family and work was interwoven with the cultural and social life of the community. The Colored Women's Club of Montreal began a pattern of helping to establish and sustain institutions.

Organizations aimed to bring all blacks together, and at to foster a culture of mutual aid. Although each organization stated and approached it differently, their aims were the same—to restore human dignity in fellow blacks, to alleviate isolation, and to help with physical and emotional needs. The Union Church was the first undertaking where race was the sole requirement for participation, and for many years it functioned as the community's only centre. The Universal Negro Improvement Association's racial advancement followed under the banner, "One God, One Aim, One Destiny." The popularity of this race advancement organization was an indictment of the racist environment which existed in Montreal. The community centre was the final achievement. The Negro Community Centre's inter-racial Board opened different outreach and funding possibilities and eased some of the Church's responsibilities by representing black Montreal, questioning the status quo, raising issues of human rights, and facilitating cross-cultural interaction. These different organizations were interconnected and had overlapping missions as well because many families participated in all three associations. The bonds were loose and interwoven. The most concrete evidence of this fact were the activities of Reverend Este—the tireless reverend was also chaplain for the UNIA and his presence there was a common sight. He was also personally involved in the creation of the NCC which was an initiative of his Church. Este represents the countless individuals who moved in and out of each community institution with ease and purpose to build and establish links in their community through their associations and interpersonal connections.

From 1897 to 1930 blacks in Montreal, like their brothers and sisters across the country, weathered virulent anti-black reaction from the government and fellow citizens. The tide of sentiment had turned. One hundred years earlier, during the 1830s as Fugitive slaves crossed into Beulah Land as free people, Canada had been a haven for American blacks. Yet, by the turn of the twentieth century Canadians made it very clear that Afro-American immigration was not what they wanted for their nation.

Undaunted, blacks worked to develop their communities. Demonstrating their willingness to be equal particpants in Canadian society, they made every effort to participate in World War I despite resistance from the Canadian Expeditionary Forces.

In varying degrees the three distinct cultures—American, West Indian, and Canadian—contributed to the success of Canada's railroads. Their labour was needed as the railroad industry supported the economic infrastructure of a young nation. In a racist and stratified labour market, black men were assigned to portering. Black ethnic divisions were accentuated by the railways' use of temporary migrant workers. The presence of temporary workers depressed wages and forestalled collective union action. The anti-union CPR sought to control their labour force through the PMBA. In the short term, however, the PMBA resulted in good employee-employer relations. But without union status most porters in this city continued to be overworked. They worked overtime without compensation, and were harrassed and fired without recourse. The CBRE's recognition for the Order of Sleeping Car Porters signalled the beginning of the trade union struggle.

Black women were also in the struggle. The transient work pattern of the railway took men away from home as often as three or four days a week, totalling perhaps sixteen days in a month. Maintaining the home alone, and caring for children in a sometimes hostile, definitely unhealthy environment, was a full-time occupation. When there was no other choice these black women used their homemaking skills in the homes of the wealthy and the middle class. Domestic paid work burdened many women and left little time to do their own homemaking. Fortunately, there were some women who had the time and opportunity to pool their resources and to respond to the needs of the St. Antoine Negro community.

The St. Antoine community survived. It eventually began to move west, and there were small concentrations of blacks established across the island. The next thirty years would bring greater changes which would affect where people lived, how and where they worked, and their status in the community.

CHAPTER FOUR

The Depression Years
[1930-1940]

The St. Antoine community was severely affected by the Depression in part because no other Canadian city suffered the same degree of unemployment as Montreal did.[1] The situation in the black community was serious—by March 1933, close to 80 percent of the Union United Church congregation was unemployed.[2] As most of the employable men worked for the CPR, this was the result of manipulation of the job market by the railway. Despite the existence of surplus labour in Canadian cities, CPR continued to import American workers. In 1931, CN informed CPR that they had sixty surplus porters, but CPR still hired from the United States, and ignored men listed in Canada's major unemployment depots, including Montreal. To support their action CPR claimed that hiring Americans was beneficial to Canada's economy in spite of high unemployment, because these new labourers purchased goods like uniforms in Canada. CPR's use of American labour ended in 1933 when the severity of the Depression was too much even for CPR to ignore.

Conditions for all blacks worsened as the Depression inflicted hardships on a community already economically deprived. Many families were forced to rely on the charity of those few who were able to hold onto their jobs, and on the tireless efforts of community workers like Reverend Este of Union Church and Reverend Ellis of the High African Methodist Episcopal Church.

Both men are both fondly remembered for their work during the Depression. Reverend Ellis is also remembered by whites in the district because following Sunday services he offered food to everyone. He established a soup kitchen and during the holiday season he gave to anyone who could demonstrate a need. Both churches canvassed for donations of food, clothing, and money for the needy.[3]

The loss of jobs often meant that rents could not be paid. This had an impact on community organizations—the Eureka Association folded when its black tenants could not pay the rent. Some blacks were forced to live on the street; others starved to death. In spite of church efforts, dislocation was inevitable for many blacks, and families who had moved away to other districts reluctantly returned to St. Antoine as their incomes dropped.

The Universal Negro Improvement Association, which was dependent on community funding, was hit hard as attendance and membership declined.[4] The fortunes of the UNIA probably had more to do with the parent organization's ongoing scandal and Marcus Garvey's problems, but the UNIA maintained a small, loyal following motivated by Garvey's belief in the importance of pride and self worth. One member reminisced that one day after hearing such inspirational history, he left Liberty Hall with the certain knowledge that no white person was better than a Negro. "In those days, that was revolutionary thinking."[5] Just how revolutionary was underscored when the UNIA encountered racism once more in St. Antoine.

In 1931 Liberty Hall had to be vacated and the UNIA planned to moved to Fulford street (now Georges Vanier). Neighbouring white residents protested, but after the UNIA obtained fifty signatures from residents who did not object the landlord relented, a lease was signed, and the UNIA moved in. The protest was co-ordinated by the district's alderman, Joseph-Maurice Gabais, who lived a few blocks west at 2407 Coursol street. Losing the fight to keep the UNIA out of his neighbourhood, Gabais, in the same fashion as Hushion, then tried to thwart the UNIA's efforts to obtain its annual dance licence. According to Gabais, the parish priest was dead set against having the UNIA in his parish. It was suggested that the priest threatened to work for Gabais' defeat in the next election should Gabias allow the license to be granted.[6] So Gabais would not be moved. This forced the UNIA membership to curtail certain fundraising plans, but despite Gabais' machinations they were determined to carry on with their regular activities, and be guided by the principles of living in harmony with their neighbours.

For the blacks who had purchased land on the South Shore the lack of money during the Depression cost some of them their properties. Some purchase agreements stipulated that a permanent structure had to be built on the land within a certain period of time—but without work this was not possible.[7] The vegetable gardens which provided food for hungry families and the shacks that people lived in even in winter were not considered to be adequate development by the mortgage holders.

The Depression took its toll on families as well. Where only one parent had previously worked, now women were also on the job market. Those unable to work the long, live-in hours of the domestics were sometimes able to find jobs in the garment industry which were accessible to blacks for the first time.[8] In families where both parents worked and were still unable to cope, children were placed with relatives, friends, or sometimes with private and public child welfare agencies.[9] Education was not free. School fees, books, and uniforms had to be purchased, which forced poor families to remove their children from school and send them to work. This perpetuated a cycle of poverty as illiterate youth found it difficult to obtain employment.

There may have been poverty of the pocket, but there was no poverty of the mind. Even during the depths of the Depression, drama and literary clubs continued to nurture young people, and by encouraging social contacts, volunteerism, and philanthropy, the whole community as a whole maintained a sense of belonging and self-discipline.

Many of the groups that had emerged and flourished during the 1920s adapted to the trying circumstances that blacks found themselves in. In 1933, the Colored Women's Club began a soup kitchen. Then in 1935, in response to tremendous need, the women raised money to purchase and maintain a bed at Grace Dart Hospital for blacks without the resources to pay for hospital admissions.[10]

Union United Church's Sunday School took pride in the fact that they had able and experienced teachers to teach elocution, public speaking, and drama. Many well-educated blacks contributed to the community's intellectual life and aided in the training of the children. These activities culminated in the production of many skits and pageants. In the community, learning to handle oneself in public was considered to be an important element of a child's education—they were skills which equipped youngsters for future leadership roles.[11]

Comportment and cultural values reflected upbringing and music was the touchstone. It was very much part of a healthy and loving family environment; one elder mused that "music was the way we showed love to each other because a house was not a home until there was a piano in it. Everybody played an instrument."[12] Music, with its roots in gospel, jazz, and show music, had always been an important aspect, both privately and publicly, of the black community.

During the 1930s, new groups focussed on the performing and literary arts emerged. The Excelsior Debating and Dramatic Club was formed in 1933 and was considered to be a revival of the intellectual and social ferment which had existed in the UNIA's heyday. Earl Swift was the driving force behind the Club.[13] He was a highly educated man who could find work only occasionally on the rails, but who "exposed the members to all of the education he had."[14] The Excelsior Club fostered public speaking through poetry readings, dramatic monologues, and critical forums.

The most ambitious artistic endeavour was the Negro Theatre Guild. Community elder Pauline Paris remembered that "it was formed because Don Holden wanted to put on 'Green Pastures'."[15] Elders in the community confirmed that the Negro Theatre Guild evoked a sense of great pride in its day and is still remembered fondly. A hallmark of perfection and excellence, the Guild mounted productions for nearly twenty-five years to acclaim beyond the environs of Montreal.[16] The fusion of its diverse talents, skills and energies coalesced into several mega-productions which launched stars, the brightest of whom was Percy Rodrigues, who went on to become a well-known stage actor. Each production called on the talents and time of many community members, including carpenters, electricians, seamstresses, and hairdressers. The Guild was a success because it created cohesiveness and was an outlet for creativity.

Creativity was expressed on a smaller scale as well. The Phyllis Wheatley Art Club focussed attention on black history and artistic activities, as well as responding to more practical needs.[17] The nine women of this club raised substantial sums for charitable purposes during the Depression. They managed to set up a scholarship fund for children who achieved high academic standing.

Philanthropic funding came in many guises. Julius Jones operated a soup kitchen, and his wife Maude Jones made an impact supporting the arts.[18] This wealthy black woman was a Christian Scientist and a staunch fighter against racial discrimination. She was an independently-minded person who sponsored and patronized many activities in the community.[19] It was also during the 1930s that Isabella Johnson, or Granny as she was called, maintained a country home in Plage Laval (now Chomedy, Laval). It became a drop-in centre for the whole community and people used country visits to Granny's as a special way to renew themselves. Each Sunday afternoon, groups of people would socialize there—the visits lasted anywhere from one day to the whole summer! This was special support that made a difference in people's lives during hard times.[20]

The Negro Community Centre began to come into its own during the Depression. In 1931 Dudley Sykes was hired as executive director, and he guided the community through the Depression and World War II. He was "terrific and liked children."[21] This is borne out by the range of child-oriented programing he instituted, including weekend and summer programs.[22] With regular funding from the city-wide Red Feather fundraising campaign and the various personal and business connections of the inter-racial Board, the NCC was not dependent exclusively upon its hard-hit community for income. During the Depression this mix of funding enabled the NCC to support programs that attracted an average monthly attendance of 1,000.

Because of the great needs of the Depression, fraternal organizations played a vital role in the community's stability. The responsibility for the welfare of members' families was taken very seriously. The Depression knit the community closer together and, despite the lack of new members, it was easier for people to transcend their difficulties and ensure the survival of their community.

Between 1930 and 1940 black immigration from the West Indies dwindled to a trickle and the composition of the district changed. The loss of jobs on the railways caused many Afro-Americans to return to the United States with their families after the Crash of 1929, exceeding a similar emigration which had occurred during the recession between 1921 and 1923.

Other factors also contributed to this exodus. Increased unemployment intensified racial discrimination, and with Canadian railway companies unable to hire, returning to the United States became a viable alternative for Afro-Americans. The Pullman Company, and even some Canadian rail companies were still hiring south of the border! Although the Brotherhood of Railway Employees was making great strides in the United States, in Canada the CBRE's policy and the non-union status of the PMBA resulted in little success at the CPR. Working in Canada was less attractive. The inauguration of Roosevelt's New Deal in 1932 promised increased economic opportunities, and the repeal of Prohibition in 1933 made America inviting again.[23]

Widespread discrimination in the United States had created two parallel societies. In their segregated society American blacks had their own black universities, businesses, lawyers, newspapers, hospitals, tradespeople, and labourers. But in Canada, where opportunities were purported to be equal, most blacks, regardless of skills, tended to fit into one level of society—*the bottom.*

Montreal blacks who wanted to improve themselves academically and professionally during the Depression found it was almost impossible because economic insecurity led to intensified discrimination. The white working class had always objected to blacks because they did not want blacks competing with them for jobs. During the Depression the professional white class began to exhibit the same type of behaviour. The handful of blacks who wanted to, or who could afford to become professionals were a threat. The white majority did not acknowledge blacks because they did not want competition in the shrinking job market.

Examples of blatant discrimination involving medical professionals in Montreal were recounted by women in the Hostesses' *Memory Book*.[24] The Superintendent of Nurses at the Montreal General Hospital, in a meeting with the Reverend Este of Union Church, informed him that although black nurses could train in Montreal, white patients would not allow black nurses or doctors to touch them, and they would never find employment, since there were not enough black patients in the hospitals. The few black families who could afford it sent their daughters to the United States where they studied and worked.

The lack of nursing opportunities was a major issue. The UNIA was also unsuccessfull in trying to place nursing students. The story of Vivian Layne-Sullen illustrates the entrenched and systemic discrimination that existed in Montreal.[25] Layne-Sullen had a brilliant academic record and wanted to become a nurse. The UNIA formed a committee to find a hospital which would accept her but were disappointed when the city's hospitals would not consider her. Este approached influencial Montrealers like John Cragg Farthing, the Anglican Bishop of Montreal, to request assistance. Reverend Este assumed the Bishop would demonstrate a desire to help, but the Bishop said that, "white people would not want black people to look after them. I can't help you. Try the United States."[26]

With no opportunities in Montreal, Layne-Sullen trained at the Lincoln School for Nurses in New York. One story was that she returned in 1935 and with UNIA assistance obtained a job in Montreal,[27] but it appears she found employment in New York. She achieved some measure of fame when she was the attending nurse for Martin Luther King Jr. when he was stabbed in New York on September 20, 1958.

As the Depression deepened, internship opportunities for black doctors in city hospitals ceased, and this situation was to continue until 1947. Montreal hospitals, unwilling to have black doctors and interns practice on their white patients, provided McGill University with the justification for tighter quotas for Canadian black students entering their programs.[28] Officially, private and public hospitals were open to black trainees and residents. At the beginning of the Depression, McGill's stance was that …

it was necessary to tell the coloured students that if the Hospital should at any time object at clinical work they will have to go to a Negro Hospital in the United States for this part of their course—but it has not been necessary to enforce it.[29]

An arrangement was made between the McGill Faculty of Medicine and Howard University so that black graduates could serve their internship in Washington, D.C. It was common knowledge in the community and a major disappointment that no blacks interned at Royal Victoria Hospital from the early 1930s until 1947.[30]

McGill University's position in the department of medicine was such that before 1930, the Bahamian legislature entertained a motion to censure and to remove McGill from the list of colleges at which Bahamian government scholarships would be available. The Bahamian legislature wrote McGill to enquire if they excluded black students at the university. The issue of racism in Quebec's university system was a topic of discussion between Premier Henri Bourassa and a Trinidadian newspaper reporter during the primier's trip to Trinidad in 1929. The premier was asked if coloured students were excluded from Quebec universities. Bourassa replied: "We French Canadians do not look at race problems from any other point of view than that of the French in France." Surprised to learn that there had been complaints of colour prejudice at one English university, he protested that "we have it not, as of course, you know." Bourassa was confident there never would be a complaint directed against French-language universities like Laval and University of Montreal.[31]

Medicine was not the only department with a quota at McGill. Long-time church worker Gwen Husband remembered that blacks were well aware of a colour bar at McGill. In the 1930s McGill's law school would not accept a black woman, Ivy Lawrence, who then went to England to study. The community was deprived of her expertise because when she returned, not having studied the Napoleonic Code which is practised in Quebec, and which is a prerequisite for practising law in Quebec, she settled in Ontario.[32]

Vivien Layne-Sullen and others like her who triumphed over the barriers were role models for the black community. Achievements of outstanding individuals were a beacon to the community in trying times. The day-to-day struggles of the Depression were put aside while blacks encouraged and supported the gifted and the brave.

The departure of black Americans from Montreal occurred at the same time as a record number of Nova Scotians and New Brunswickers arrived in Montreal looking for work. They were mostly young, poorly-educated men and women who possessed few marketable skills. New Brunswickers came to Montreal during the Depression attracted by the possibility of greater opportunities and expecting less prejudice and discrimination.[33] Black Nova Scotians, marginalized in Nova Scotian society, also wanted jobs, but they also sought an improved life in Montreal.[34] This influx continued throug the Depression, and at the same time Canada's racist immigration policy kept immigrating West Indian and American blacks low.[35]

During the 1930s another population shift began to adversely affect the black community—black women from twenty to forty years old began to outnumber black men.[36] This was related to American men leaving and to Canada's immigration policy. From 1897 to 1929, black American men who entered Canada generally outnumbered Afro-American women four to one, while West Indians entered Canada at an average rate of fifteen men to one woman.[37] Americans chose to live in Ontario six times more often than in Quebec, while West Indian immigrants showed no discernible preference between the two provinces.[38] Therefore, as American men left, West Indian men did not enter the country in sufficient numbers to replace them. The situation was exacerbated by two other factors. Approximately 40 percent of the black males on the island were either married to, or living with, white women.[39] When the American men left with their white wives, black women did not leave the city at the same rate as black men. When Quebec-born males reached employable age in the 1930s it was difficult to find work, even on the railroads, as scores of permanent workers were replaced in favor of temporary workers. And many of them left the city searching for gainful work.[40]

One other result of the departure by the Americans was the alteration of the railways' work force. By the mid-thirties there was an increase of non-American men seeking employment on the railways. By 1940, West Indian and Canadian men were displacing Americans and this trend would to continue into the 1940s. There were few jobs and the money was less than it had been in 1920s, but the railway offered some financial security which was non-existent in other jobs. This was counterbalanced by the inordinate amount of on-the-job harassment and management abuse. Blacks

recall the false accusations which arose out of minor personality clashes with white conductors who filed reports against them which resulted in several demerit marks or firings; conductors also filed reports claiming that porters became familiar with women passengers and this accusation was often filed against a porter who was close to retirement, as a means of getting out of paying him a pension. These conditions in particular caused porters to live in constant fear, and after a porter's arrival back home from many a trip he wondered how he made it without incident of some sort.[41]

The westward residential movement of blacks in Montreal continued during the Depression. As the older, easternmost part of the St. Antoine district deteriorated into a slum, absentee landlords sold the land to big businesses. Residents kept moving west as housing gave way to factories. Eventually Mountain street became the eastern boundary of the community. As it had been three decades earlier, the first blacks to move west were West Indians who could afford to move.

The alternatives to St. Antoine were still the southwest sectors of the island: Verdun, Ville Émard, and Côte St. Paul. They had attractive housing, a good image, low taxes, and the trickle of blacks into these areas did not threaten white neighbours. Few had the means, but many blacks were determined to break away from the negative social and economic labels that the St. Antoine district represented. For most it would take a world war, unionism, and urban renewal to shatter those labels.

The despair of the Depression was not unique to blacks in Montreal. Its impact was felt by everyone in the marginal classes of society. What was different during the Depression was the degree of hardship. In Montreal, living in decent conditions was the exception rather than the rule for the poor citizens. Financial insecurity and chaos forced people to move and caused the breakup of families. Despite this, people reached out to each other to maintain their institutions, and with determination they developed a rich cultural life.

The Depression caused significant changes to the population of St. Antoine and to the pattern of male employment. Along with the diminishing American population, the loss of Quebec-born males had serious repercussions because when they reached working age, jobs were scarce for even the elders of the community. The railroads ceased to be the primary source of employment and advancement—never again would the railroads employ 90 percent of the adult male population.[42] Even at the end of the Depression not everybody was working and the unemployed still had to find jobs. From a position of 'last hired, first fired' blacks continued to deal with the lack of long-term employment.

CHAPTER FIVE

The War Years
[1939-1954]

In direct contrast to the Depression, the war years brought many positive changes to Montreal's black community. Increased employment opportunities improved conditions for Montreal blacks and postwar benefits helped to reduce their marginal status. In the words of one community member: "Many Montreal blacks thanked God for World War II."[1]

The war brought about numerous changes that were to be of long term benefit to Canada's black population. Many of the negative patterns so evident in the 1930s were reversed. Social programs were, for the most part, created for all Canadians regardless of race or religion as provincial and federal governments began to take over more and more of the social services which had been provided by private organizations and institutions.[2]

In addition to factories which required workers, the Canadian armed forces desperately needed recruits. Despite this need, black Canadian volunteers were rejected by the armed forces solely on the grounds of race. British West Indian men who had come to Canada specifically to serve in the army were not allowed to enlist if they were black. West Indian students attending school in Montreal were not allowed into Canada's officer training programs because they were not considered British subjects. The bureaucrats interpreted British to mean white. White West Indians born in the Caribbean were able to immigrate with fewer problems and were met with more open acceptance by Canadians.[3]

West Indians were not the only blacks who could not find a place in the service. Frederick Phillips, the first black to be admitted to the Quebec Bar Association, remembers trying to enlist in the air force. His application was refused—the reason being that he did not have the necessary qualifications. Since he knew that former schoolmates were being accepted into the Officer's Training Program he continued to apply until he was finally admitted and assigned to general duties such as washing dishes.[4]

Unfortunately, Phillips was not alone—it was the usual pattern for black enlistees across the country. Blacks were never placed in the elite branches of the armed services. There were no separate black units in the army but blacks in regular units were often shunted into service jobs as cooks, orderlies, and batmen, with extended latrine and kitchen duties.[5] This stereotype, that the black man was suitable only for service work, or that black men were lazy and unreliable, kept them from positions of responsibility. Though there were no separate units or battalions for blacks, it was apparent as in the World War I, that the Canadian Armed Forces, particularly in Montreal, still suffered from negrophobia.[6]

In 1941 the the black community, under the auspices of Reverend Este, formally protested the racist policy of Canada's military. As the war accelerated and protest within the black community mounted, blacks in Montreal found it easier to enlist in Canada's armed forces. Their acceptance resulted in the long-term benefit which allowed ex-servicemen to bring their children to Canada after the war.[7] Black servicemen were now able to have their children join them in Montreal

As they did during World War I, the black community mobilized to aid the war effort—women volunteered at the Red Cross; fund-raising and clothing drives were organized, and and bandages were rolled for the men overseas.

As Canada's war effort intensified, the government took over the regulation of the private business sector because the war effort required "the most efficient use of the national resources in supplies and man power and productive facilities." This required central planning and direction of the national economy.[8] Federal wage and price controls and collective agreements resulted in uniformity in wages. Black workers were no longer subject to the whims of individual employers, and many blacks worked in jobs previously barred. For the first time employment opportunities expanded for blacks in Quebec.

Unemployment in the community was reduced when blacks enlisting in the army. Nearly all the porters who had been laid off enlisted.[9] In 1941 the percentage of black men working as porters hovered around 50 percent[10] and the majority of working black women worked as domestics. As the war began there were essentially two job options for black men—traditional railway jobs or military training.

For much of the 1940s the war dictated job availability and working conditions. It was one of the first opportunities for some blacks to use their education and demonstrate their competence. As in other communities across the country, there were job opportunities in Montreal which had not existed before the war, particularly in industry. However, these opportunities were still not generally available to blacks. Henry J. Langdon remembered that "[whites] were probably still wanting to be unscrupulous and prejudiced, but circumstances dictated otherwise…they had to look to others."[11] Blacks knew that it was necessity that forced white society to change the rules about hiring black people during the war.

There were hard won modest gains. In the fields of nursing and medicine, Reverend Este's persistant lobbying paid off during the war years. Queen Mary Hospital finally accepted black nurses as trainees and interns and the Montreal General Hospital integrated its training as well—accepting individuals for their skill, not their race or ethnicity.[12] In 1947, after many years, McGill and Howard universities ended their arrangement for Montreal blacks to intern at Howard.[13]

In Montreal's retail sector, employment was still closed to most blacks—at least to those who could not hide their blackness.[14] A campaign was launched by the Negro Community Centre to convince major retailers to hire blacks. Eaton's department store was the first major retailer to change its policy, though this occurred after the war. The turnabout happened as a result of the NCC's intervention over a candy bar carried by Eaton's called "Negro Snipes." The NCC board sent a letter to Eaton's expressing the community's displeasure that they were carrying a product with such a derogatory label. The letter also pointed out that despite the patronage of blacks, the department store did not have a single black on its staff. Eaton's agreed to withdraw the candy bar and agreed to hire anyone recommended by the Centre—and this eventually took place.[15]

Discrimination continued to be a barrier even within the National Selective Service which was established in 1942 as a government agency to control enlistment and all aspects of employment throughout the country. It had the power to tell people where and when they could work, which ensured that both the military and industry had appropriate manpower. From the beginning of the war until 1942 an office of the Department of Labour already functioned in a similar manner in Montreal. After 1942 the Montreal office of the Selective Service continued to accept racial restrictions from prospective employers and automatically placed blacks in menial jobs, regardless of their qualifications.[16] The Montreal director of the Selective Service was reported to have told community leaders that black workers were "unreliable, worthless," and of "low IQ."[17] In response the community held a mass meeting, after which a protest deputation was sent to Ottawa. As a result, the National Selective

Service placed several blacks in office jobs almost immediately. Even though the Service implemented less discriminatory employment policies, racial restrictions were still a reality.

The fact that blacks were a visible minority continued to prevent their access to a wide range of job opportunities.[18] Only a handful of black men, those who had highly skilled technical and engineering backgrounds, were able to take full advantage of the existing labour shortages[19] because such skills were scarce even in the white population. Older black men with less training remained in the pre-war service jobs of waiter, porter, doorman, and mechanic. In spite of the poor working conditions endemic to the railroad industry, many of the skilled and professional men who had worked on the railroad for many years would not accept alternative employment and risk losing their hard-won seniority and pensions from the railroad.[20]

Nevertheless, between 1941 and 1948 there was an overall change in the general character of black youth employment. The 1941 census recorded 1,718 blacks in Montreal. Of this total, 419 men and women worked in nearly eighty occupations.[21] The war years brought significant change. By 1949 there were between two and three thousand blacks engaged in a wide range of occupations, ranging from professional and junior executive levels, through artisan and clerical employment to semi-skilled and unskilled jobs.[22] This major shift was generational in nature and confined to two groups—black youths who came of age during the decade, and women in their twenties who were able to make the transition to new opportunities with greater ease than had their parents and older siblings.

Openings in women's employment were a result of the enormous, rapid growth in the service sectors during the war. White women who left jobs in hospitals, restaurants, and hotels for higher paid jobs in the war plants made room for black women. Some young black women got work in industries manufacturing goods for the war effort, including munitions factories and the office at the basic training army base on Hochelaga street.[23] This did not mean that there was less racism—these black women were hired for expediency's sake. It was becoming obvious that everyone's labour was required to win the war. As the war continued, the National Selective Service defined nearly every industry as an essential part of the war effort.

Comparing the income derived from domestic work with factory jobs clarifies why the factory and the assembly line were the preferred choices. Domestic workers' incomes ranged from $15 to $39 a month. Working conditions for domestics included sixteen-hour days, having to forego time off, receiving goods like clothing in lieu of of money, and being subjected to arbitrary demands. By contrast factory work permitted anonymity, a steady wage, and fixed hours. The freedom it represented was a boon for black women. Afro-Canadian feminist Dionne Brand asserts that black women "grabbed on to the industrial wage and hung on for dear life."[24]

Although black men were experiencing a changing labour market in the 1940s, the most radical shift from traditional jobs occurred with young women. Their transition from domestic work to factory and office jobs created a positive climate of change that affected the overall status of blacks.[25] On the average, only 14 percent of the black female population worked in 1941. West Indian and older Canadian black women made up the majority of domestic workers; Canadian-born men and women generally worked in factories. The persistence of several black women did lead to hirings in the retail industry and in the white-collar sector, which required more skill compared to washing floors and taking care of white babies, and higher financial status.

Some of the younger women, particularly teenaged girls, viewed the shortage of domestic labour as an opportunity to earn money. For a three dollars a week, one woman recalled, that at age fourteen, "I told them [employers], I didn't do ironing, the washing, walls, or windows." Giving half of what she earned to her mother was a source of great pride—being able to contribute to the household was a sign of adulthood. She had greater earning capacity than her brothers of the same age. Nevertheless, she said, "everybody knew the boys had to stay in school longer to get a decent job."[26]

The 1941 census established that there was a low, but statistically significant, positive relationship between place of origin and occupation.[27] Those who worked in the traditional service jobs continued to follow the pattern of previous decades: older West Indian and American men still tended to be concentrated in the railroad industry. The reason for the ongoing link between the West Indian male population and the railroad industry at this time was connected to colonial identity:

> The displacement of American sleeping car porters by West Indians is related to the claims the latter had as British citizens, at a time when such claims were being used to create employment opportunities for white British immigrants on the Canadian railroads. At one time considerations of citizenship overrode considerations of group experience, psychological aptitude, and training opportunities, in

determining who was to become a porter.[28]

As the war dragged on, the CPR reinstituted its policy of hiring Amercian blacks. CPR reasserted its previous anti-union stance by firing workers who tried to organize union locals. The men at CPR attempted to move the Porter's Mutual Benefit Association away from its role as a mediator and looked elsewhere for union representation.

In 1939, the chairman of the Porter's Welfare Committee requested that the American, A. Philip Randolph, now international president of the Brotherhood of Sleeping Car Porters, assist in organizing the buffet, sleeping, dining and parlour porters of the CPR. His efforts got a boost with the introduction of national wartime labour legislation that protected workers' rights to organize. Membership in the Brotherhood of Sleeping Car Porters union at CPR grew rapidly, from 153 men in 1942 to 620 members in 1943.

With factory work came union membership. During and after World War II the Canadian union movement experienced a renaissance, and unionism in Quebec improved the situation for Montreal's blacks. The gains were not only financial—from World War II onward labour unions led the fight against discrimination.[29] Blacks employed outside the traditional jobs gained union membership, obtained higher wages and increased job security alongside white co-workers. The most significant development in the union movement in this decade for blacks was the unionization of the Canadian Pacific Railway porters in 1942. The struggle for railroad unionization had been long and bitter, the resulting wage increases, though not immediate, were welcomed.

In 1942 the porters of the CPR were finally organized by the International Brotherhood of Sleeping Car Porters, an affiliate of the American Federation of Labour. The first contract between the Brotherhood and the CPR was negotiated and signed in February 1945. Arthur Blanchette, who was appointed International Field Organizer in 1947, was transferred to Montreal in 1949 to establish the Canadian headquarters in Montreal.[30] The activities of locals in Toronto, Winnipeg, Calgary, and Vancouver were co-ordinated from the Montreal office.

This arrangement formalized the long standing links porters had themselves developed across the country. Montreal, the national rail centre, had been the hub of porter activitity for decades. Porters on their runs moved from assignment to assignment, from station to station, getting to know each other and making contacts. This movement from east to west and north to south, contributed to the cosmopolitan, urbane outlook that blacks in Montreal were known for. Many accounts of these men and their families reveal that their stays in Montreal had been the final link in a chain that stretched the length of the rails.[31]

The three years between the establishment of the union and the actual signing of the contract with CP were stressful for many families. The company was opposed to union representation and tried to intimidate the organizers. The fear of reprisal hung over everyone's head, including the porters approaching retirement who felt particularly vulnerable:

> …although the porter's grievances were many and serious, the feeling persisted that portering was a good one and some porters were fearful of disturbing one of the largest employers of blacks. Some families, by the 1940s had been working with the CPR for two or three generations.[32]

The signing of a contract with CPR created a new work environment. Salaries jumped and overtime was recognized and paid. Porters enjoyed shorter work hours, an agreed grievance procedure and a greater measure of self-respect. A regular porter with a good run (meaning good tips) could adequately support his family if he did not have to support two homes, one in the United States and one in Canada. For individual black workers, unionization brought job security and less fear of suspension, loss of pensions, and offered the possibility of advancement. Blacks were better able to plan their futures. Job security meant better living conditions, savings could be used to rent or purchase better homes, to set up young married couples, and to finance the higher education of their children. The post-war redemption of war bonds was another factor that placed blacks on a more secure financial standing, and many were able to purchase homes outside the St. Antoine area.[33]

The unionization of the railroad workers in the mid 1940s in Canada also resulted in the creation of the Ladies Auxiliary of the Brotherhood of Sleeping Car Porters. The Canadian affiliates of this American organization provided women with a variety of social activities: games of whist, bus trips, the annual Mother's Day Tea, and the ever popular, New Year's Dance. The Ladies Auxiliary was a structured support group which helped women sustain each other during times when their families were affected by the vagaries of the railroad.

At this time Canada's immigration policy towards blacks was confusing and contradictory. Blacks were constrained by stringent entry requirements—there were preferred or appropriate job categories, and black women were channelled into domestic service because the war did not reduce the demand for domestic help. Some blacks worked for other black women who were working in the wartime industries. With a high demand for domestics which the local and European market was unable to meet, the federal government took steps to recruit from the West Indies.

At the same time the government was encouraging the immigration of domestics it discouraged the immigration of other female black labour. The inconsistency of the government's policy was evident in 1942 when the director of immigration, in response to a request for domestics from the Caribbean, wrote:

> Canada's coloured population has not increased rapidly and while that is to some extent due to our climate it is also due in no small measure to the immigration policy that has been pursued for years. The Immigration regulations reflect the immigration policy and while there is not what one would call a colour line, there is something that comes very close to a racial line...I did not make the regulations that I have to administer and yet I recognize that these were framed with the purpose of encouraging certain types of immigrants and discouraging others and among the latter is immigration of the negro race.[34]

Such anti-black statements and policies underscored the department's approach to black immigration in the forties and fifties. Prime Minister Mackenzie King stated in 1947 that immigration policy should exclude those people who would "make a fundamental alteration in the character of our population," and his Minister of Immigration, Walter Harris, interpreted this undesirable group to include "persons from tropical or sub-tropical countries."[35] The inconsistencies of Canada's policies continued throughout the years of conflict. Years later, in the mid-1950s, Jack Pickersgill, the Minister of Immigration, declared that Canada benefitted from the fact that "the West Indies gave to Canada a higher percentage of educated immigrants than any other country." This acknowledgement changed nothing about Canada's immigration policy until the sixties.[36]

The 1941 census recorded a black population of 1,157 in the three St. Antoine wards. The black population for all of Montreal was 1,718. These figures are not accurate because the census significantly undercounted the black population. However, the census figures do suggest certain trends. We can ascertain that about 25 percent of the black population lived outside of the St. Antoine district. The census also indicates that 29 percent of the blacks were Caribbean born, and sixty-three percent were born in Canada.[37] While there is agreement that the cultural composition of the community had changed, the figures pertaining to the American population are another example of inaccuracy in the 1941 census. From an estimated high of 50 percent in the 1920s, black Americans living in these wards were purported to make up less than ten percent of the total black population. Perhaps this was a result of the fact that Americans were not listed in the census because they retained American citizenship. Most blacks at the time agreed that the number of Afro-Americans in the community had decreased, but the figure of six percent was considered much too low.[38]

The war and the rapid social and economic changes that resulted during the 1940s had an impact on the type and number of blacks living in the city. During the 1940s and 1950s an elite, French-speaking Haitian group comprised of a few hundred or so began to settle in the province. It has been assumed that their assimilation was remarkably quick due to their high levels of education and the need for their skills in the medical, educational and technical fields.[39] By 1949 the English and French-speaking population in the greater metropolitan area was close to 3,000.[40]

The 1941 census indicated for the first time that the percentage of Canadian-born blacks far exceeded that of other nationalities in the Montreal black community and this trend continued into the next decade. Nova Scotians had become the third largest group in Montreal. In 1946 the community gained new members when some of the young West Indian men discharged from the Canadian Expeditionary Forces settled in Montreal.

Other trends of the 1930s continued into the 1940s. There were very few men between twenty-five and thirty-five, but there were a great many between forty and sixty.[41] The young men who left Montreal during the Depression exaggerated the male-female imbalance endemic to the community. In some cases, Montreal men enlisted in the United States because of recruiting obstacles encountered in Montreal.[42] Although the number of women nearly doubled relative to the number of men between the ages of twenty-five and thirty-five, there were still a relatively small number of women of this age group in Montreal.

There was an imbalance in the older population as well. From age forty-five onward, men outnumbered the women. Does this mean that women in the older age groups left the city? Did domestics who came into the city prior to the 1920s leave, or is this the result of errors in the collection of the census data? The answers are not readily available but we do know that the shortage of men before the end of the war was acute. The exodus of males during the thirties contributed to a loss of child-bearing women during the 1940s. Stories would suggest that in response to the lack of men in their own age group, women left the city seeking husbands—most moving to the United States rather than the Caribbean.[43]

Overall, the two largest age groups were those under twenty and those over forty. Of the under-twenty group, the majority were born in Quebec, ten percent elsewhere in Canada.[44] This suggests that during the war there were few West Indian or American-born black children living in Montreal. There is no doubt that many West Indian children had arrived with the immigration of hundreds of West Indians in the early post-war years. On average, West Indians immigrated to Canada at a rate of over 300 people a year during this period. Montreal was the destination of choice: throughout this period roughly 60 percent of the West Indian immigrants settled in the Montreal area.[45] Unfortunately children were lost in these statistics because immigration officers did not note age as a demographic characteristic, and interprovincial migration figures of West Indians would not have taken minors into account.

The small number of Quebec-born blacks between the ages of twenty and forty was probably due to the fact that the first four decades of the twentieth century were characterized by acute hardship, a significant transient population, financial insecurity, underemployment, and unsanitary conditions. Such conditions resulted in reduced marriage and birth rates. This situation was much improved during the 1940s.

Another significant change was in the local black student population which more than tripled between 1944 and 1948. Unlike their counterparts in the 1930s, these black students had better opportunities to finish their elementary education. It is difficult to determine whether the increase in the school population was the result of migrations of families to Montreal, the general improvement in the standard of living for the poor and working class blacks, or the result of the provincial Compulsory Education Act of 1943 which abolished school fees.[46] All of these factors contributed to the dramatic increase in the number of blacks in the schools. This change did not mean that the educational environment had improved for this generation. As one parent remembers, some students opted to quit high school rather than suffer the ongoing racist encounters with teachers and students.[47]

Black students during the 1940s were generally Protestant and English speaking. At this point the enrollment of black youths in the schools did not create severe institutional problems as the entrance of other immigrant groups coming into Quebec school systems did because blacks were numerically insignificant.[48] Those living in the West End went to one of three elementary schools: Royal Arthur, the English Protestant school; or the two English Catholic schools—the all-girls St. Anthony's, and the all-boys Belmont. Since the majority of blacks attended Royal Arthur, it became known as the Negro school.

Contributing to the improvement of blacks were the benefits acquired by black war veterans. The black veterans returned to take advantage of many privileges which other blacks did not enjoy. Extended university training at little expense, land grants, and loans for the purchase of houses helped blacks in postwar Canada to achieve a standard of living which most of them would never have been able to attain.[49] These material benefits which look so good on paper were overshadowed by the daily effects of racism on the lives of these veterans. Some of the gains made against discrimination in the military during the war were lost after the war. In Montreal white veterans did not want to associate with their black comrades. The Canadian Legion segregated its members and established Colored War Veterans branches as it had after World War I.[50]

By 1947 a significant change had taken place at the Negro Community Centre. The Interracial Board of Management had become a 20-member board comprised of ten black men, one black woman and nine whites.[51] The community had changed radically since the centre was established in 1927, particularly in the increase in requests for memberships from the non-Negro population of the community. As a result, in 1949 the Board agreed to delete the word 'Negro' from the by-laws, but not from the name of the centre. The emphasis on racial matters in the centre's programing gradually changed to an emphasis on the inter-cultural aspects of its program. Still, many members felt that retaining the word 'Negro' in the name was important for identity and that changing the name would be a move towards a loss of control.[52]

In July 1949 the Board of Directors chose their third executive director, Stanley Clyke, originally from Truro, Nova Scotia. An intelligent, educated man, Clyke was passionate about the youth and the elderly, and made regular visits to shut-ins. Although Clyke was committed to change, he demonstrated great respect for his predecessors who had worked so hard building and helping the community.[53] He trained in social work at McGill University, and the new programs he instituted reflected his background—the centre's group activities focussed on aiding the individual. This-social work approach was adopted by the Board of Directors and in the NCC's 1952 annual report, Clyke outlined what this strategy would mean:

> Besides a meeting place for community activities, the NCC is a social agency concerned with adjustment of people to each other and to their environment. Because social agencies are designed to deal with people's feelings, attitudes and behavior, to interpret values, rights and privileges, to promote personality change, to develop citizenship responsibility, our work here with groups becomes an increasingly important tool in human growth and development.[54]

The incorporation of these modern social techniques did not sever the NCC's ties with Union Church, but marked the beginning of an informal dual leadership. For the next several decades Stanley Clyke led the community in partnership with Reverend Este—each with his own mandate to improve the conditions of their people. As a new world opened up for the community in this postwar period, Clyke and Este were called upon to create programs, sometimes jointly, that were responsive to these changes.

In keeping with Clyke's vision the NCC increased its committment to social action. At his urging the NCC received its Letters Patent in 1949. As an incorporated body with by-laws and a charter it was now able to respond to the greater community and to define itself as the clear representative of all blacks. Its main functions, as outlined in the NCC's Constitution and By-laws, were to "provide facilities and leadership for educational and recreational, and health opportunities for members of the community it serves; and to encourage a better spirit of understanding between races."[55]

With new members, and the adoption of new approaches, the mandate of the centre was broadening as it responded to the changing St. Antoine community.

Two new branches of the Elks became active in the black community during the war years. Elk's Victory Lodge #1088 Inc. was established in 1941, and three years later it received permission from the parent organization in the United States to start a women's auxiliary called the Eastern Temple #779.[56] The humanistic precepts of "Elkdom"—brotherly love and charity, encouraged blacks to join for protection, mutual aid, and recreation. More than a social venue, their social activities were designed to raise money for worthy causes.

By establishing fraternities, blacks discovered that there was strength in numbers, and that the existence of the organization increased their credibility outside the black community. The federal government favoured immigrant sponsorship backed by the resources of the fraternal associations. One woman sponsored thirty immigrants on the basis of her membership in a fraternal organization.[57]

The UNIA began the decade mourning the death of their leader, Marcus Garvey, who died June 10, 1940. The question of his successor created serious divisions and diminished unity within the global organization. The Montreal Chapter was determined to support Garvey's family and focussed much of the organizations energy on the rehabilitation of the UNIA. The UNIA's worldwide internal power struggles in the early 1940s involved many factions and led to charges of corruption. To quell the revolt that followed Garvey's death the Montreal division supervised the Rehabilitation Committee of the parent organization. Contact with other divisions encouraged the Montreal group to maintain ties with the greater UNIA organization. In Montreal the UNIA's summer activities were suspended during the war years but after the war the UNIA continued their youth and business programs and new continuing education courses were launched. Even these endeavours could not stem the inexorable decline of the organization. With Garvey's death the UNIA became a social club, far removed from its past race activism.

Another lasting legacy of the war was the new opportunity to improve living conditions in the black community. By the end of the decade many blacks had taken advantage of veteran's benefits and either bought land or a home, or moved into rental property designated for veterans and their families. Veteran's housing also played a crucial role in determining where blacks would settle, in and around the island, into the 1960s. For some blacks improved mobility meant moving from the old, eastern part of the St. Antoine district into the better housing west of Fulford Street (now Georges Vanier).

In the forties, the West End was the more familiar name for St. Antoine, which related back to a time when St. Antoine was the western extremity of the city. Unlike St. Antoine, which took in all of St. Henri, the designation West End meant the area west of Old Montreal to Atwater avenue.[58] Between 1931 and 1941 the total population of blacks and whites in the poorest, easternmost St. Joseph ward in the West End had decreased by almost five percent. The movement west affected all residents in this ward. While French-

Canadians and Irish Catholics were still in the majority, the proportion of French-speaking people in the ward increased from 42 to 46 percent. Conditions for francophones had not improved much;[59] they were not in a position to move from the ward, and blacks were in the same situation. Sixty-six percent of all blacks enumerated in the 1941 census lived in the West End. This was a reduction from the 1920s where St. Antoine was home to 90 percent of Montreal's blacks. Despite the ravages of the Depression the number of blacks who had moved outside of St. Antoine increased steadily.

In the 1940s, 84 percent of the blacks in the West End lived within the area bounded by St. Antoine street to the north, the CNR tracks to the south, Versailles to the east, and St. Martin street to the west. The population shift westward was almost complete. By 1941 the census enumerated only two blacks in the area that was once the original porters' quarters—the old subdivided homes of the first blacks in the nineteenth century.[60]

Blacks concentrated in the eastern St. Joseph ward and the central ward of Ste. Cunégonde were salaried and self-employed. Most depended on black clientele for their employment. Those who earned higher incomes generally lived in St. Henri ward. The poor who worked for subsistence wages in the white community, were scattered through all the three wards of the West End. The differences in income among black workers was great—ranging from two to thirty-six dollars a week.

Blacks lived in the West End for of a variety of reasons. It was close to work and to the major black institutions and not far from uptown (Ste. Catherine Street), downtown (Nôtre-Dame and the market), and good transportation. The people living near the railroad terminals could not afford the higher rents and increased transportation costs of living in more desirable neighbourhoods because they did not have steady employment, or they had low-income jobs.

Many porters had homes in areas such as Verdun, far from the railway yards. Despite the fact that housing was better in Verdun, and in other areas south of the tracks, it was considered an undesireable location—moving there was not considered an improvement, like moving west or north of St. Antoine would be. Any move north of the escarpment was an improvement, and anything south a loss in status, so in the twenties and thirties Westmount was considered ideal.[61] Ville Émard had the same low status as Verdun. Other up-and-coming districts were Lachine, Montreal East, and the South Shore. Blacks, those few who could afford to, were slowly moving into Nôtre-Dame-de-Grace, Montreal West and Côte St. Luc.

During the 1940s and and into the mid-1950s, the district of Nôtre-Dame-de-Grace (NDG) was considered a better area to live in than the West End, Verdun, or Ville Émard. This sentiment was not limited to the black community. Writer Terry Copp who grew up in NDG, fondly referred to it as "that refuge for those who made it."[62] This sentiment was shared by the white English-speaking working class population at the time. Blacks struggled to move into these districts for the status that it offered. However, discrimination in these better districts was widespread, ensuring that for a long time to come the districts in the southwest sector would continue to have more black residents than those in the northwest.

After the war Montreal experienced a housing shortage. In some cases, due to escalating rents, it was cheaper to buy homes than to rent, so inexpensive property on the South Shore again became attractive again. Homes...

> were considered security against racist landlords and high rents. Some women who married in the 1940s immediately bought land on the South Shore and on weekends and layoff periods they would build homes. In the meantime the newlyweds would live at their in-laws until they could move into their new homes.[63]

Even poor families tried to pool money to buy a home if they could. Blacks wanted to avoid the frustrations of renting inadequate housing and the stigma of living in the West End. Remembering the homeless of the Depression increased their determination to move out of the St. Antoine area. What was only a dream in the thirties became a reality in the 1940s.

At the other end of the scale were those blacks who wanted to stay or to move to the West End. Many were poor and living in districts adjacent to St. Lawrence boulevard—the major reception neighbourhood for immigrants before the war. Cheap rents, which reflected the quality of the housing, was its major attraction and St. Lawrence was seen as a stepping stone to better neighbourhoods. Compared to St. Lawrence, housing in the western section of the West End around Ste. Cunégonde was an improvement.

This was the case for blacks from the Maritimes and for a number of newly-arrived West Indians. With their meagre resources they could not afford to move from the St. Lawrence area. It would take several years, complicated by the city-wide housing crisis, before they could make the move into the West End.

There were a small number of blacks who chose not to move from of St. Antoine even when they could and owned their own houses. After two or more generations they felt at home there.[64] In later years, when they put their houses on the market, they would try to sell to another black because they remembered how difficult it had been to purchase a home when you had a black skin.[65]

Although the overwhelming majority of blacks in Quebec lived in rented accommodations, their desire to own a home encouraged the growth of another unique real estate broker. The Spathodia Association, formed during the 1940s, was a community organization that did what the Eureka Association had done in the 1920s. Members of the Association started buying property in Ville Émard so that blacks could build homes there. One of the main reasons for the re-emergence of a realty group like Spathodia was that, except for veterans housing, blacks in the 1940s usually had to put a double down payment on a house that they wanted to purchase. This discriminatory practice which had previously kept home ownership out of the reach of all but upper middle class blacks.[66]

The movement out of the West End district towards home ownership in Ville Émard was so noticeable that in 1960 the Negro Community Centre's *Board of Directors Report* stated that:

By 1949 the movement of Negro families from what was considered the Negro district became an important factor in the social service functions of the Negro Community Centre. Although there has never been any actual Negro district in Montreal...most...found this area close to their work...after World War II, Negro families moved to suburban and rural districts in and around the Metropolitan area to such an extent that the Board of Directors of the Centre expressed some concern about the future location of the Centre.[67]

From 1939 to 1954 life started to improve for Quebecers. Government legislation provided protection against discrimination in some areas, and brought economic benefits to most Canadians. A few of the benefits which affected blacks included the federal Unemployment Insurance Act of 1940 that gave employees financial protection against involuntary unemployment, the Compulsory Education Act which made education accessible and mandatory for all youngsters in the province, and the Family Allowances of 1944, that provided monthly payments to all mothers.[68] Quebec blacks were also able to take advantage of an improved economic climate which the war had created.

The nature of work changed and women could more easily work outside of domestic service. Prices rose, but on the average, so did incomes. Many blacks remained in the poorer housing of the predominently French and Irish Catholic West End. These wards were characterized by low incomes, low rents, a high birthrate, high death rate, and the prevalence of tuberculosis. Still, the two-income family's increased financial and job security raised the expectations of a large segment of the black population. Improved housing also increased because of the federal government's veteran's housing programs.

However, the most important change that World War II brought to the lives of Quebec blacks was the organization of unions. Aside from the obvious benefits of decent wages and job security, unions across Canada were catalysts for human rights activism and anti-discrimination movements. In Montreal black labour activists, mainly those involved with the railway unions, struggled to establish anti-discrimination legislation. In the 1950s, blacks in these unions played a large part in the removal of barriers to West Indian immigration—from 1946 to 1950 there were 947 black arrivals, less than half of one percent of the total number of immigrants entering Canada.[69] The results of the half decade following the war demostrated that lobbying and mobilization would be necessary.

Better employment opportunities during and after the war permitted many blacks to change their lives. Overall there were greater improvements in living standards and in education from 1939 until 1955 than there had been since the beginning of the black presence in Montreal. As conditions continued to improve blacks increased their buying power and their sense of security. Decreased housing discrimination in some sectors made it possible for families to move out of the West End and begin the exodus to the suburbs. The result was a new awareness of community and new associations to represent it.

CHAPTER SIX

The Domestic Scheme
[1955-1965]

The period from the mid-1950s to the mid-1960s was one of consolidation for Montreal's black community. The standard of living and job mobility increased dramatically. It was also a period when community associations and human rights organizations proliferated.[1] Changes would occur in the late 1960s as the result of immigration from black and developing countries which would irrevocably change Montreal's black community.

Like many black communities in North America, the differences between the old and the new blacks were becoming apparent. In Montreal old stock blacks were those who had survived the First and Second World Wars and the Depression, and who ascribed to the values and ways of an earlier time, regardless of their ancestry.

A new wave of post-war immigrants, arriving in relatively prosperous times, helped to repopulate the black community and make up for losses incurred during the Depression and the war years. These new immigrants brought different values which did not quite mesh with Montreal's old stock black community, and eventually, as their numbers increased, these newcomers used their energies to refashion old community associations and create new ones.

New immigrants, mostly from developing countries, were not attracted to the Union United Church, and instead jointed Anglican, Baptist, and Catholic churches in increasing numbers. For these poor immigrants, Union United, the only black church on the island, no longer represented racial pride, but instead stood for integration, and the fellowship of all peoples. This was an anathema to many of the new immigrants and a sign of "the weakness of Oldtimer immigrants and Canadian Negroes."[2] The existence of a black church emphasized negritude and a lack of and social mobility—and they wanted to avoid this church at all costs.

Union United Church had 300 participating congregants in 1964, 60 percent of whom were women. Only 20 percent identified themselves as West Indian.[3] Union United had become the church of the old stock families whose lives had shaped the church for decades.

In some ways the same could be said about the Negro Community Centre, except that it was undergoing profound structural changes which would affect its membership and activities. The centre provided a broad range of services and activities that included after-school programs, a dental clinic, counselling, music, crafts, movies, and parties. All of the programs took place in two rooms behind the Union Church and in the gymnasium of Royal Arthur School, which the centre rented several nights a week. There was not enough space to accommodate all the programs. The lack of space came to the attention of the Montreal Council of Social Agencies as a result of a study conducted in 1955. This precipitated a merger of the membership and programs of the Iverley Community Centre, an English-speaking white community centre, and the NCC. With support of the white members of the NCC Board, it was agreed that the NCC would take over the building that was owned and used by the Iverley Community Centre. The Negro Community Centre Inc. took possession of the building at 2035 Coursol, situated in the centre of the community, in July 1955.[4]

After the charter was formalized, the membership of the NCC visibly changed. In 1954, just before the merger only ten percent of the NCC membership was white—immediately after the Iverley merger the ratio was 50-50. By 1962 white membership had dropped to 35 percent of the total membership, but they still had significant influence. The black majority who were members lived mostly in the West End. Steps were initiated to adopt "Interracial Community Center" as the official name, but on September 11, 1956, at a membership meeting, this proposal was once again defeated.[5] With the loss of white membership over the next five years the total membership decreased and in 1962 there were 904 members. The NCC's role in the 1960s was similar to what it had been a decade earlier. As Stanley Clyke elaborated, it was still

one of broad training; [using] available resources for educational purposes; [creating] learning experiences in which the people we serve act maturely and responsibly in the exercise of becoming good citizens. If we have to use social activities to achieve these goals, then we use them.[6]

A program for hungry children was instituted shortly after the move to Coursol street and the children from nearby elementary schools went to the NCC each weekday for a hot lunch.

The merger with the Iverley Centre highlighted, for the first time, that the NCC's mandate included a community centre, and that it was an island-wide black resource. Membership was now open to blacks living anywhere in the greater Montreal area and non-blacks who lived within the east-west boundaries of Windsor (Peel) and Atwater, and the north-south boundaries of St. Catherine and Nôtre Dame.

The merger also increased the NCC's contacts with other community agencies and with service clubs such as the Kiwanis Club, the Canadian Program Club, the Northmount Lions Club, and the Jewish Junior Welfare League. From these groups and the efforts of others, the money was raised for a gymnasium. The inter-racial, integrationist stance of the NCC began to attract the attention of many people. In 1957 a CBC movie, "A Community Within," portrayed the members using the many programs and services of the Centre. It was aired nationally and increased the exposure of the NCC.[7] Under Clyke, the NCC's approach to programing, and its philosophy reflecting new social work methods was becoming a model for other community centres.

The Universal Negro Improvement Association had, for all intents and purposes, ceased to operate after World War II. Most of the membership was old—members had passed away and those remaining did not have the energy to sustain the organization. Young members of the organization

> tended to look upon the UNIA as a club for senior citizens . . . there was no conspiracy, as it were, to keep out young blood...The leadership continued to view the problems...in precisely the same manner in which Garvey had perceived them.[8]

Society had changed but the moribund leadership of the UNIA was ill-equipped to meet new challenges. The first and most important challenge was the concept of integrationism which was sweeping North America, and Montreal was no exception.[9] For many blacks and whites integration was now the solution to the race issue and it became the focus of their activism. For supporters of the NCC and other like-minded people, the community had not ended in its fight for acceptance—it had just changed its tactics. Montreal's Garveyites, however, remained unrepentant about the UNIA's undisguised and militant philosophy of the primacy of race. They did not believe that society could ever move towards an integrated colour-blind society. Sticking to this unpopular philosophy caused the fortunes of the UNIA to continue to fail.

In 1951, reacting to the pain and frustration of those around him, Donald Moore created the Negro Citizenship Association (NCA) in Toronto.[10] Within two years a branch organization was set up in Montreal. This was a social and humanitarian association which fought against discrimination and which was dedicated to assisting black West Indian immigrants and their relatives. The Negro Citizenship Association, particularly the Toronto chapter, formed a coalition of labour, church, and fraternal groups to lobby the federal authorities. With immigration as its focus it is not surprising that the many of the groups that worked with the NCA had substantial black representation. The NCA created a cadre of members that was familiar with the intricacies of Canada's immigration system, and they advised immigrants how to complete forms, how to deal with immigration officials, and how to circumvent the bureaucracy where possible. In 1955, when the federal government created a new immigration program for domestics, the NCA redoubled efforts to have immigration processing dealt with fairly. This became the focus of the NCA struggle for several years.

Around 1960 the NCA responded to a growing tide of racist incidents in Montreal and expanded its mandate to include fighting job discrimination. The aim of the NCA and a coalition of community groups was to lobby for provincial legislation for fair employment practices which corresponded to the legislation in Ontario. In Quebec the principal job related issue was tied to the racial integration of the taxi industry in Montreal.[11]

Regardless of its battles against racism, it was not easy to maintain the NCA. The Montreal division had difficulty recruiting and keeping members. The community, though aware of the organization, was not willing to significantly support the NCA. At its most committed period there were fifty active members and the organization was in constant threat of collapse.[12] At its zenith in the mid-sixties, the NCA produced *Expression* a local student-created newspaper. *Expression* was not a community news publication—its focus was national and it addressed the federal government's immigration policy. Created by students, it catered to progressive postgraduate students who took pride in their black consciousness. Seven issues were published. The writing was serious with footnoted articles of analysis and criticism of government policies which affected blacks.

At the beginning of the sixties the black community's institutional landscape

underwent fundamental changes, due in part, to the emergence of island associations created by blacks from West Indies which dealt with the basic needs of
the new black residents to Montreal. Their main objective was adapt to the
new Canadian situation. Accommodation became a primary ideology for a
broad spectrum of Montreal's resident West Indian population.[13] These island
groups helped members find jobs and survive the cultural shock of their new
environment. The members visited people who were sick and conveyed
messages to relatives back home, thus strengthening links between families
and friends here and abroad.[14]

The first island association was the Jamaica Association in 1962, which
was followed by the Guyanese Association in 1963, the Trinidad and Tobago
Association in 1964, and then the St. Vincent Association in 1966. Despite
their popularity in the 1960s island groups were not completely accepted.
Within some intellectual circles students denounced and ridiculed the whole
concept of island associations. It was during this same period that black students
were developing the basic concept of blackness—of being perceived as being
black regardless of country of birth. The students felt that the racial problems
every black person experienced bound them together and were not based on
place of birth. They believed that one voice and a united strategy was the best
approach to solving problems within Montreal's black community.

Immigration issues continued as one of the most important issues in the black
community. Racist immigration policies of earlier governments continued into
the immediate postwar period. Official West Indian immigration to Canada
had not exceeded 3,400 between 1905 and 1955, and until 1955 there were
only 7,000 West Indians in all of Canada.[15] As late as 1950, after Canada's
Department of Citizenship was created, "white if possible" still remained the
rule for selecting potential immigrants. Even the new Immigration Act of 1952
did nothing to demonstrate that Canada was willing to accept non-whites on
the same basis as white immigrants. Prospective immigrants could be refused
for reasons of nationality, citizenship, ethnic group, or origin. After decades of
being shut out, blacks here and abroad were forced to act against Canada's
restrictive immigration policies.

In 1953 pressure from Caribbean governments forced Canada to drop
"climate unsuitability" as a criterion for refusing immigrants entry into the
country. The position of the Canadian government towards the immigration
of non-whites reflected the discriminatory attitudes and racist behaviour of
Canadians. As late as 1955 legislators such as the Minister of Immigration,

John W. Pickersgill, stated categorically that because the nation preferred whites, "the policy of preventing or strenuously limiting immigration from non-white countries would continue."[16]

Considering the realities of the booming Canadian economy and the needs of the population, this desired policy could not always be adhered to. During the post-war period, when servants were in demand, the Canadian government recruited white women in Europe. But in 1949 when their were not enough white European servants available to meet national requirements, black Caribbean domestics, already working in England, were targeted. However, they did not remain domestics for long—they moved on to other jobs which could be termed institutionalized domestic work—nursing attendants, health care aides and other service sector jobs. Though their education was not recognzied, these women studied nights and on their days off to qualify for these new jobs. As a result an ongoing loss of servant labour persisted in Canada. The Domestic Scheme was created by the federal government in 1955. Under Canadian government classification, European nannies were now replaced by black domestics, and black domestic immigrants were now under contract for a pre-determined period. The contract conditions were difficult but immigrants wanted employment so Canada was able to capitalize on the strong demand, particularly from middle-class black women immigrating directly from the West Indies who wanted to escape the depressed economies of the region.[17]

Then in 1960, as England was undergoing a major overhaul of its labour and immigration policies, the Canadian government extended the criteria to allow the admission of hundreds of skilled black workers. Many blacks came directly from England as job opportunities there closed, and Canada opened its doors to accommodate skilled workers into its own booming, labour-strapped economy. The process became easier in 1962 when racial criteria were removed from immigration policies. Independent immigrants, having no relatives in Canada, were admitted based on their capacity for self-reliance and potential productivity and contribution to Canadian society. This real change in Canada's immigration policy also stimulated an increase in direct West Indian migration. Unfortunately this shift in policy did not help the thousands of blacks who were already in the country and who wanted to bring their relatives to join them. Their histories in Canada were not considered, for unlike the independent immigrant, sponsored immigrants were subject to restrictions. On the strength of these two regulatory changes, up to 1,000 government-sponsored adults per year entered Canada between 1960 and 1967.

These new regulations emphasized education and skills. For the first time in Canada's history racial discrimination was not included. The change was called as a major breakthrough by non-whites living in Canada and was seen as a watershed in Canada's immigration policy. This liberalization of immigration regulations was an improvement, but the anticipated increase in immigration did not occur. Non-white immigration increased from less than four percent of the total in 1961 to nine per cent by 1965. The new regulations did not solve the problem of subjectivity—individual immigration officials still had the final say about what skills and what education were desirable, and the ultimate decision on who would enter the country. Ironically, Canadian officials concentrated on skill requirements knowing (or with the expectation) that immigrants would be directed into unskilled jobs. The skill and education requirement was used to severely curtail black admissions into the country.

Between 1961 and 1965, 11,835 West Indian immigrants entered Canada—about 2.5 percent of the immigrantion total.[18]

By 1955 Canada had processed 25,000 European domestics.[19] As conditions improved in Europe, the supply of these preferred domestics diminished. Faced with continuing demand for household workers, the government signed bilateral agreements with Jamaica, Trinidad, and Barbados in 1955 and established the Domestic Immigration Service.[20] Despite the small numbers of West Indians who entered the country under this program, many Canadians were still concerned that too many blacks would be admitted. So "the domestic scheme began very cautiously in the fear of upsetting the character of the Canadian people" with only twenty domestics arriving in Montreal that first year. From 1955-1962 only 2,690 English speaking West Indian women emigrated from the Caribbean islands.[21] These hand-picked women were sponsored by their governments and by the Canadian government. Most had to be retrained to work in domestic service because many came from the Caribbean urban middle-class and had been educated for clerical, teaching, and nursing positions.[22] Though their high level of education was not a consideration for their integration into the labour market once in Canada, the federal government was certain that the chance of the women leaving domestic employment for higher wages in industry was small. This was because the opportunities for black women in industry were limited—and the government belived they were best suited for domestic service.

Forty percent of the domestics had received matriculation or high school leaving diplomas, and over half the domestics had some secondary education. One third had additional technical or commercial training. In the West Indies the women had had good jobs and their children were well educated. Only 12 percent had worked as domestics prior to emigrating. Some gave up comfortable jobs as teachers, teachers' assistants, nurses, nurses aides, secretaries, and clerks, to come to Canada to work. Others had grown up in middle-class homes that even had servants. Considering their social standing, the incentives to migrate must have been powerful.[23]

The women who came to Canada as domestics did so primarily as a means to escape boredom, and to travel. Their middle-class, urban backgrounds had exposed them to cosmopolitan values, and they

> had built up glorified expectations visualising a country of great wealth, where work and life would be easier and where it would be simple to advance financially. They were unprepared for their working conditions…and for the length of time involved in further studies and training…half expressed disappointment in the Canadian people…finding them unfriendly, ignorant and prejudiced.[24]

For a minimum of one year the women were essentially indentured servants for well-to-do Canadians. Technically, after one year the domestics were free to remain in Canada to pursue other careers or to continue their education and training, but after their first year few had the opportunity or the time. The work they were required to do was a shocking experience for many; they were expected to perform all of the domestic chores, including cooking, cleaning, and the care of children. Their adjustment to Montreal was even more difficult because they found "no group with which to identify, their numbers [were] insufficient to create any in-group within themselves, and society… [was] little concerned with their absorption." Seventy-two percent were lonely, unhappy, disgruntled, obsessed with their future, and hoped to return home. [25]

The women were experiencing the downward mobility experienced by many immigrants. However, there was a stronger dynamic at work because they were not ever accepted by Montreal's West Indian community. Middle-class blacks saw the domestics as a blight in their community: "They come from the lower classes and they have lost us face…A domestic could not be a friend of mine..they are not typical; they are not the best we have to offer" The fear was that "Canadians will clump all West Indians into one category on the basis of color and treat them accordingly."[26] What this middle class, white collar worker did not comprehend was that with or without domestics, this would have happened anyway. The porters' experience years before had made that clear.

Men in particular, looked down on the domestics, regardless of their background. Domestic service in West Indian culture was perceived as a sign of low class standing. There is little wonder that these women felt no sense of belonging or acceptance. They were invisible in their own community, and by the very nature of their work—with its long hours—made it impossible for them to participate in community events. This exaggerated the isolation that most immigrants experienced.[27]

Community groups attempted to counter their loneliness and reduce their isolation. The NCC responded by supporting the establishment of the Pioneer Girls in 1955—an informal group of domestic workers who met weekly on their days off to cook together and to socialize. Eventually it became a federally funded, structured program in 1957. The Pioneer Girls lasted only five years because it didn't solve the problem of isolation, it was neither co-ed nor activist, and recreational activities were quite narrow.[28] The long term benefit of the program was that it helped create networks between these women and exposed them to other associations. When Pioneer Girls was disbanded in 1960 the women had made other organizational connections.[29]

One year after arriving these workers were allowed to become permanent residents. Those who gained this status also began the arduous process of trying to sponsor their families. Women who applied to bring their fiancés or boyfriends were under pressure to marry them within thirty days of their arrival.[30] Female immigration from the West Indies was higher than male immigration even during the 'open door' period.

The arrival of sponsored relatives was the major benefit of the Domestic Scheme program. Though less than 3,000 women came to Canada, it was the arrival of hundreds of their relatives and friends that began the expansion of black communities in major cities across the country, including Montreal. Exact numbers are unclear, but eventually hundreds of black families immigrated from the islands and many more families were started in Canada as a direct result of the women in the program.

Trying to acurately determine the total black population in Quebec is difficult. The 1961 census reported that 3,858, or 90 percent of enumerated Negroes lived on the island of Montreal.[31] One independent researcher suggested that Montreal's black population was just past 4,500 in 1963.[32] Given that the accepted view in the black community is that there were 6,000 to 7,000 blacks living in the city around 1950, and there was a lack of any evidence of a substantial of population loss in the intervening years, the census figures, and those of the independent researcher for the early sixties, appear to be much too low. The Department of Citizenship and Immigration in 1961 estimated that close to 7,000 blacks lived in Montreal. Like the community's estimate this would seem to be a far more realistic figure.[33]

There have been numerous overestimates of Montreal's black population; the most outrageous by Boubacar Kone, a visiting journalist. Citing estimates given to him from community members, he claimed that in 1968 Montreal's black population ranged between 40,000 and 50,000.[34] This would have meant that at least two hundred thousand blacks had to have come to Canada in the first eight years of the 1960s! The most realistic estimate of the total number of English speaking blacks living in Montreal by the end of the sixties is probably closer to 15,000.[35]

Other researchers avoided the question of numbers and tried to describe Montreal's black population during the 1960s in terms of its class and cultural diversity. Harold Potter and Daniel Hill, in their 1966 survey of black settlement in Montreal, categorized six classes of blacks: West Indians, students, Haitians, Americans, domestics, and non-confessing blacks.[36] The first two groups consisted of the core population of blacks in the 'Negro district' and of a dispersed population of blacks on and off the island. Those who lived outside the district fared better even though some remained in traditional jobs.

The most traditional railway jobs had long been altered. By 1951 the sleeping car porters' job qualification was no longer restricted to coloured men. After the railways acknowledged the right of porters to form unions (independent of the companies), wages were greatly increased, making portering more attractive to whites. During the 1960s, the main concern of the rail unions was the amalgamation of the divided unions. An amalgamation of the waiters, supervisors, and other non-skilled labour (Group I) with the porters' unions (Group II) meant that the seniority lists would be combined. Group I rail workers did not want to lose their closed shop exclusivity and the economic advantage they had over the Group II porters. This struggle continued until the Canadian Brotherhood of Railway, Transport and General Workers (CBRT) amalgamated four locals in 1964. When the seniority lists were combined it became possible for a sleeping car porter to rise to a higher position in the industry. The union's caste system which had existed since 1921 was broken. For the first time real gains were made in the rail industry.[37]

The black men involved in this struggle for equality and justice did not stop with the success of the rail union. They influenced the other unions and brought human rights issues into the unions themselves to ensure that anti-discrimination issues and human rights would be fought for. In Montreal, unions redirected funding into coalitions of civil rights groups that focussed on housing discrimination. With this support these groups conducted surveys and wrote briefs that were brought directly to the door of the Premier of Quebec. "This kind of cooperation was necessary for us because we alone could not have financed the survey or rounded up the signatures. The Human Rights boys are affiliated with the Unions; the Unions finance it and they have plenty of money."[38] Unionized blacks in Montreal used the vast resources of the unions in order to further the civil and human rights agenda—blacks did not lack leadership but funding.

Before 1967, because of the federal government's 1962 selection policy, most blacks who immigrated to Canada were men employed in service industries, as well as clerical and skilled groups. Like the domestics who immigrated at the same time, these men were expected to fill jobs that whites would not do. They competed with unskilled white males in the job market and blacks were forced to work in the most menial jobs— dishwashers, janitors, and ushers. With low income and status, this early 1960s wave of immigrants often experienced temporary unemployment, underemployment, isolation and discrimination, and worst of all, culture shock.

The majority of West Indians that had come into Montreal in the 1960s were

> primarily in occupations like school teaching, junior business posts, clerks, the civil service, secretaries and stenographers, or they are small landed proprietors. They are highly class-conscious, self-assertive, and striving for higher social status. They are aggressive, touchy, and sensitive. These are the socially mobile people...it is very difficult for individuals of this class to act together as a group and to accept leadership or direction; they are highly individualistic[39]

They were determined to make a place for themselves, and they responded to the socio-economic situation in Montreal quickly. They tried to ease their loneliness by opening cultural and ethnic organizations and social clubs. By 1965 thirteen organizations were created to meet the specific needs of the

West Indian population, and within ten years there were over forty. Many of these groups such as Barbados House and the Jamaica Association were reflections of island and/or ethnic affinities. The need for a sense of belonging was so important that the emerging island nationalism would eventually dominate the institutions of black Montreal.

There were others who did not fit in, as many as 4,000 to 5,000 blacks were transient immigrants who did not "intend to settle in Montreal but (were) trying to make a stake to take them to Toronto, Vancouver, or some other city where they hope to find a prosperous future."[40] Like the nineteenth century Refugees who fled American civil strife, and the educated blacks of the 1920s, many of these early immigrants could see no future for themselves in Montreal.

Newcomers who chose to make Montreal their home upset the status quo and a situation where there was progress in civil rights and immigration.[41] The newcomers felt they could make a difference, so like the West Indians in the 1920s they took the lead. They headed numerous human rights organizations and became involved in the publication of the many progressive newspapers which proliferated in the late 1960s and early 1970s.

By 1964 Montreal's black community had undergone significant change. It was once one community where blacks, regardless of origin, lived in close proximity to each other, sharing the same organizations and struggle against discrimination. Now blacks were leaving the core community to rent in Nôtre-Dame-de-Grace and Lasalle which became the black immigrant reception areas. Contact between established blacks and the West Indian newcomers was minimal. Many of the recent immigrants never met a black Canadian.[42] When they looked at the number of blacks in traditional jobs, and the poor facilities and poor housing in the black community, they believed that Canadian blacks had embraced accommodation and done little to improve their status. These new immigrants had no desire to share the marginalization of the established black community.

Marginalization affected groups in different ways. The black student population was one important group that lived on the fringes of the community. They were on student visas from Africa, the Caribbean, and South America. Unlike previous decades, their numbers were no longer insignificant. The majority of the students were men, and in 1965 as many as 3,000 were living in rooming houses scattered throughout Montreal. It was not unusual for them to move several times a year to avoid the threat of deportation, and the harassment and intimidation they regularly experienced from their white landlords and neighbours.[43] Their attitude, rather than where they lived in the city, kept them on the fringe of the black population. Many students felt that black Canadians were docile, accommodating, and conformist. To long time residents, the students were radical and 'too forward.' For several years these students remained distinct from the greater black community and created their own organizations and newspapers that promoted black power ideology.

This gap between the students and the community narrowed during the late sixties over a series of events which occurred at Sir George Williams University in Montreal.[44] Because large number of black students were involved, individuals and associations put aside their differences to support the students.' This solidarity helped students establish roots in the community. As a consequence, Montreal became home to many students, though immigration rules made it very difficult for some of them to remain in Canada. They applied for landed immigrant status after graduation, but many students remained indefinitely and illegally. They went underground in the West End, the McGill student ghetto, Côte-des-Neiges, and in other districts with a substantial black population.

The first French-speaking black Haitians, 3,539 affluent, highly-educated professionals, arrived in Montreal between 1963 and 1972. Many found teaching positions in Quebec's French-language schools and universities.[45] Not only were the Haitians linguistically and culturally different, they were generally from a much higher economic bracket than the majority of English-speaking blacks.

Many of these early Haitians immigrants considered themselves to be in self-imposed political exile.[46] This, and the fact they were French-speaking, might explain why there was little social interaction between the two groups. This small core of Haitians aligned themselves with Quebec's nationalist movement and were the first immigrant group to be attracted to Canada primarily on the strength of the Québécois influence.[47] Nationalistic sentiments at this time were not attractive even to the radical element of the educated English-speaking blacks.

In 1968 another group of Haitian immigrants began to arrive in Montreal. Though not as highly educated as those who arrived before them, they had more than fourteen years of schooling. This segment of the Haitian community was predominantely blue collar, despite their education.[48] It is this working class population that formed the bulk of the Haitian community as we know it today.

There were black Americans who temporarily lived in Montreal while playing for professional Canadian sports teams. Relatively well off, these men and their families were usually American citizens who lived across the island, outside of the black community. As a result of the Vietnam war, Montreal became home for a small number of Afro-American draft dodgers and deserters. Most of these blacks from the United States went to Toronto and Vancouver. In addition to fleeing from the military they had hoped to escape prejudice and poverty, yet they lived on the fringes of the black community. [49] Montreal's black community, once dominated by black Americans, now had only token representation.

By the 1950s the boundaries of the West End shifted west and south to the Lachine Canal. The residential center was now St. Martin street. This southward push resulted in a polarization along linguistic lines. Most of the English-speaking residents of the West End lived above the tracks while the majority of French-speakers lived below. As blacks moved further into the western part of the district, housing improved. After decades of absentee landlords, the nineteenth century housing stock east of Guy street had badly deteriorated. Houses in the western areas were in much better condition because they had been sold recently by their original owners.

Living conditions had improved dramatically for Montreal's black community in the post-war period. Increased stability unified families—they grouped together so that certain streets, even whole blocks, became home to large extended families. Neighbourhoods in the West End took on a clannish atmosphere as grandparents, in-laws, and cousins found housing close to each other. Rows of houses became the domain of individual families and leases were passed on from one generation to the next.

Another consequence of improved housing conditions during the 1950s was the arrival of new residents from other areas. Some West Indian and black Canadians moved into the West End. One reason was that the housing in the western section of the district, though more expensive, was of better quality than in the St. Lawrence Boulevard corridor. Still the movement to other districts continued as blacks were attracted to newer refurbished districts.

Lasalle, a working class suburb of Montreal was one of the new areas blacks were moving to from St. Lawrece boulevard and the West End black community. Public housing projects in Lasalle Heights became home to many black Canadians, including some from the Maritimes. They were pioneers because they were isolated by distance and did not have easy access to the churches, associations, and other institutions of the downtown black community. Housing projects like the Heights were welcomed by blacks because they were comfortable and the rents were reasonable. In Ville St-Laurent blacks purchased lots from the municipality and built their homes while they lived in rented apartments—in some cases the building process took years. This pattern was very similar to what had happened in previous decades on the South Shore.[50]

Housing in most of these areas was new and expensive compared to the housing of the West End but many families were willing to spend more of their income on higher rents in order to gain central heating, hot running water, modern kitchens, more space, and privacy—amenities lacking in much of the shabby housing of the West End.[51]

When it was possible during the 1950s families left the West End with its poor living conditions and the stigma of poverty. "Blacks moved out of downtown because they wanted to better themselves."[52] This remained true for those who left during the 1960s as well. Some moved to be close to family and friends,[53] still others moved because of the poor schooling at schools like Royal Arthur or because of the bad reputation of the district.[54]

By the end of the 1960s small numbers of blacks, including West Indians, lived in the various municipalities on the South Shore, but few blacks lived on the West Island, the area extending west from the city of Dorval to the end of the island. Families who moved to these areas intended to buy homes rather than to rent. Those who did move to the West Island were either the few Canadian blacks already living in upper middle class areas or homeowners in the older Montreal suburbs of Verdun and Côte St. Paul. English-speaking blacks with varying incomes had moved to areas such as Montreal East, Lachine, Snowdon, Lake of Two Mountains, and Rivière-des-Prairies.[55]

The most significant black movement in Montreal was during the late 1960s when large numbers of West Indians settled in Côte-des-Neiges and Nôtre-Dame-de-Grace (NDG). NDG and St. Antoine were perceived as black districts by Montrealers, although blacks have never been the majority in any district in the metropolitan Montreal area. Like Westmount in the 1920s and 1930s, and NDG in the forties and fifties, Côte-des-Neiges became the preferred district for blacks to live in throughout the 1960s.[56]

The availability of government-subsidized housing was a major reason that blacks relocated to other districts.[57] The once-inaccessible NDG became possible for blacks when the Benny Farms development was created for veterans. This project broke down the barriers for black veterans and their families to have decent housing in that district.[58] Other areas like Ville St-

Laurent and Montreal North had large housing projects for veterans in the 1950s and several black families left the West End to live there in the early 1960s. To take advantage of the good housing and reasonable rents a few families opted to relocate to Central Mortgage and Housing Corporation (CMHC) projects in Point-aux-Trembles and Montreal East.[59]

The major drawback of CMHC-funded federal government housing projects was their distance from downtown but they were an attractive alternative to downtown neighbourhoods and were generally free from discriminatory renting practices.

The most important reason for widespread black mobility between 1960 and 1969 was the destruction of a large section of the West End when the City of Montreal initiated a sweeping urban renewal program in the West End. There were extensive expropriations in the district which was razed and renamed Little Burgundy.[60] The boundary for Little Burgundy became Atwater to Guy, St. Antoine street to the Lachine Canal.

The official purpose for the renewal was the building of decent housing for low income families.[61] Around 1966 the City of Montreal began to buy property in the district, much of which was slated for demolition and new construction.[62] Over 75 percent of the land and dwellings was acquired over a period of years; in effect the City controlled who would live there.[63] Blocks of tenements were demolished and scores of families were forced to move out of the district. Fed up with the uncertainty—some families relocated two or three times in the district as a result of the demolitions—they looked outside of the district for housing. Over a nine year period, 1968 to 1977, thousands of people were uprooted and many voluntarily left Little Burgundy. As vacant lots remained undeveloped for years, the number of people who could or who wanted to return to the area dwindled. Hundreds of blacks never returned to the original community—by the time housing became available, they were comfortably settled in other areas.

Although the housing was modern, situated on new streets with refurbished parks, and with rents scaled to income, people were not attracted to the new Little Burgundy. They did not want to move again and they did not wish to deal with the municipal housing bureaucracy with its rules governing the size of apartment one was allowed and the number of people permitted per dwelling—people were not comfortable with this level of control.

Coinciding with the movement of hundreds of black families out of the area that became Little Burgundy was the arrival of thousands of blacks, particularly West Indians, in Montreal. These new residents chose not to live in Little Burgundy because more desirable areas were now available.[64] Thousands of these newly-arrived English-speaking black immigrants moved directly to Côte-des-Neiges and NDG where many already had relatives living. Seventy-seven percent found their first apartment in this manner.[65] This pattern, which reinforced and maintained family ties was also evident in other Montreal districts.[66] Through this process, immigrants were introduced to sympathetic landlords, and blacks did not, at least initially, have to worry about acceptance.

In the French-speaking black community a similar pattern was emerging. From the beginning the small Haitian population lived outside the core areas where English-speaking blacks lived. In the late 1960s the first wave of Haitians settled in Montreal North. There were few English-speaking blacks living in Montreal North at that time and there was little contact between the two groups.[67] For the first few years the Haitians lived in flats situated in the working class part of the district. By the late 1960s and early 1970s things had changed. The Haitians had established themselves and moved into the middle-class section of Montreal North, and few had moved to the West Island, Laval and the South Shore. Many lived in Rosemont, St. Leonard, Plateau Mont-Royal, and as far west as Ville St. Laurent and Côte-des-Neiges.[68] By avoiding the typical immigrant pattern they bypassed the downtown core and Little Burgundy and quickly established communities in non-immigrant areas.[69]

As Little Burgundy and the southwest sector ceased attracting new residents, it became a minor appendage to larger districts. After 1968 the island's black community was no longer solely centered downtown.

The Domestic Immigration Program of 1955 was important for Montreal blacks because it was the first post-war program designed to bring blacks to Canada. Prior to the mid-fifties, immigration to Canada had been a difficult process for the unskilled black woman and doubly difficult if she was skilled![70] The Domestic Immigration Program was the only opportunity for young, childless black women willing to work as domestics to enter Canada on a permanent basis. The sponsorship of these domestics and their relatives in the program resulted in the immigration of hundreds of men and women.

In the early sixties non-white immigration into Canada continued to expand dramatically because the bullish Canadian economy required a cheap labour supply, and because Canada faced international condemnation over its non-white immigration restrictions. Bending to pressure, and under the guise of humanitarian motives, Canada eliminated certain racially discriminatory regulations from its Immigration Act in 1963 and also later in 1967. After several decades of exclusion, the easing of restrictions heralded an unprecedented rise in non-white migration to Canada.

The number of West Indians settling in Montreal stimulated the proliferation of island organizations which represented unique ethnic and cultural identities. This wave of black immigration introduced a variety of new skills into the community as the job market expanded. Many were teachers, lawyers, doctors and nurses whose professions gained them access to a better lifestyle. Downtown Montreal was not attractive to them and they chose to move into other areas, in some cases following the white suburban movement to the West Island.

Due to government policies and an improved standard of living, new clusters of blacks had developed across Montreal during the fifties and sixties. Echoing earlier immigrant patterns, blacks in the fifties and sixties moved into new areas as soon as they could. From NDG to the east end of the the island, the Canadian black population, augmented by blacks from the Maritimes, had grown more slowly than the English and French-speaking West Indian immigrants of the mid and late sixties. Successive waves of black immigrants followed. Despite the presence of the Union United Church, the UNIA and the NCC, the majority of blacks in the Montreal Urban Community have never lived in Little Burgundy. With its reputation, many would not live there, even if given the opporunity.

CHAPTER SEVEN

The Sir George Williams Affair
[1966 -1980]

The sixties was a volatile period for Afro-American activism as Canadians tuned in to the day-to-day struggle of black communities in the United States via the media. To assume that only the American model influenced black Canadian political activism would be incorrect because there was was a natural evolution towards a new consciousness of race that emerged in Montreal's black organizations in the late sixties.[1] Montreal's expression of blackness was not an American derivative or a product of the student protest era but a homegrown activism which was the culmination of years of black expression and grassroots activity in Canada.

Montreal's modern activist roots emanated from a series of conferences on West Indian issues which took place at McGill University. The first conference in 1964 was a student-run affair which focussed on the "going home" debate. The conference organizer was the Canadian Conference Committee, (CCC), a student group which eventually evolved into an umbrella organization of volunteer groups called the National Black Coalition of Canada (NBCC). Since about 1960 this subject had divided the black student populations of both Sir George Williams and McGill universities. There were students from Africa and the Caribbean who planned to return home after the completion of their studies and others who wanted to make Montreal their home. The 1964 conference was created by members of the "going home" group who felt that they should be knowledgeable about events in the Caribbean, and that they should develop a broad understanding of all black people and their concerns. Caribbean speakers were invited and the workshops had a Caribbean theme.

Community criticism of the Caribbean focus convinced the students to expand their approach the following year, and members of the Montreal black community were invited to participate. The first of many debates was over the issue and extent of non-student input, and the balance between Caribbean and Canadian issues. By the 1967 conference the CCC had unilaterally decided that the 1968 conference would be held in the West Indies. Divisions deepened even more between those going home who saw the CCC as a means to re-enter Caribbean society, and the Canadians—the organizations, ex-students, and other students—who did not want the CCC to move in such a direction. They formed a coalition and during the conference ousted the going home leadership.

In October, 1968 this committee organized a conference at Montreal's Sir George Williams University with the focus, "Problems of Involvement in Canadian Society with Special Reference to Black People." The conference was unique in several ways. For the first time the whole black community participated, and for the first time the black Canadian leadership spoke out against the incursion of the radical tactics of the American Black Power movement.[2] This was also the first time the conference's emphasis centred around issues affecting blacks in Canada.

Stanley Grizzle, the prominent human rights activist from Ontario, called the transformation

> an awakening of the West Indian groups in Canada to the fact that whether they are here as students, domestics or immigrants, their development is greatly affected by the fact that they live within the social, political and economic framework of Canadian society.[3]

Almost immediately there was a counter response to the national orientation of the 1968 CCC conference. In October McGill University hosted the Black Writer's Conference—an event that had Pan-African international solidarity as its theme and which was controlled by the going home faction. The West Indian organizers of the conference believed in the empowerment of blacks and the affiliation with blacks worldwide. To reinforce their stance they invited black revolutionaries Stokley Carmichael from the United States, Michael X from England, and Walter Rodney from Jamaica to promote the international revolutionary movement. Despite, or perhaps because of its vocal anti-white tenor, the conference enlightened and galvanized the black students and provided a context for what would occur at Sir George Williams University.

Sir George William University is a large university situated in downtown Montreal. During the regular 1967-68 winter session enrollment was close to 20,000 day and evening students. The university grew out of the educational work of the YMCA which began in 1873 by offering evening courses. This developed into the YMCA schools which in 1926 became Sir George Williams College, and subsequently a university in 1948 when it received its charter from the province of Quebec.[4] In contrast to McGill, many Sir George Williams students came from a working-class background, many of them holding day jobs, and attending school at night.

In 1968 Perry Anderson, an assistant biology professor at Sir George Williams, was accused by many students, including six black students, of grading them in a discriminatory manner. The complaint, lodged with Dean of Students, Magnus Flynn, became the catalyst for a series of events which culminated in the destruction of the university's computer centre on February 11, 1969.

Unhappy with how the university administration was handling their complaint, the students made it a public issue in the fall of 1968 and demanded that a Hearing Committee be established with appropriate student representation. The university agreed to the creation of the committee but the students were displeased with the nominations to the committee and began a series of sit-ins and other pressure tactics which lasted through the fall. Following the breakdown of negotiations, on January 29, 1969 over two hundred students, black and white, staged a sit-in on the ninth floor Computer Centre of the Henry F. Hall building. On February 10, after several days of demonstrations and negotiations, a proposed agreement between the students and the administration disintegrated at the last minute and students barricaded themselves in the Computer Centre. On February 11 city police were called in and a fire broke out in the computer centre which caused about $2 million damage.[5]

The number of students who had participated during the occupation at any given time varied between 100 and 300, and included people from Trinidad and Tobago, Jamaica, Guyana, the Dominican Republic, Barbados, other Carribean countries, and various African countries. Though not all of the demonstrators were students at Sir George Williams, in the end only 97 were arrested, including 30 women.[6] The next day, on February 12th, Professor Anderson, who had been suspended during the crisis, was officially reinstated. On June 30, 1969, the university's Hearing Committee found Anderson not guilty of racism.[7]

Forty-two blacks were arrested, less than half the total of 97 arrested, yet the Sir George Williams Affair remains, in the eyes of the public and the black community, a black event. For the black students involved the episode was "a rebellion against a negative history" of oppression and discrimination in Montreal.[8] Twelve criminal charges were laid including charges against sitting-in. Until this point, staging a sit-in had not been a criminal act anywhere in North America and this was the first time the police had even chosen to lay charges for this manner of protest. For several days bail was denied to those arrested, and when it was finally accepted on February 19th, property was not accepted for bail, which was unusual. The bail amounts, ranging from $3,000 to $14,000 were considered excessive. The municipal court also demanded that the foreign students hand over their passports or visas.[9] For the rest of the community the excesses of the authorities over the years—beatings by the police, threats, deportations, and exorbitant fines—validated the students' militancy. The immediate result was that the incident "produced a community-wide feeling of belonging to one people…it did not matter where you came from or who you were."[10]

The black community, despite mixed reactions, defended the students, although support declined over the long term. Those who supported the students from the beginning continued to do so regardless of what happened subsequently in the courts, or in the press, but there were individuals and groups who disagreed with the students' tactics. Support within black organizations for those charged in the Sir George Williams Affair was mixed, and the students faced every reaction. One student activist recalled that the NCC and Union Church leadership, perceiving themselves as spokesmen for the community, were antagonistic. The old guard community leadership was gradualist in its approach to change. They did not openly oppose the student actions at Sir George Williams, but they did not approve of the tactics or the independent, radical mind-set of those involved. From the students' perspective, it was abundantly clear that the old guard did not support them. "It never occurred to us to even have the Thursday night rallies in their [NCC or Union] buildings"[11]

There were students and citizens in the black community who did not support, even in principle, the role of the black students during the Sir George Williams Affair. Others viewed the 'affair' as a West Indian event—these were immigrants who strongly identified with the students but felt insecure and afraid, and "thought they were going downhill with them."[12] The activist students and their supporters responded to these negative reactions with a grassroots approach. In several districts of the black community they canvassed door-to-door, trying to convince people that the students were not the ogres they were made out to be. This action raised the political consciousness of the community and generated goodwill and support. So the long term benefit of the Sir George Williams Affair was a convergence of goals—the fight against discrimination.[13] It also awakened the leadership in the community. They became aware of the need to be more active in shaping policies and in creating organizational structures which could deal with issues in a relevant manner. Clarence Bayne, a professor in the Commerce department at Sir George Williams, remembered that "the way we saw it was that the students made decisions for the whole black community and that was not the way a community should have its strategies worked out for it in a development situation."[14] The community was annoyed that plans which had an impact on the black community were being enacted with no consultation. It was strongly felt that the students were placing the community in a position of being forced to support their plans.

This consensus hardened during discussions held among the students, the NBCC, and community members at the regular Thursday night meetings at the UNIA. Community members became angry when the students were reluctant to answer questions about the events at Sir George Williams. The atmosphere became even more tense when the students intimated that the people present might be their enemies. The community was in a dilemma. They wanted to support the students but they lived the reality of facing the public every day on the bus, or at work where they would be asked questions. Some admitted that they were scared. Although the community expressed how upset they were that the students acted without consultation they offered their general support.

The community had not been aware of student issues and the leadership was determined that this would never happen again. Serious attempts were made to restructure institutions in the black community and other institutions which had an impact on blacks throughout Montreal.

The events at Sir George Williams University in 1968 and 1969 affected more than the students who were directly involved—uncommitted blacks in the community at large became more activist. One individual said that the Sir George Williams Affair opened his eyes to "wonderful opportunities for us [blacks] to develop and grow."[15] It became more than a focus of support for students and the leadership and it had a powerful effect on many of Montreal's black residents. For Clarence Bayne, the crisis "also sensitized Montreal to the rights and needs of minority people and showed the black community that the development of structures to deal with racism were too slow."[16]

Out of this very concern the National Black Coalition of Canada was formed in October 1969, eight months after the Sir George Williams University incident. Although it was initially situated in the NCC, the NCBB was conceived as a national organization which would fight racism. With the support of twenty-eight Canadian black associations, chapters of the NCBB rapidly opened across the country. The Black Coalition of Quebec (BCQ) was the Quebec chapter and its members worked to respond to the problems affecting Montreal's black students.

The establishment of the Quebec Black Board of Educators (QBBE) was another example of how the community took steps to make institutions more responsive to its concerns.[17] Although the QBBE was born in the aftermath of the Sir George Williams Affair, Sir George Williams students were only marginally involved. The impetus for the organization originated at McGill. As the black students of McGill and SGW established links they began to realize that—with three exceptions out of perhaps three to four hundred black students on the two English campuses—all the blacks attending the universities were directly from Africa, the Caribbean, or United States. Few among them were from Quebec's black community. The fact that only a handful of all black students attending Sir George Williams and McGill were native Montrealers, begs the question of why Montreal's black youth were not going to college.

Under the Black Education Program (a name coined by the newspaper *UHURU*), meetings were held by student activists who conducted their own independent research at McGill throughout 1969. They established contact with young blacks in Montreal-area high schools and attempted to discover why Montreal's black students were not entering college.[18] The story they heard often was that most of the young people in the education system became so frustrated in the schools that they eventually lost the drive to complete high school and to go on to college or university. The student researchers heard stories that "black students at the secondary level were actively discouraged by administrators and teachers from continuing their studies."[19] The researchers did not realize that this was a decades-old scenario in Montreal's school system.[20]

Their research revealed that there were very few black teachers, no black professionals at the administrative level, and none directly involved with the promotion of education for black people in the system. They concluded that the system itself was blatantly racist. This was the catalyst for the student movement's involvement in education issues in Montreal.

By fall 1969 interested black students had created a subcommittee on black studies to encourage McGill University to institute a black studies program.

In November 1969, black students met with Dr. Michael Oliver, vice-principal of McGill, to discuss the proposed black studies program and to set up a summer project for high school students which would enable them to enter university. They continued to build a case for remedial studies and on April 23, 1970, the Academic Policy committee of the McGill Senate was convinced.[21] McGill accepted the remedial program. Successful graduates of the new black education program would be accepted into McGill as if they had graduated from a Quebec high school.

During this period the Board of Black Educators (eventually becoming the QBBE, an association of black teachers and related educational professionals) was taking shape. The students opened discussions with the universities and the Protestant School Board of Greater Montreal (PSBGM), the body responsible for most English-language elementary and secondary schools. The institutions which were responsible for the delivery of education were being sensitized to the particular arguments and the needs being identified by the university based student body. At this juncture the students expanded their collaboration to include educators and other professionals.[22] The purpose of the collaboration between students and professionals was to sensitize the black community about the drop-out issue. After some dialogue off campus between the universities, the QBBE, and the PSBGM, the idea developed to create an organization to provide opportunities for black youth to advance their education. All the English-language educational institutions in Montreal had become more aware of the lack of educational opportunities for black children.

At the point that the QBBE coalesced, but the collaboration between the students and educators was not smooth. In the initial stages of the organization's development there was a confrontation between the so-called student radicals who had initiated the research and the more conservative professionals. The final confrontation occurred at a meeting at the NCC when the two groups clashed around issues that were rather pertinent and sensitive to that period. The radicals believed that real and relevant education should include African history and heroes, and material about other non-eurocentric peoples. Perhaps the most contentious issue was whether the QBBE should refer students to Sir George Williams University, given the negative feelings that blacks had about the university. The teachers, who were generally conservative, wanted to stream black youth into Sir George Williams. Since less than one year passed since the Sir George Williams Affair, such a position was completely unacceptable to the militant black students who had been involved in new educational projects.

The students and their supporters preferred to stream black students to McGill, especially since Sir George Williams had refused to reinstate students involved in the sit-in. Sir George Williams also would not authorize the release of student records, despite the fact that these students had not been found guilty of anything, so that they could apply for admission elsewhere.[23] The students active in the Black Education program believed that promoting Sir George Williams University negated everything they had been working for. The views of conservative forces prevailed and as a result, many of the student radicals withdrew from the grassroots education movement.

The work of the QBBE continued with vigour throughout the 1970s. The PSBGM remained the target of negotiations. In 1970 four demands were presented to the Board with data which demonstrated that:

a) its schools streamed black childen automatically and systematically into technical programs because of their perception that black children did not have the intellectual capacity to do advanced studes; b) there were very few black teachers in schools with high concentrations of black children; c) there was a lack of black administrators within the school board; d) classroom school books and other pedagogical materials had very negative images and concepts of blacks.[24]

In an attempt to deal with the racist educational system which was ignoring the needs of Montreal's black youth, the QBBE's ongoing negotiations with the PSBGM resulted in concessions which included the establishment of tutoring programs and the introduction of black guidance counsellors. One of the first changes was a Black Liaison Officer at the school board level. Over time, other changes included the establishment of black schools and, where appropriate, a black core curriculum.

In July 1970 the QBBE set up and ran Da Costa Hall, a post-secondary tutorial and summer school to stream young adults back into schools and eventually into university. Later the BANA remedial program was established for elementary students. (BANA means child in the Chiluba language of Zaire). Montreal's educational institutions agreed to accept students who graduated succcessfully from the Da Costa Hall program. Carl Whittaker, an early organizer of Da Costa Hall, believed that its summer program had a significant effect on the self-esteem of the black children it touched:

It provided students, some for the first time, [with] a learning environment where they were a majority, where learning was not oppressive, in a positive, non-racist environment. There they could not even misuse racism as an excuse not to perform. It did remedy some of the weakness in some of the courses, and it did stream the kids positively out of the system.[25]

For the first time, after several decades of frustration and obstacles, blacks found themselves with the opportunity and the expectation of higher education. The number of Canadian blacks entering post-secondary institutions began to rise. Dawson College in Montreal is a prime example. In the 1971-72 academic year, black student enrollment was 138; in the 1972-73 it was 254; and in 1973-74 it had grownto 314.[26] The QBBE, Whittaker asserted, had been key to this change: "I believe that if the organization did not exist, and if this movement did not occur, that these opportunities would not have been opened."[27]

The crisis at Sir George Williams affected the established institutions of Montreal's black community in clear-cut ways. The leadership of the Universal Negro Improvement Association believed that the obvious failure of the integrationist approach by blacks which was revealed during the Sir George Williams Affair was nothing less than the vindication of Garveyism. On February 11, 1969, and for several weeks after, the UNIA basked in the fall-out of the Sir George Williams Affair—it injected new life into the UNIA.

The UNIA made its facilities available to student protestors—Liberty Hall became the meeting place of the February Eleventh Defence Committee which was established to raise funds for the defense of the 97 students who were eventually charged. This Committee held fundraising events across the city to generate funds for the high fines levied by the court. Historical lectures combined with social meetings became regular features of Thursday night meetings as the radicals joined other blacks who were indignant and angry about the events at Sir George and the subsequent trials and deportations. The purpose of the programs was to "strengthen and extend the unity that already exists among black people...develop the feeling that we are one people... cultivate a sense of national consciousness...[as] Africans at home and abroad."[28] With fundraising in mind, it was no coincidence that Thursdays also happened to be the domestics' regular day off in the city, so the Thursday evenings became a regular West Indian event.

Still, the rallies were more than social events. In the heady days of February, and for the few months after, it was standing room only at Liberty Hall. But as the year wore on sometimes only ten people would show up for the Thursday events. The lack of participants may have been a reflection of a change of direction by militant students and of a redirection of their energies. The establishment of the QBBE and other community-wide organizations, stimulated the students to direct their energies towards creating venues for realizing their ideals.[29] Diverse activities such as the Congress of Black Women, Black Youth TV, and Cultural Youth Workshops developed as blacks began to expand their institutional horizons. The rebirth of the UNIA was short-lived in the long-term, but while the Affair occupied the headlines and the talk shows, Liberty Hall was revitalized.[30]

The Negro Community Centre (NCC) was also affected by the events at Sir George Williams. One of the first changes resulted from a direct challenge by students involved in a group known as the Black Action Party (BAP). Initially BAP members were uncommitted black students who met and talked about the repercussions of the events at Sir George Williams and how McGill students could create change in a different manner. During the 1969-1970 school year their meetings on the McGill campus became more structured, and they decided that it was important to work behind the scenes. This did not mean inaction—they were committed to knowing what was going on in the community.

At a meeting on campus shortly after the declaration of the War Measures Act in October, 1970, BAP learned that the NCC needed volunteers.[31] After some discussion, they concluded that because the NCC was the centre of the community and the place to initiate change, that six McGill students would volunteer at the NCC. They received some support at the NCC from the white workers and volunteers, but many blacks at the NCC protested because they were threatened by the changes the students were proposing. According to Leslie McLaughlin, a BAP organizer, the main reason for this reaction was the staff's planned re-orientation of the NCC. Multiculturalism was the buzzword for government funding at the time, and the students feared multiculturalism would be another way to maintain the status quo. According to BAP there was nothing about blacks or aboriginals yet included in Canada's multicultural history; and the history and contributions of many non-European peoples in Canada had been ignored.[32]

As BAP's outreach extended to the NCC, their membership grew to include a group of high school students from the High School of Montreal who were mostly from Little Burgundy. Beginning in 1968 the students experienced significant consciousness raising at the newly-established Afro-Canadian Club in the High School of Montreal. The club program included discussions on African history, black history in the diaspora, liberation movements, and the unspoken history of blacks in Canada.[33] The black student movement which began at the High School of Montreal later spread to other high schools where there were many black students. The Afro-Canadian Club was quickly connected with the race consciousness that was growing at Sir George Williams University, and to a lesser extent at McGill.

The BAP volunteers at the NCC decided that education would be their focus, and on January 12, 1971, under the aegis of the BAP, a series of black history lectures was inaugurated as part of the NCC program.[34] Black high school students were ready for a new kind of education:

> We showed them the politics of the world—which included neo-colonialism, slavery to the present times. We made them read, write and study. It was an education for all of us because in educating these children we educated ourselves to the point that we (the teachers) learned something. We always took note that we were living in a white community. This was unlike the States where blacks could cordon themselves into isolated, segregated communities. The purpose was not to tell them to go out and kill whites but to give them a sense of pride. To show them the complexities of the colonial relationship that they lived under—through slavery and colonialism Africans, (they) were in the Americas and remain here today. We taught them to challenge authority with knowledge.[35]

For several months the BAP volunteers worked to establish good relations with the NCC and to convince the parents of the students that afro-centric programing was important. The struggle between their afro-centric stance and the NCC's official multicultural approach remained. The Black Action Party organized a community rally for April 10, 1971 at the NCC. The BAP was looking for strength in numbers and wanted to involve the community in the debate about change at the NCC. Few showed up for the rally and the NCC doors were locked. The city police who had been shadowing some BAP members were cruising around the area in unmarked cars.[36] One policeman, intent on harrassing everyone on the scene, succeeded in creating an incident involving a passer-by on her way to a convenience store. His agressive action towards her caused other blacks around the NCC to come to her assistance, which resulted in the arrest of four black people.[37]

To many Montrealers, both black and whites. the Black Action Party was a replication of the American Black Panthers. Although the BAP felt that American blacks were struggling to assert their civil rights—rights that the BAP believed Canadian blacks did not enjoy in their own country—the BAP did not sanction subversion or violence to achieve their goals. BAP's ultimate goal was to create black pride. Marcel Green, a BAP member recalled that we

> were trying to put forward an alternative style of living that would point out to people what their community was. We realized this was a community that didn't know itself. Black people were ignorant of what was around them—of their own history in the city. Blacks had moved all over the island to many different parts, they did not know their Little Burgundy history.[38]

The 1960s had seen a gradual modification in the composition of the NCC's Board so that by the time of the Sir George Williams crisis only two white members remained on the Board of Directors.[39] One of the BAP demands for change in the direction of the Centre, was for an all-black board. For many BAP members even one white board member was an insult because it did not represent of the city's dynamic black community. There were blacks from many different backgrounds who could bring their expertise to the board and the NCC no longer had to rely on the economic and social connections of its white members. BAP's demands where eventually brought before the members of the Centre for a vote. The first was the removal of all white members from the Board; the second was that the Negro Community Centre's name be changed to the "Community Centre." The board agreed to the first but the membership refused to yield to the second proposal.

Retaining the word 'negro' in the centre's name was a defeat that the students refused to forget. They believed it was time to discard this respectable turn-of-the-century appellation. Negro was passé and indicative of an old mentality—when being negro meant you were a third class citizen and you thought of yourself, and were treated, as such. The students were proud of being black and they revelled in the confidence and power that 'black' gave them. They turned their backs on the Negro Community Centre in disgust.[40]

This issue went to a vote over two basic views of history. To those who argued to retain Negro,' the change was a denial of their history and the history of the community they had built in Montreal. This was particularly true for many members who were proud that the NCC was extending beyond a black context and becoming part of Montreal's larger service network. Evidence of this acceptance was the turning over of the deed of the NCC building to the NCC by the St-Laurent Association (formerly the Iverley Community Centre before they moved to Ville St-Laurent).[41] The Negro Community Centre was, in the eyes of members who wanted tor retain the old name, part of a proud legacy that blacks had worked hard to maintain for generations, and it could not so easily be abandoned or forgotten.[42]

The other perspective was intimately tied to the legacy of the computer riot at Sir George Williams University and the black cultural renaissance of the period. To the student activists history had taken on international proportions, and blacks in Montreal were part of a global historical movement that all blacks, regardless of where they were living or where they had come from, had to participate in. History meant returning to one's roots—except those roots were African by definition. They believed that history should not be limited by regional identities. The students were committed to their beliefs and Montreal's black organizations felt the repercussions.

Bob White, director of the West End Sports Association, recalled that the "best thing about [the Sir George Williams Affair] and the civil rights marches was [the creation of] Black Studies."[43] Through the seventies, during day camp and regular weekday and weekend programming at the NCC and other community associations, this group of young adult volunteers and staff made it a point to teach black history to the children in their charge. Africa became central to this teaching. This was not only historical Africa but contemporary Africa that was struggling to throw off the mantle of European colonialism. The children learned about apartheid, and about Nelson Mandela and other imprisoned black activists. Connections were made with the ANC, SWAPO, and freedom fighters in other countries. In its own small way, through its annual African Liberation Day marches Montreal's black community raised funds for black liberation movements.

This afro-centric approach permeated the social and cultural dynamics in black instututions and it continued to affect the NCC's programing and direction during the seventies. When Lawrence Sitahal became the new Executive Director of the NCC in 1970 after the death of Stanley Clyke, the restructuring of the centre's programming and direction continued unabated. This change was also due to the centre's response to a situation In Côte-des-Neiges.

By 1971 white response to the growing number of blacks in the Côte-des-

Neiges area had begun to cause problems. Black youths and some adults were in conflict with small merchants in the area, other visible minority youth, and with each other. The media focussed on a few incidents and started to talk about long hot summers in reference to the long hot summers of race riots in American cities. Côtes-des-Neiges area organizations worked quickly to find solutions. The first of several task force meetings took place in Côtes-des-Neiges on March 3, 1971. Black groups, the Montreal Police Department, members of Montreal's city council, the PSBGM, and other concerned citizens and groups attended the meeting.

In May 1972 eight groups formed the Quebec Black United Front to develop a community response to City of Montreal police director Jacques Saulnier's assertion that there was no racial discrimination or harassment of blacks by police.[44] Without support from the police hierarchy, blacks knew the situation in Côte-des-Neiges would not improve. Director Saulnier's public remarks increased the difficulty and made co-operation more awkward.

The Quebec Black United Front presented its position at a press conference on Friday, May 5, 1972:

(1) The problem with the police is not restricted to the CDN area. It is a city-wide problem.

(2) Since this is the case, and since we are representative organizations with the community we feel that:

a) Saulnier's statement is completely wrong and out of place

b) the deep-rooted racist attitude of society is reflected by police actions

c) there should be human rights legislation in Quebec (it is the only province in Canada without it)

d) the groups should present their case as a united front

e) there is police harassment of blacks in general, but there is an open tendency of police to pick on black youth because they are more defenceless and less able to stand up for their rights.[45]

In the early seventies the Negro Community Centre evolved through contact with groups such as the BAP and the Quebec Black United Front. When Lawrence Sitahal was appointed director of the NCC it was a sign of the end of a once successful, but now dated model. This was exemplified in Sitahal's appointment of Carl Whittaker in May 1971 who was able to use the newly-popular techniques of grassroots organization in Côte-des-Neiges. Aware that others were dealing with problems affecting teen-agers, he focused on preteen issues and met the black residents of the district in their homes. After much study there and in other neighbourhoods his report to the NCC in 1972 confirmed that the problems of Côte-des-Neiges were endemic to the island of Montreal—lack of services for blacks, welfare rights, delinquency, and poor education. With blacks moving into many districts the explosive nature of Côte-des-Neiges reflected a city-wide problem.

Whittaker's report presented a five-year plan which emphasized the use of neighbourhood associations. They would be volunteer-directed and be designed to help each specific district. [46] The Whittaker report included three recommendations:

a) There should be a representative structure put into areas where there is a significant numbers of black people; b) the NCC should make an attempt to involve existing organizations in what they were doing; c) the NCC should evolve from social work to a new cultural form called the Black Community Central Administration of Quebec (BCCAQ). [47]

Given the structure of the NCC and its philosophy, Whittaker knew that his proposal was radical, so he elaborated on the concepts behind the recommendations:

1) Functional independence: an attitude to adopt to deal with other organizations in the community, in order to co-ordinate or interact without duplication to maximize the benefits from the two efforts and, 2) an operational unity—one that had to be structured, not just talked about. [48]

Following acceptance of the report, local organizations were established in September 1972 in areas with significant black populations: NDG, Côte-des-Neiges, and Lasalle. [49] The Black Community Association of Lasalle, the NDG Black Community Association, and especially the Black Youth Committee of Côte-des-Neiges, were based on the neighborhood association model, and targeted black youth. The programs were educational, cultural, recreational, social, or involved communications such as Black Youth Television, Black Community Media Inc., Black Community Radio, or "Black Is." These neighbourhood groups were designed to have as important impact in their neighbourhoods as the NCC had had in its neighbourhood.

The three satellite centres functioned autonomously but were to be co-ordinated through the successful council structure of the Black Community Central Administration of Quebec.[50] Where previously an event would attract hundreds, it was not unusual for an event sponsored by the BCCAQ to now attract tens of thousands. Under the umbrella of the BCCAQ were a host of other organizations—the Black Studies Centre, the Black Is Youth Television Workshop, the Walker Credit Union, and the QBBE. It was decentralized services within decentralized neighbourhood functions, all under a centralized administration. The goal of the BCCAQ was to subsume the NCC's role and re-direct its mandate to the three neighbourhood organizations. The centre would exist under the BCCAQ rather than in its former paternalistic, overseer capacity.

The structure was solid from 1972 to 1978, though it had some detractors. The focus of debate was about whether it was in the best interests of the NCC to have strong satellites in other districts. Another area of contention concerned the centre's dominance of other districts, which was neither efficient nor acceptable, given that economic control was solely in its hands. Others argued that the Board and its executive director should be replaced for a true black leadership to emerge.

A decision about the type of acceptable community leadership was part a larger debate over "Rip van Winkle" Canadians. The Canadian black writer Lyle Talbot, stated that

> blacks in Canada were a bunch of Rip Van Winkles who slept, not for twenty years, but for a hundred and twenty years after they landed on Canadian shores…and didn't wake up until our brothers and sisters from Caribbean countries began to arrive in significant numbers during the wave of immigration…of the 1960s.[51]

The Rip Van Winkle viewpoint gained credence in Montreal and in many black communities across the country during the early sixties, when new black immigrants arrived and saw what they perceived to be stagnation, 'Uncle Tomism,' and a defeated, impotent, black leadership. The Rip Van Winkle sentiment was a flashpoint and an insult for Montreal blacks who understood their long struggle in the city.

By 1977 strident voices on both sides of these debates attracted the attention of the *Montreal Star* which reported that the NCC board chairman Vere Rowe had "called for an end to the 'debilitating civil war' tearing apart the community with rightists versus leftists, old guard against new guard."[52]Perhaps the call was too little too late for the forces of division and independence eventually overpowered the forces of unity. From 1978 the BCCAQ began to crumble under the weight of competing internal and external forces.[53]

For Carl Whittaker, the disintegration meant lost potential:

> Those seven years were an effective period—a movement toward a constructive effort, despite the limited resources in the community…If we could have hung onto the level of organization; even plateaued at that level, (even if a period of years had passed before we could had moved on from that point)…we would have laid down a constructive framework [for future]…community development in the black community.[54]

In 1980 the community associations of Côte-des-Neiges, Lasalle and NDG were incorporated separately. In September the Negro Community Centre's new bylaws signalled the end of the NCC's centralized administration of the BCCAQ.[55]

The Côte-des-Neiges Project developed, in part, out of media reports of "the long hot summers" and an attempt to find solutions. By 1972 the project was set up as a new type of organization in black Montreal. The groundwork was laid after the Sir George crisis (when students had gone door-to-door in Côte-des-Neiges to explain what the students were protesting about). These encounters identified what the problems were and people in the district initiated group activities to try to deal with them. This grassroots approach was matched and encouraged by the philosophy of a group of student organizers which included Leroy Butcher. Butcher had a vision for a dynamic organization based upon a new model of programing. The popular model at the time was "animation" which Butcher believed was static one "where they would go out and get people and organize them for an action… but once the action was finished that was the end of that."[56] Butcher believed that the needs of the black community were more profound and that they could not be effectively met using the animation method.

Capitalizing on the groundswell of grassroots politicization which had begun to build in CDN due to the student movement, Butcher's idea was to expand on the political philosophy and social vision which had been embodied the Thursday night rallies. He tried to run his organization as a socio-political unit. Ironically, Butcher recalled that the most political move to come from the Côte-des-Neiges Project was actually the inauguration of the festive Carnival parade. He lamented that:

> we started the carnival here not because we wanted to carnival in the street but because we wanted to get involved in an activity that would bring together the masses…from which we could speak to the powers that be. Though the 40 to 50 thousand black revellers caught the attention of blacks and whites in power [politically] it was a mistake…without having it [our own support base] concretized.[57]

Besides its recreational and advocacy aims, the Project branched out into non-social service areas. It developed business ventures and supported the establishment of a garage, a day care centre, children's store, and meat buying and packing business, to name a few. For a short time they owned a residential building.[58] The impetus for these projects was to develop new funding sources. Butcher was motivated by the belief that "by getting organized and standing up and doing something positive, society's view was bound to change—it was a question of changing the discriminatory attitude of society at large toward blacks.[59] They also served another purpose, which was to encourage the black populace to obtain goods and services from blacks, which promoted self-sufficiency. Self sufficiency was the new principle which guided policy at the Côte-des-Neiges Project. It was in opposition to the reliance NCC had on funding from the wider community.[60] In this regard it was a unique organization for its time.

The Côte-des-Neiges Project continued until 1978. At its zenith it commanded great respect in the community and was affectionately called The Organization. Butcher put the Project in context:

> If a community does not have these experiences it is a dormant community—our community is not dormant. However some force needs to come up and we never ever really know where the force will come from or how it will develop that will take all that energy and perhaps coalesce it and move it along another step. What we have been able to do organizationally and on a community basis is take it from one step, one method of organization, one way of viewing the world, to another level. Somebody else or some other group will take it

another step forward but the community has moved in that time and I feel we have been able to contribute significantly to that movement.[61]

At the end of the sixties Montreal entered a new era of exchange with its black citizens. The black press became a significant mediator because of its role in educating individuals, while simultaneously creating community consensus and building a sense of community. The press which emerged immediately after the Sir George Williams Affair provided an alternative to the mainstream version of events as they appeared in the Montreal *Gazette* and the Montreal *Star* during the court proceedings and trials.

Yet it was much more. The black press also became the tool to foster community education. The emerging black identity in Montreal of the late sixties and the seventies was not accepted by the thousands of recent black immigrants. The black press was a dynamic instrument which enabled a changing community to keep in touch with the issues of the day, including the world-wide struggles of international liberation. In the pages of the black press readers were introduced to historical and contemporary black heroes, and concepts of blackness and African ancestry were debated and digested.

> Blackness is the end point of the process of becoming. Blackness is black power..[it] replaces the dying concept of Negroes and we must have a revolutionary consciousness of being to replace it. Blackness must stress black culture to inspire, educate, delight and to give identity, purpose and direction of the black man's passage...Blackness must be the channel, the strengths, and the beauties of black people to bring all Afro-America spiritually, emotionally, and historically in tune with the power-culture consciousness.[62]

When *UHURU* (Swahili for freedom), hit the streets June 4, 1969 almost four months after the Sir George Williams Affair, it caused a reaction. It was started by several students who had been involved in the Affair. It was a bi-monthly taboid initially funded by eighteen people who each contributed ten dollars. Teacher and amateur historian, Roy States said that *UHURU* had a devastating impact on both blacks and whites and States remembered how valuable *UHURU* was following the events of February 11, 1969:

> If I were to tell you the story about that newspaper now it would probably be mild but I wrote [about it] the night the paper was born,

and I have all the feeling and the excitement. Everything was shown in that [first issue]. Even though white people couldn't read it, it disturbed them. You'd see young blacks telling white people, "Oh no it is not your paper. Only black people could buy this paper."[63]

The content of UHURU was anti-white and extremely Afro-centric in its orientation. Each issue contained articles on African history and black studies at the national and international level and included articles and editorials about symbols of blackness, what it meant to be black, and tips on how to shed one's whiteness. The objective of the paper was to "develop a political level of consciousness based on a unified acceptance of the politics of Pan-Africanism."[64]

UHURU also functioned as a watchdog by analyzing community activities and the institutions serving its black readers. It became a buzzword as students fanned out across the city, selling the paper to blacks in the streets and on campuses, and engaging in debates on street corners. The paper's headquarters on St. Antoine street became another meeting place for students, or just a place to hang out. More importantly, UHURU functioned as an informal clearinghouse about student-related events and as a chronicle of the on-going judicial process for the students being prosecuted as a result of the computer riot at Sir George Williams University. This was particularly important to the foreign students who had been involved in the protest. They had lost their passports and visas had been withdrawn—they had no legal status and could not work. Many of these students were also suspended from Sir George Williams, their Canadian student status was suspended, and their situation was complicated when the university refused to issue their records to other universities. Without student status, support by their country of origin was in jeopardy and many were obliged to leave. A number of articles articles in UHURU criticized the colonial policies of the governments of the Caribbean nations which did not support their students.

Towards the end of 1969 many who had worked on UHURU moved on. Some students returned to the United States or the Caribbean. The publication closed down as militancy waned and the core militants left the city. The ideology of UHURU was never adopted by the black community's mainstream organizations and institutions,[65] but once it was gone, some black institutions took initiatives to create a new publication.

The demise of UHURU on November 9, 1970 left the black community without press for four years. Carl Whittaker, working at the NCC, initiated the idea of a monthly newspaper. With the help of Yvonne Greer from UHURU,

Focus Umoja began publication in November, 1974.[66] The black press in the city was reborn to educate a black constituency that now numbered in the tens of thousands. *Focus Umoja* was the voice the BCCAQ and it informed the whole community about the BCCAQ and its operations. *Umoja* covered important aspects of community life, with emphasis on culture, politics and, education. The tone of *Umoja* was less strident than *UHURU*. It was not Pan-Africanist, or anti-white. But Whittaker remembered that *Umoja* was perceived as a descendent of *UHURU* ; where 'Uhuru' meant freedom, 'umoja' was defined as unity. Both were vital to the growth of black community, and unity was the concept that the BCCAQ was promoting for the whole community.

The energy and ideology of the students which had been maturing throughout the sixties was put to the test during the Sir George Williams Affair—the black community's watershed event of the post-war era. As a result of the Sir George Williams incident some members of the black community felt more vulnerable—the event had created the sense that they were no longer welcome or safe in the city. The positive result was that the incident generated activity rather than apathy in the community.

The aftermath of the Sir George Williams Affair forced Montreal's black community to examine its problems anew and to experiment with new forms of institutional structures. It was the catalyst that brought West Indians (who normally would not have become involved in the Canadian community) together with Canadian-born blacks (who normally would not have become involved with West Indians). For a while the events at Sir George Williams prompted collective efforts like the Black Action Party, the BCCAQ, *UHURU*, and *Umoja*. The West Indians worked to establish new black organizations and demanded changes to the old structures and institutions which were ineffectively serving the black community. There was a push toward creating umbrella organizations which reflected the institutional centralization which was occurring throughout the social service system in Quebec. This co-operative activity contributed to a new sense of black awareness and pride

CHAPTER EIGHT

Building Together

As a result of the expansion of the black population across the island of Montreal during the 1960s it was clear by the early 1970s that the black community could no longer be defined by the limited boundaries of the old community. This did not mean that blacks and other visible minorities were welcome everywhere, for the most part, blacks still routinely suffered from discrimination in housing.[1]

Although blacks lived in many parts of Montreal, services provided by the NCC and the church were still largely confined to Little Burgundy and southwest sectors. After long deliberation, by 1972 black organizations responded to the situation with branch services—counselling, daycare, and after school programmes—opened in districts with a large black population. This expansion occurred in the older English-speaking black section and in the newer French-speaking Haitian sectors as well. The Haitian population's needs resulted in the creation of community centres with objectives and services tailored to meet their unique needs.

The arrival of large numbers of black residents into mostly white districts created friction. The areas of real concern went beyond the problems of racist neighbours. As the role of government and para-public institutions such as hospitals and universities expanded, the focus in the black community shifted to the struggle against discrimination in these institutions. In response to Quebec's endemic racism, new black organizations emerged.

Quebec's institutions—the courts, law enforcement, education, government departments, and the media, had many problems. The racism that existed in these public institutions resulted in an increase in the number of racist incidents. Many blacks believed that discrimination at the institutional level could best be fought at the grassroots level,[2] while others believed that strong and united institutions were the most effective tool. People no longer relied on organizations which had existed for decades—new leadership was required to serve and speak for the community.

The Negro Community Centre passed new by-laws on September 11, 1980, which for all intents and purpose disbanded the Black Community Central Administration of Quebec (BCCAQ). Two years later associations in NDG, Côte-des-Neiges, and Lasalle regrouped under the Black Community Council of Quebec (BCCQ), now centered in NDG. One of the reasons for the creation of the umbrella group was to correct the perception of funding groups that there were too many black institutions straining the system with requests for funding.

The BCCQ developed out of the ashes of the BCCAQ and its mission was similar: "It was mainly involved with the launching of community development initiatives and with co-ordinating and promoting the growth of the neighbourhood associations."[3] The three original associations in NDG, Lasalle, and Côte-des-Neiges form its core but many organizations operate under the BCCQ umbrella and groups such as the West Indian Canadian Day Association, Miss Black Quebec Pageant, ACCES, and Drew Society have received technical and administrative assistance from the BCCQ.[4]

The BCCQ was a multifaceted organization that provided a forum for the discussion of community issues in addition to culturally-sensitive services to the black community "on a global, as opposed to neighbourhood basis." It also initiated co-operative arrangements related to community development with government agencies.[5]

The BCCQ's membership consisted of affiliated organizations which was similar to the original BCCAQ board structure. Eventually the BCCQ membership expanded to include individuals in the community interested in participating and supporting its aims. Both the BCCAQ and the BCCQ embraced an ethno-cultural viewpoint based upon unity and community development.

> Mutually reinforcing…was the genuine desire among some leaders in the Black Community to promote a sense of unity and community among African Canadians of diverse national origins, and to use resources in collective ways in order to affect a constructive program of community development. This was in harmony with the philosophies of identity that were pervasive in the black community.[6]

The BCCQ attempted to strike a balance between its institutional initiatives and its own centralized community services, while other groups like the NCC discovered that defining a constructive program of community development could become a quagmire which threatens much sought after unity. When the BCCAQ dissolved, the NCC adjusted its mandate to reflect two radical changes: the growth in immigration and the drastic urban development in Little Burgundy. The district did not benefit from the upsurge in new black residents— urban renewal resulted in fewer blacks remaining in the district which was still reeling from the city's demolitions and forced expropriations. The NCC's new mandate was to:

1. Provide opportunity, facilities and leadership for its members to engage in cultural, social, educational and recreational activities.

2. Provide representative intervention for its members in particular and the black community in general with various government and other decision-making bodies.

3. Foster the development of community structures that respond to the localized needs of their respective communities.[7]

4. Collaborate in the representations on issues that affect the black community as an ethnic minority.[8]

The NCC was changing because it still had a role to play despite the demise of the BCCAQ and despite the fact that 50 percent of its membership no longer lived in Little Burgundy. The NCC had never experienced such upheaval and its new mandate signalled its willingness to work within the new institutional landscape and after the demise of the BCCAQ, efforts were made to offer limited services in the satellite districts, particularly in Côte-des-Neiges.

For many blacks and mainstream organizations, the NCC's shrinking influence did not change the status quo—the centre remained the voice for the English-speaking black community even as associations regrouped under the new umbrella of the Black Community Council of Quebec. The NCC enhanced its role by establishing another community newspaper. In 1981 the board gave its approval for the *Afro-Can* to be the publication arm of the NCC. The mandate of the tabloid was to report NCC activities—in many ways it was a hybrid of *UHURU* and *Umoja*. Many of *Afro-Can*'s articles were historical, promoting pride of race and highlighting Garveyism. Blacks of exceptional merit from Montreal and elsewhere were featured and most issues of *Afro-Can* included a feature on Canadian black history. *Afro-Can* ceased publication in 1987.[9]

In May, 1975 when Centraide was created to succeed the United Red Feather

Services, which had been the NCC's main funding source, pressure was felt by the NCC to eliminate, or justify duplication of services in Little Burgundy and in the other sectors of the black community on the island. From 1985 onward this was an all-consuming exercise for the NCC's directors as its new mission for the NCC was being debated.

On March 28, 1987 the NCC suffered a major setback to its building when a section of the stone wall at the back of the building collapsed. Repairs were completed months later but NCC was confronted with the need for complete renovations of the 100-year-old property. Due to funding restrictions related to the board's redefinition of the centre's role, the collapse of the wall at this time was a disaster for the centre. These events eventually led to a permanent reduction in direct services, staff, and programs in the Little Burgundy area. In September, 1989 the last of the full-time employees were released and for the next six years volunteers staffed the building. In 1995, while waiting for funding from Centraide, the board of directors closed the centre while community associations situated in NDG and other city districts continued to serve the majority of the black community. For the first time blacks remaining in Little Burgundy were forced to go to white institutions in their district for assistance, or to the satellite centres whose services extended to the old neighbourhood.[10]

To maintain its relevancy, the Universal Negro Improvement Association (UNIA) set up the Garvey Institute in spring 1983. For several years this institute developed programs to promote black culture. Some members began to co-ordinate with the provincial government to set up an officially-recognized school in Little Burgundy. They wanted to teach an afro-centric bilingual curriculum to children ranging from kindergarten to grade six. In 1991 a permit was granted to Quebec's first black private school, where black history, civilization, and culture are celebrated.[11]

During the 1970s the new wave of women's groups in Canada again witnessed a split based on racial differences—white and black—and of different agendas. In 1973 black women from across the country attended a three-day conference of the Canadian Negro Women's Association (CANEWA) in Toronto. The Colored Women's Club of Montreal obtained funding so that a Montreal contingent could attend. On their return, enthused by the solidarity and the power of black womanhood that they had experienced at the conference, these young English-speaking women formed the Montreal chapter of the National

Congress of Black Women.[12]

The focus of the National Congress of Black Women (NCBW)[11] has changed over the years, but it is interested mainly in issues relating to education, health and welfare, youth immigration, the black family, day care, human rights, and racism. The Montreal chapter has hosted national conferences and has concentrated on the issues affecting black women in Montreal.[13] The philosophy of the NCBW has influenced the structure of black women's groups across Canada. The Congress is not based on national heritage, skin colour, marital status, or any other factor. It was established to be accessible to all women of African descent and to encourage bilingual exchanges on a national level.[14] Montreal's chapter, with strong bilingual leadership during the 1980s, worked hard to integrate Haitian women into the Congress. A bilingual format was used at regular meetings, but as the Montreal chapter grew its membership divided into two natural groups—English-speaking members and French-speaking members, mostly Haitian women living in east Montreal.

In 1972 the Haitian population banded together to form the Maison d'Haiti— Montreal's first Haitian community organization.[15] Its mandate differed from that of the English-speaking organizations at that time. Maison d'Haiti helped Haitians to integrate and adapt to Quebec society while stressing the maintainance of their original culture. During the 1970s the Haitian population perceived themselves as an exiled people sojourning in this province until they could return to the homeland. This was in contrast to most English-speaking blacks, in particular the West Indians, who came to Montreal to make it their home. The Haitians, particularly the early French-speaking immigrants, expected that they would live in Quebec, raise their children here, and preserve a Haitian way of life until they returned to Haiti. Montreal's Haitian community is unique among the city's black communities in that the majority of parents and their children consider themselves as foreigners in Canada![16]

The Maison d'Haiti provided services to the community for unemployment assistance, legal matters pertaining to housing, and immigration. Its dual mission was to teach the culture of Haiti and to provide services to assist adaptation to Quebec society. The Maison believed that boredom, delinquency, and help-lessness that Haitian youth experienced was the result of the lack of any refer-ence to the history or culture of Haiti.[17] To address this, the Maison d'Haiti initiated courses in history and culture, including the teaching of Creole. As with other ethnic groups that teach their mother tongue, learning Creole, made people feel proud and made learning French even easier.[18]

For more than twenty years these goals have helped Maison d'Haiti maintain its premier role and leadership in Montreal's Haitian community. Although a few of its founders returned to Haiti, the large membership and the staff have fostered continuity.

The Maison has been responsible for the bi-cultural education of two generations of Montreal's Haitian youth. As one woman on the staff of Maison d'Haiti stated: "I learned about my country through Maison d'Haiti."[19] Haiti or Canada—perhaps this duality explains the pattern of social and institutional distance that began to form between the two communities, especially during the turbulent period following the Sir George Williams Affair. Now there are two black communities with two very different ways of handling their adjustment to Quebec society. Nevertheless, Haitians as a community have aligned themselves with English-speaking blacks when collaboration has been required to fight racism and discrimination.

Racism and discrimination within the Montreal taxi industry, with its origins in the 1960s, continued into the early 1980s. This conflict had parallels in another decades-old struggle—the unequal unionization of the porters at CPR. The union caste system set up in the early 1920s reflected the unwillingness of white male workers to accept black workers on the railways. As the result of deals with the employer, a formal system of exclusion was put in place solely on the basis of race, ensuring that black men could not compete with white males for jobs in the same rail industry. Forty to fifty years later, it is this same objective that fuelled the actions of whites who wanted complete control of Montreal's taxicab industry.

More than any other issue, police relations define the existence of racism in a society and Montreal has been no exception. Blacks, particularly young men must cope with the unexpected, unprovoked danger directed at them by the police. The response by black institutions to racism can create tensions within the community because black institutions have dual roles—they must press for change and yet calm people down in times of crisis.

In the early 1960s, as the result of collective agreements which improved salaries and working conditions, the railways began to hire white men for jobs which had traditionally been reserved for black men. Although the railway was no longer the only employment opportunity for black men, many remained working in the transportation sector in Montreal. Porters who left the railways to find work in other transportation-related jobs, had "difficulty in transcending the barriers to other areas of employment such as bus driver..."[20] In the 1960s the taxi industry became an employment choice for blacks, many of whom were ex-porters and students. Haitians did not begin to enter the field until early 1974. Like the porters before them, they suffered discrimination from their white employers, white cab drivers, their customers, and from the police. Individual actions, and sometimes the collusion of these groups, conspired to deprive the black taxi driver of his ability to earn a decent wage.

During the 1960s and into the 1970s incidents increased and evidence began to point to serious and systematic discrimination. Incidents included forbidding access to lucrative taxi stands—including Dorval Airport—accepting discriminatory calls from clients who requested white drivers, refusing to accept black owners or drivers, and using racist propagands to steal business from competitors who hired blacks. Black groups joined the Negro Citizenship Association (NCA) to pressure the taxi industry. When it was alleged that one company, SOS Taxi Ltd. had fired all its black drivers and it seemed that other taxi companies were going to follow suit, protests from the black community were finally noticed by the media, which began publish reports on the "shocking" practices of the taxi industry. On July 16, 1982, the Quebec Human Rights Commission announced that it would investigate allegations of racism in the taxi industry, including the racist behaviour of the customers.[21]

Even before the final public hearings, on December 9, 1983 the commissioners were surprised at the prejudice expressed by the people who came before their tribunal. Some members of the public spoke freely of how they did not want to be served by a black taxi driver and that no black driver could ever meet their expectations. An alarming one-in-four Montrealers admitted to "some racial prejudice vis-à-vis black drivers."[22] The Quebec Human Rights Commission concluded in its final report released in November, 1984, that white taxi customers contributed to the development and perpetuation of racial discrimination. The Commission also discovered that the industry had many techniques to exclude and harass black drivers.[23] Through the 1960s and 1970s, though the forms of discrimination varied from one taxi company to another, all were based upon racist values and on the fear of competition.[24] Fifty years after black railway workers took collective action to improve their situation, black taxi drivers were in a similar situation. Once again white men felt threatened by competition from black drivers.

The taxi owners refused outright to hire blacks and established taxi stands reserved for white drivers only. Taxi dispatchers would make phony calls to victimize and harass black drivers. In addition ,a next in line practice permitted dispatchers to bump blacks for the next available white driver. When black drivers successfully integrated an area, white drivers launched campaigns to have stands revert to White Only. They threatened to leave companies which hired white and black drivers and they were caught discouraging white customers from using black drivers. The public unwittingly assisted in the racism against blacks. It was acceptable, even encouraged, to request white only drivers. The 1984 report of the Quebec Human Rights Commission reported that direct and systemic racism permeated the taxi industry, which embarrassed the Quebec government into a major overhaul of the laws and regulations controlling the taxi industry.[25]

Quebec was experiencing profound social change in the 1970s, and even before the election of the separatist Parti Québécois in 1976, political debate focussed on the primacy of the French language. Beginning in 1969 with the Union National's Bill 63, successive governments passed language legislation to acquire control over the linguistic assimilation of immigrants. Demands from the French-speaking population for stronger linguistic legislation caused Premier Robert Bourassa's provincial Liberal government to pass Bill 22, Loi Sur la langue officielle, in July 1974. This bill made French the language of government and the workplace. For Québécois nationalists and labour unions the law did not go far enough; for anglophone and ethnic citizens, the law was too severe, and they did not support the Liberal government in the 1977 provincial election.

During its first mandate, Premier René Lévesque's separatist Parti Québécois (PQ) passed Bill 101, Charte de la langue française (1977) which made French the official language of the state, the courts, schools, and business. Despite objections from Quebec's anglophones, the Charter has been accepted as the mechanism for Quebec governments to control the province's unilingual evolution.

Language legislation during the mandates the Liberals and PQ was butressed by the subsequent hotly-contested 1980 referendum held by the Parti Québécois government. The language-related legislation and the referendum created anxiety and uncertainty among English-speaking blacks as they attempted tried to define the black position in this great political debate. There were some blacks who felt that the the language debate did not concern them because it reflected the concerns of two white, European groups, and that blacks should sit on sidelines of the debate and await the outcome. This was in contrast to other blacks who perceived language as an integral issue and that blacks should take the opportunity to gain recognition of the civil and humanitarian rights for blacks in the province. Despite different perspectives, the result was a convergence of action in the community at the same time blacks were encouraged to promote bilingualism. The passing of the language acts produced a strong negative reaction in the English-speaking black community. The French-speaking population was generally sympathetic to "the goals being pursued by Quebecers to acquire political instruments."[26]

There were several points of view in the English-speaking black community during the decade before the 1980 referendum, but until the election of the Parti Québécois and Bill 101 there was little reaction from the community. The leadership of the commmunity avoided taking a public positions on issues, wishing to avoid being used by either side in the debate. [27] In 1976, prior to the election of the Parti Québécois, Professor Clarence Bayne of Concordia University, speaking on behalf of the BCCAQ, defined the situation as a problem between English and French Canadians. For blacks the question was—would there be more benefits in a federal Canada than in a separate Quebec?[28] By 1977 the continuing language debate had prompted some ethnic/island associations, and several old guard organizations to create a new umbrella organization called the Montreal Alliance of Black Organizations (MABO), to speak on behalf of the more than twenty groups in the alliance on the language issue. [29]

Reverend Frank B. Gabourel of Union United Church, representing MABO at a news conference on April 8, 1977, changed the tenor of the debate in the community first by asserting that the "protection of civil rights [was] much more important than language."[30] He proposed a new black agenda by suggesting that if the provincial government was to assure human and civil rights that blacks would be prepared to support the Parti Québécois' separatist platform. His comments were seen as a major strategic blunder. Other leaders of the BCCAQ called Reverend Gabourel's assertion "political madness" and even equated it with murder. [31] This galvanized the black leadership to act. Four days later on April 12, the BCCAQ released a public statement to clarify the issues as they saw them.[32] The BCCAQ denounced the ethno-centricism reflected in the Parti Québécois' White Paper on Language, and refuted the assertion that language was inseparable from culture. The BCCAQ predicted a severe reduction in immigration from English speaking countries and anticipated that the government's language policy might be used as a basis for employment discrimination. This significant national story from Quebec was carried in the black press across Canada[33]

The community found itself ideologically split into two camps. The two factions were described as the difference between

> those who believe that a threat point must be first established in negotiations with the government before any meaningful concessions are gained, and those who naively believe that in politics one operates in an atmosphere of goodwill…to [just] politely ask… government to observe their human rights in return for black support for that government's policies."[34]

This distinction was both tactical and political, but these differences did not cause a rupture because there was fundamental agreement that French was necessary. Community leaders repeatedly stressed their support for the protection of the French language. Black organizations petitioned the government for funding and other resources for French-language training.[35] There was a groundswell of support in the the community for French language instruction—many families sent their children to French immersion classes or into the French-language school system, hoping to provide their children with an edge in the workplace which their non-French-speaking relatives did not have.[36]

The debate on language issues in Quebec evoked memories of old battles in the black community. The historical relationship between power and language was one that blacks had become all too familiar with. Their original African languages had been suppressed by the English, French, and Spanish colonizers of Africa. Acquiring one language rather than another is a matter of circumstance and not of choice. All people of African descent in Canada live with this legacy; their language of expression is now a European one. The Afro-Canadian experience of employment marginalization which began during the slave period when the language they spoke was French.

Anticipating the future of a predominantly French work milieu, a 1979 editorial in *Focus Umoja* expressed the dilemma black Quebecers might encounter despite their intent on becoming bilingual or trilingual:

> …the indispensable condition of the blacks' survival…will be the acquisition of a fluent knowledge of French. Yet, the bureaucrat will be always too happy to remind you:"Your Mother Tongue [sic] is not French! Moreover…another hurdle is placed in your path. You're

neither Québécois nor French Canadian. The frustrations continue…
your visibility will be given a negative mark as is so often the case
whenever blacks seek employment generally and especially in
competitive fields.[37]

As more and more English-speaking blacks became bilingual, being a visible
minority in Quebec would continue to be a disadvantage. Youth workers
confirm the despair black French or English-speaking youth experience as a
result of the interplay of language and race.[38] A 1992 study of Montreal's
English-speaking blacks by Alberte LeDoyen analyzed the dynamics between
race and language, and concluded:

> Leur vulnérabilité au desavantage socio-économique pourrait provenir
> du cumul de deux facteurs menant potentiellement à l'exclusion: la
> couleur et la langue…La discrimination envers la population noire
> anglophone ayant été décélée dans d'autres domaines que le travail, il
> n'y a pas lieu de se surprendre outre mesure des écarts socio-
> économiques observés, ni non plus du fait que la deuxième génération
> soit soumise elle aussi à des obstacles freinant son intégration égalitaire,
> nonobstant sa connaissance fréquente du français.[39]

On Remembrance Day, November 11, 1987, a nineteen year old unarmed
black, Anthony Griffin, was accused of non-payment of his taxi fare. He waited
for the police peacefully, but was taken into custody on an unrelated outstanding
warrant. Once in the parking lot of police station no. 15 he ran from the
police car, then obeyed the police order to stop running, turned to face the
officers and was shot once in the head by a sixteen-year veteran police constable
AllanGosset.

The reaction was quick and explosive, filled wiith disbelief and outrage.
Meetings within the community took place as the leadership found itself
balanced delicately between the need for constructive action and the need to
channel the outrage and fear of their community. On November 19, 60 people
held a short candle-light vigil which ended at station 15. On Saturday,
November 21 the black community leadership, including the NCC, organized
a major two-hour demonstration that wound its way from Phillip's Square to
the municipal courthouse on Nôtre-Dame street. Thousands of supporters,
including members of the city's ethnic communities, participated to express
their concern and to share the grief of Griffin's death. Similar marches of

solidarity were held in Vancouver, Toronto, and Québec City.

Allan Gosset was charged with manslaughter on November 20, but the charge itself caused controversy and outrage. Manslaughter implied that Gosset shot Griffin because his life was threatened and Griffin intended to harm him. The facts indicated that neither situation had existed. Demands for justice centered around the type of inquiry—public, royal commission, coroner's inquest-that would be established to look investigate the case. On November 24, responding to the demand for accountability, the Quebec Justice Minister Herbert Marx announced that the Quebec Human Rights Commission would hold an inquiry into relations between police and racial minorities. The irony was that the Commission's mandate was limited—the inquiry could probe the Allan Gosset case because it was before the courts!

On July 3, 1991, Marcellus François and two other occupants of the car he was driving were mistaken by the police for two murder suspects. Police tailed the car and surrounded it without warning when it came to a stop. Marcellus François was unarmed but he was shot without cause by Sergeant Michel Tremblay, a ten-year veteran of the MUC police. The reaction in the black community was again swift and strong. The police admitted to bungling the operation.[40] Marcellus François died on July 18, 1991. Though one leader called for civil disobedience, the majority of the city's leadership balanced between constructive action and coping with the outrage and fear of constituents. On Saturday, July 13, 1991 the black community leadership organized a major demonstration and thousands of supporters from all communities marched from Place d'Armes métro station to Premier Robert Bourassa's downtown Montreal office, and then back to the Court House on Nôtre-Dame in Old Montreal.[41]

Police violence against blacks has a long history in Montreal. Police relations have changed over the decades; today there is less familiarity between police and citizens. Bob White of the West End Sports Association remembers that in the 1940s and 1950s:

> there was a better relationship then [between blacks and the police] because you had few English cops and there wasn't much crime amongst the blacks. The police knew the black criminals—they knew them all. Were most of them in jail? No...they lived on the periphery. They had no visible source of income but the police knew them. The police weren't as vicious with them because they were criminals.[42]

Suggestions that it was the black population explosion, or the negative image of blacks as portrayed on American television, or a change in the type of men who became police does not explain why the 1960s witnessed a fundamental change in police relations with the black community. White described it best when he said "now the police are vicious with blacks who aren't even criminals."

On-going conflict between the police and English-speaking West Indian blacks in Côte-des-Neiges was a reality in the early 1970s, as it was between the Haitians and the police in 1979. These were the incidents reported in the press but most of the encounters with the police were not as public.[43] Reported police actions included calling "dirty nigger," assaulting groups and individuals verbally and physically, even telling blacks "to go back to [their] country if [they] weren't happy with…treatment here."[44] As early as 1982 scores of incidents had been recorded at the Quebec Human Rights Commission and the overwhelming number prompted the Commission to launch an investigation into police conduct.[45] The results of the Commission's study in 1988 confirmed that in "the police force, the trivialization of racism sometimes takes the form of denial of the racist character of certain incidents. Lack of awareness of the issue of racism is much more marked at the lower levels of the force…and sometimes goes hand-in-hand with overtly racist or dubious attitudes."[46]

The eradication of racist views with the MUC police force has been identified as an internal police [hiring, training] matter, while the black community has been empowering itself by creating legal and judicial programs. The community's overwhelming grassroots reaction to the Marcellus killing forced the BCCQ to set up a legal clinic and a 24-hour black crisis line. An uneasy truce keeps the black community and the police at bay, though the boundaries of that truce are often strained when past incidents are remembered.

Unlike any previous period, the scale of black migration to Montreal dramatically increased in the mid-sixties—although any attempt at gauging accurate figures is difficult. During 1966 Canada admitted nearly 5,900 blacks, about 45 percent of whom arrived from England and about 45 percent from the British West Indies. Other figures put the number closer to ten or twelve thousand. There were claims that by 1967 immigration from Africa, the West Indies, and Brazil surpassed the 10,000 mark, just below five percent of all immigrants in that year. There is also opinion that in 1967 a minimum of

35,800 immigrants had registered from the larger area of the Caribbean Basin, including West Indies and Antilles.[47]

Nineteen sixty-seven was a pivotal year in Canadian immigration history because of the inauguration of a non-discriminatory immigration policy by the federal government. The policy contributed to a massive nine-year influx of West Indians to Montreal. For the first time the precise criteria for selecting immigrants were defined. Intended to be nondiscriminatory, it was based on a points system where the prospective immigrant earned points based on education, skills, health, and other attributes. Non-white racial groups were, for the first time, theoretically placed on an equal footing with whites.

West Indians immigrants were well-educated, middle-class, and professional or skilled, but this did not ensure that they received automatic acceptance from Canadians. By the mid-sixties their presence and contribution was beginning to be acknowledged. The rapid expansion of government jobs, the explosion of technology, and the post-war baby boom, put their job skills demand—these upwardly mobile blacks were "ambitious and status conscious."[48] Their attitudes, expectations and orientations, were quite different from other West Indians already in Canada and "their approach to social and political problems tended to be more activist" in orientation. Due to their sheer numbers this new generation brought with them different social and institutional links.

Another category of eligibility for immigrants created by the federal government were nominated relatives who were "midway between sponsored dependents and independent applicants." This category enabled relatives in Canada to sponsor family members for immigration and it accounted for the marked increase in immigrants. As many as 115,000 West Indians migrated to Canada from 1967 to 1975, as a result of the changes the Canadian government instituted beginning in the mid-sixties.[49] The high point of black immigration in the 1960s was in 1969 when blacks reached eight percent of total immigration. Of the total black immigration between 1967 and 1974, over 70 percent was from the West Indies, but only between 20 and 30 percent of West Indians entering the country opted to settle in Montreal.[50]. This influx was so large that by 1968, West Indians once again had numerical dominance in Montreal's black community.

During the peak years of Trinidadian immigration between 1973 and 1974 over 600 managers and professionals, 1,500 clerks, and 2,000 skilled and semi-skilled workers came to Canada. Thousands of Barbadians immigrated to Canada during the latter half of the 1960s and the early 1970s and between

1973 and 1976 approximately 14,082 Guyanese. In 1973 and 1974, the peak years for Jamaican immigration, 3,000 immigrated to Quebec.[51]

This high level of emigration of mostly managerial and professional people significantly depleted the educated population of many Caribbean islands. In some quarters, particularly at the governmental level in the West Indies, concern was expressed over Canada's role in the systematic brain drain of the Third World.[52] The United Nations responded to their concerns by 1971 and a study was undertaken to asess the extent of damage caused by the loss of skilled and educated manpower. The educated elite of the Third World came to Canada for economic and political reasons,[53] but the viability of the professional class structure on the islands was at risk. The rapid increase of West Indian migration to Canada in the early eighties evoked "fears that the Dominion would denude the islands of their most highly educated stratum," particularly as "the proportion of skilled and professional people from the West Indies entering Canada [was] among the highest of any migrant group."[54] Ten per cent of West Indian immigrants were classified in the managerial, professional, or technical categories, 14 percent were clerical, 20 percent in service commercial, or transportation occupations, and 12 percent in skilled occupational categories. Less than three percent were classified as laborers. The remainder entered as wives, students, or children of migrants, along with a very low percentage of unskilled workers.[55]

The benefits of this migration to Canada were obvious, and contrary to the popular view, the non-white immigrants did not take away jobs from Canadians. Canada gained the benefit of educated citizens without having had to pay for their education. Such contributions were needed because Canada's population lacked specialized skills in some fields. These immigrants brought skills and money.

Canada gained enormously from immigrants. Out of the three largest recipients of immigrants between 1961 and 1971—the United States, England, and Canada, Canada had the largest net capital value of immigrant labour . In precise figures, Canada gave 2.3 billion (U.S.) dollars in "aid" and received 11 billion (U.S.) dollars worth of skilled labour. This was almost five times what Canada gave. England did not fare nearly as well; it contributed 4.4 billion (U.S.) dollars to Third World development and got back 5.5 billion (U.S.) More surprising is the United States which spent 39 billion (U.S.) dollars on development aid and received only 33 billion (U.S.) worth of skilled immigrant labour.[56] This group of West Indian immigrants were an integral aspect of Canada's economic health during the sixties.

While the English-speaking black community benefited from the West Indian immigration, there was increased demand by Haitians to emigrate to Canada. Quebec's desire for French-speaking immigrants caused large numbers—93 percent of the total—to settle in Montreal during the early seventies.[57] They came to Quebec to escape the repressive Duvalier regime. They also came because changes in laws governing the admission of immigrants to those countries traditionally favoured by Haitians were tightned up. This was true of Zaire, the U.S., the Dominican Republic, and the Bahamas. Another reason was Canada's relatively tolerant Canadian immigration laws, and the Eden-like image of Canada painted by Haitians in Quebec to their friends and relatives in Haiti.[58]

Historically Canada's economic health has relied on immigrants and imported labour. From slavery to the building of the railroads, and from domestic service to the classroom, blacks have been used to fill gaps in the labour market. Professional and skilled black immigrants whose credentials were not accepted or recognized by Canada were forced to work in jobs which Canada needed filled. Canada, like other modern industrial states has had less need for unskilled immigrants.[58] Canada's new immigration policy still constituted a type of discrimination based on expertise. Immigration policy is "a national consequence of the policy of selection based on the skills that were needed and could be absorbed," and immigrants added "to the fund of skills so essential to economic progress, for an expanding economy called for a labor force that was adequate not only in numbers but in quality."[60] The government's approach is "one of manpower and immigration acting as a sort of regulator for the working population : a faucet that could be turned on and off depending on the prevailing state of the economy."[61] The black population in Quebec had known this type of direct intervention before. The Haitian experience, though on a larger scale, echoed that of the English-speaking West Indian and American blacks decades earlier.

Quebec and Ontario received the majority of Canada's new black immigrants. Of Quebec's non-white immigrants, 76 percent chose to live in Montreal.

Montreal's black population was composed of three main cultural/linguistic groups. In order of size they were French- and Creole-speaking Haitians, English-speaking West Indians and black Canadians, and trilingual Africans. The African population was divided into English-speaking (14%), French-speaking (78%) and other (8%) language groups.[62]

The fastest growing black cultural group between 1970-1980 was the Haitian community. From an insignificant minority of a minority population in the late sixties the Haitians eventually made up half of the total black community in the greater Montreal area.[63] By 1977, there were an estimated 17,000 Haitians.[64] The first group of Haitians had relatively little impact on the black English-speaking majority because their numbers were small, and because they came from a professional Haitian population.[65] The second wave of Haitians were Creole-speaking with less education, but even so, from 1968 their numbers grew steadily. In 1975-76 Creole-speaking Haitians made up 70 percent of the working Haitian population.

Estimates by statisticians and demographers reveal tremendous inconsistencies when attempting to define the Haitian population. This is similar to the problems that have plagued other black groups, particularly those from the Caribbean. The tracking of the Haitian population during their greatest period of immigration was hampered by the criteria utilized to document them. For instance, the official Quebec and Canadian statistics for the Haitian population did not include the total working population of Haitians, since they included neither the non-immigrant individuals, (those holding a student, not a resident visa), nor illegal alien or clandestine workers. Moreover, these statistics ignored all the children born in Quebec of Haitian parentage because they were listed as Canadian.[66]

The 1981 Census registered 25,850 Haitians; yet by 1979 the most reliable figure in the community had already been estimated to be closer to 35,000.[67] What the statistics do not reveal is the huge numbers of Haitians wanting to come to Quebec, during the 1970s and 1980s. The potential was so great that if immigration had not been curtailed "there would be as many as 100,000 Haitians in Montreal..."[68]

From 1973-1975 the majority of Haitians who had already obtained their landed immigrant status began to sponsor their relatives—first their children and then their elderly parents. As a result the Haitian population mushroomed although there was a decline in the numbers of working Haitians entering the city.[69] At the same time, the Haitian birth rate increased as spouses were sponsored in increasing numbers and families were reunited.

The 1967 Immigration Act permitted anyone who entered Canada on a tourist visa to apply for a resident's visa or landed immigrant status. Many "tourists" assumed that this was an automatic procedure and they began to settle in Montreal. Many of them did not meet the immigration department's selection criteria and were deported. On November 3, 1972 the government changed the law so that prospective immigrants could no longer use their tourist visa. As the word spread that the laws were changing, the number of Haitians rushing to enter Canada before the November 30th deadline rose dramatically. Haitians with resident status made frantic arrangements to bring in relatives and close friends. Thousands of Haitians continued to enter as tourists even after the deadline.[70] Even though they knew the law had changed, travel agencies and airlines continued to promote Canada as a country where immigrants could arrive first as tourists.[71] Not aware that they were contravening the law, these tens of thousands of "tourists" from many countries were considered to be illegal immigrants and were now threatened with deportation. The outcry that resulted forced the Canadian government to set up an amnesty program on July 31, 1973 called Operation My Country. The program allowed anyone who had entered the country on or before November 30, 1972 to apply by October 15, 1973 for automatic acceptance. The Minister of Manpower and Immigration, Robert Andras, also made it clear than anyone not taking advantage of Canada's amnesty offer, would "run the risk of being sought out and deported without right of appeal."[72]

The response was impressive. At shopping centre storefronts across the country close to 50,000 immigrants from many countries registered during Operation My Country. The federal authorities were puzzled that hundreds of illegal Haitians refused to take advantage of the amnesty. What the officials did not understand was the overwhelming distrust they had for the authorities. Being desperate and having sold everything they owned to get here, they were not going to take any chance that the amnesty program was a ploy to deport them.

Scores of community organizations and other agencies spoke on behalf of those Haitians who came forward or who were caught after Operation My Country ended. This put the organizations at risk and at times their offices were monitored or searched, and workers were questioned by immigration authorities and the police.[73] Realizing that at the appeal level, nine out of ten Haitians were being expelled from Canada, out of fear of expulsion some Haitians preferred to remain underground in Montreal's Haitian community. The Appeal Board considered the Haitians to be economic, and not political refugees.

> According to some observers…these two thousand Haitian immigrants [were] harshly treated by Canadian immigration authorities because they [were] Francophone and black, while federal immigration authorities [were] predominately English.[74]

The Appeal Board refused to invoke its discretionary humanitarian powers. Even the Québec Minister of Immigration intervened on humanitarian grounds. But, again and again, Haitians were sent back to Haiti without any recourse.

The plight of the Haitians galvanized community groups into action. An Anti-Deportation Committee, composed of seven organizations, drew up petitions, set up street demonstrations, and blitzed the media. Unanimous support was received from the print media which encouraged the Appeal Board to grant special redress (or a favourable decision) for economic reasons. As the issue faded from the front pages, by 1974 Haitians were finding their own ways to circumvent the threat of deportation. Some married Canadian citizens or those who had resident status, or had children. Two hundred managed to acquire a ministerial permit from the Minister of Immigration.[75] Unlike the West Indian population a large number were not sponsored by relatives or institutions, because as refugees they did not have to meet the same stringent terms as regular "working" immigrants and did not have to wait long either. In less than ten years the impact of Haitian immigration—most had arrived in the last ten years—was being felt in Quebec society.[76]

Despite the prevailing belief within the English black community that the Haitian community has fared better, the Haitian community itself has been held back by social and economic barriers that also restricted their movement in the workplace—race, not language was the issue. The ascendancy of the French Quebecer has been to the detriment of the minority populations in its midst.

The majority culture is believed to have rights above and beyond those of the individual or minority cultures. Premier Robert Bourassa said that the notion of equality is a residual benefit that arrives to the minority after the insecurities of the majority culture are satisfed.[77] Nowhere is this more evident than with Haitian youth. Almost two decades of francization had created a stronger black community awareness among the younger Haitian population. However, language has not been the stabilizer it was supposed to be. Discrimination, high unemployment and violence continue to cause widespread suffering, and feelings of social dislocation for other blacks in the province. Like the black youth in other communities, Haitian teens do suffer in spite of their language. "They know there's a double standard used to judge them. They know it doesn't matter whether they were born here or born in Haiti. They're black, that all that counts."[78]

By 1986, 38,000 Haitians lived in Montreal yet, the 1986 census demonstrated that, despite their education level, 25 percent of the Haitian population was unemployed. The working population found themselves ghettoized in the manufacturing (50%) and the services sectors (20%). The same census revealed that high educational levels did not produce a higher living status—average income for a Haitian was only half that of the average Québécois.[79] The Haitian population's occupational attainment did not correlate with their educational attainment.[80]

One consequence of being unable to find work is that today's youth cannot see a future for themselves when their siblings are unable to find jobs. With an unemployment rate (for fifteeen to twenty-four year olds) at 45 to 50 percent, youth and community workers express the same concern—how to motivate youth given the black employment market in Montreal. This is a full-time concern for Liesel Albino, Director of Maison des Jeunes:

> we work with kids with no direction, no place to go. They see themselves in an environment where there are ten other kids ahead of them for every job…It is a scary world for them. When they say "I'll go to school and get a degree and then what…" How do you answer them?"[81]

Concerned for their young people, their drift towards crime and self-destruction, and following major police incidents involving blacks, in 1991 members of the English-speaking black community asked the city of Montreal to take steps which would legitimize the presence of blacks in Montreal. In partnership with the city, it would be possible to make black youth, and the community as a whole, proud of its culture. Later that same year, the Mayor Jean Doré made the commitment to have City Hall declare February Black History Month.[82] Since then, Montreal's Black History Month has been a source of pride and unity which has spread throughout the city. With a focus on youth, the black community works together for several months of the year to create a month-long celebration. Black History Month has become a forum for the appreciation of black culture and arts, black cultural diversity, and history, especially local black history.[83]

The majority of Haitians embraced what Quebec had to offer and called Montreal home. Not surprisingly, it was the youth who adapted most quickly—although aware of their Haitian origins, they feel part of the fabric of Quebec—"ils finiront bien par découvrir qu'eux aussi ils sont noirs".[84]

Domestics form an increasing percentage of the Haitian non-immigrant workers or, temporary workers with a work visa and who are often exploited:

> The standard weekly salary of $70 for five working days…is in fact reduced to scandalous levels. It becomes $100, $50, or even $25 per month for seven full working days…under humiliating conditions: the use of the telephone, sitting at the dinner table, communication with relatives or friends, the keeping of a passport… are forbidden. In short it is the replay of domesticity at its worst, as traditionally practiced in Haiti.[85]

Still, one does not have to go far to find parallels. The conditions that the Haitian domestics worked under corresponds to the experience of thousands of other Caribbean domestics since the turn of the century in Quebec.[86]

Domestic work was not the choice of all Haitian women, but it usually was the preferred means of income for those without resident visas. There was a working ghetto in the garment factories for other working women. In their early years in Quebec, the mother in Haitian families was seldom able to stay at home even if she had three or four children. There was a chronic need to supplement their husbands' low wages. This changed the lives of these women and their families because working outside the home was new to the Haitian woman's experience[87]

The birth rate in the Haitian community was high, and despite the sponsorship of elderly relatives, contributed to a population that was actually becoming younger.[88] By the 1991 census the gender ratio of the community had change and women now constituted 56 percent of the population. It appears that the increased entry of domestics to Canada affected the gender balance in the Haitian population in much the same way it had affected the English speaking West Indians several generations earlier.

Adding to the youthfulness of the community was the university and college student population.[89] In the sixties and seventies the majority were from outside the province. They were on student visa and entered Quebec through a circuitous route. Many obtained visas through the large Haitian population in New York. Having lived in the U.S. these students attended school in Quebec to learn French. Others came directly from Haiti in order to obtain a technical skill in electronics, mechanics, hairdressing or secretarial training.

West Indians were by far the largest group of English-speaking blacks in Quebec, comprising 80 percent of the population—about half had come from the

Caribbean since 1966, to join those who had arrived between 1945 and 1966.[90]

In the 1970s and 1980s the majority of immigrating black professionals actually worked in accordance with their training and education. One of the most important benefits for the black community had been the acceptance of West Indian educators. By the mid-seventies, a large number of these teachers were working in schools with high black student populations. They were dismayed at the high rate of failure among black students in Quebec's public schools. The PSBGM, with the largest number black students, found that "out of a hundred blacks regardless of their background, only one percent make it to university while 70 percent fail."[91] The numbers were staggering. What was happening was clear to the community—institutional racism continued to create barriers to academic success.

This conclusion was not shared by everyone who studied the problem of failure. Some believed that "there was no indication that they fared worse or better in school than their white lower class fellow students."[92] In other words, race was inconsequential when compared to the class variable.

The community did not accept this interpretation as the final say on the issue. The Quebec Black Board of Educators responded to the worsening problem of academic failure and created the Black Community Work Group on Education. In 1978 the Work Group submitted a report which tried to explain the high failure rate.[93] The QBBE saw it as a consequence of adaptation problems, pervasive negative stereotyping, pigeonholing students, and a result of an inherently racist curriculum which reflects white Canadians' historical and current perceptions of blacks and the non-white world. Not everyone agreed with this conclusion: "It cannot be said that blacks in Quebec have been, until recent years, consciously or unconsciously rejected outside the realm of historical or sociological studies because of the use of a dominant "white" paradigm..."[94] This view does not take into account the long history of blacks in Quebec, the effects of slavery and racism.

The inherent racism and the damage it causes to black youth was evident to many, particularly in Little Burgundy. Support began to build to move beyond activism on a school-by-school, issue-by-issue basis. In 1977, when school board elections took place, Carl Whittaker decided to run and was elected as a school commissioner to the PSBGM. The vast area he represented included Little Burgundy and Pointe St. Charles. Without a party machine to attract votes, his win in June 1977 was achieved by the work of dozens of black people, young and old, who staffed phones, and canvassed door-to-door. He was the first black to enter the administrative structure of the PSBGM and his election heralded a new relationship between the community and the Protestant school system.[95]

In the business sphere West Indians were succeeding at the managerial level, and were engaged in a renaissance of black enterprises on the island. The limited opportunities were available in a way that had not been possible in the black community since the pre-Depression era. Blacks cited the lack of economic diversity as contributing to their marginalization. During the late 1980s several concerned blacks with various and business skills approached the government to set up a fund for the promotion and support of black businesses. The provincial government responded and with one million dollars, and in 1992 the Mathieu Da Costa Business Development Corporation was inaugurated.[96] The hope is that the MCBDC will kickstart an economic resurgence within the community, as black businesses hire, train and invest in black labour.

" Canadian" blacks made up only 20 percent of the English-speaking black population in the MUC, or roughly 12,000 thousand.[97] Fifty per cent of the Afro-Canadian population were first, second and third generation descendants of Canadians who had lived in Montreal prior to 1930. Another 10 to 20 percent were probably descended from, or were born in either Nova Scotia or New Brunswick.[98] The remaining 30 percent were first and second generation descendants of West Indians who migrated after World War II. These two culturally diverse groups, since the forties, have comprised the bulk of the black community in Montreal. Only recently have Canadians and West Indians been out numbered by the Haitian population.

Africans, the newest addition to the black community in Quebec, numbered about 5,000.[99] From 1975 to 1978, 27,252 Africans immigrated to Canada, mostly from the English-speaking countries such as South Africa, Kenya, Tanzania and Egypt.[100] There were 6,717 francophone Africans from Cameroon, Côte d'Ivoire, the Congo and Zaire, who mostly settled in Quebec.[101] (148 Africans were allowed into Quebec with refugee status). The African immigrants were highly highly educated. A 1983 study indicated that more than 80 per cent had studied at the university level,[102] but in spite of this, 64 percent were without work for periods of between one and five years. Even more telling was the fact that 90 percent of respondents had an annual income of around $9,000. Only 5 percent had incomes averaging $20,000.[103]

The size of Montreal's black population has always been in question. By 1970 the accepted figure for the black population of the Montreal Urban Community (MUC) was 15,000. Yet there are published figures that range from 55,000 (in 1974)[104] to 200,000! In 1977 Clarence Bayne lowered that figure to 75,000,[105] and Pastor Frank Gabourel of Union United Church lowered the estimate even further when he stated that Montreal's black population was 60,000 including 16,000 French speakers.[106]

One year later, in 1978, the Work Group had reported that the Consultative Committee of the Ministry of Immigration of Quebec estimated that there were 85,000 blacks, including anglophones and francophones, in the province.[107] This was followed up in a 1979 report to the Public Security Council of the MUC wherein the NCC Board of Directors had placed the level of blacks in Montreal at 80,000. That same year The *Gazette* quoted Dr. Fortas of the Afro-Canada Conference who claimed that there were 200,000 blacks in Montreal,"[108] and in 1981, Marcil wrote that 100,000 blacks in Montreal should be considered a conservative estimate.[109] One thing is evident from these various estimates, an accurate count of Quebec's black population has yet to be achieved.

Montreal's English-speaking black population was in flux during the late sixties and early seventies, and two definite patterns emerged.[110] In the late sixties West Indian blacks left the inner city districts for Lasalle, and in the early seventies these upwardly mobile blacks left Lasalle for the West Island or the South Shore.[111] This accelerated movement reflected the benefits of a higher level of education and gains made in income from better jobs. An improvement in financial status resulted in better homes in better neighbourhoods. The housing stock of the old districts was not adequate and the transition into white middle class areas was the goal of these blacks who sought the visible privileges of the white middle class. Also, when poor blacks began to move into the districts where management level and professional blacks lived, the elite moved out to newer more expensive districts. This was a pattern often repeated.

One consequence of this pattern was that it affected the viability of community organizations in the core districts. For instance, the Dr. Gaspar Branch of the Colored War Veterans suffered terribly when many of its members moved to the suburbs and other parts of city where they joined integrated Legion branches closer to where they lived. The loss of members forced the branch to close.[112]

During the early seventies there was a movement of poor and working-class blacks out of the southwest sectors of Montreal, including areas like Little Burgundy, Pointe St. Charles, and St. Henri. Like the middle class blacks, the poor wanted to leave the negative reputation and stigma of the older neighbourhoods—this was particularly pronounced during the the period of urban renewal in the early seventies. As the new uptown black communities of Côte-des-Neiges and NDG were established, rivalry was created between the uptown and the downtown youths. According to the uptown teens, living in Little Burgundy was the ultimate putdown, and youths from downtown were held in disdain—little wonder that they wanted to leave the district. Years later some would return to live permanently in the community they remembered so fondly.

In the 1980s in an effort to remove the stigma associated with Little Burgundy, some individuals and groups began to refer to the area as Quartier Georges-Vanier, perhaps encouraged by successive municipal administrations which also wished to eradicate the negative associations of Little Burgundy. Quartier Georges-Vanier exemplified all that was new in the neighbourhood and heralded a new period in the old community. Georges P. Vanier, one of the district's most prominent native sons (born on St. Antoine street in 1888), was Canada's first French-speaking Governor General from 1959 to 1967. A subway station and a municipal library in this area now bear his name.

During this period, from the 1960s to the mid-1970s, large areas of Little Burgundy were under development, and forced the relocation of thousands of citizens. Vacant lots became condominium projects, rows of triplexes, and blocks of semi-detached housing. In addition, there was a further refurbishment which included fountains for renovated parks and new widened streets, to the extent that few of the former residents would recognize Quartier Georges Vanier as the West End or as the St. Antoine community it once was. Not only were the changes dramatic, to some they were threatening as well.

Blacks living in low income public housing and co-op housing projects could not dream of living in buildings constructed by the private developers—for those on fixed incomes, rents could represent anywhere from 80 percent to all of their monthly income. Since the City of Montreal was no longer building low income housing, available housing stock for low income families was at a standstill. Within a very short period of time the new residents—white middle class ex-suburbanites and well-to-do-immigrants from developing countries[113]—would outnumber the old. There was little contact between the two groups, either by adults or the children who played on their own streets . Since there was no longer an English-language school in the district, there was an absence of the interaction that takes place in the class and in the school yard. The only school in the community was the French-language École Petite Bourgogne, the former St. Joseph parish school. All of these deveopments increased the isolation of the remaining residents of the black community.

With the arrival of newly-constructed condominiums and triplexes, new parks, and a new subway station, came high property tax evaluations and high taxes. Changes in the rental controls also gave the city far more leeway in adjusting rents. These factors forced up rents throughout the area while at the same time public housing tenants were left without protection—it was not unusual for tenants to receive rent increases of 20 to 50 percent in one year. There was a feeling among the public housing tenants that the city was trying to squeeze out the poor to make way for other, more desirable residents.[114]

Despite these changes, blacks stayed in the area for economic reasons and because their family history was tied up with the history of the West End and St. Antoine, even though their children are bussed to schools outside the area.[115] They had been a part of the black community in the area for generations—regardless of income or status, leaving the district meant leaving part of one's family history behind. This was why many have felt threatened by the changes.

The population of blacks living in Little Burgundy was considerably less than it was in the late 1950s. There were probably 3,000 blacks living in the area in the mid 1980s.[116] One study found that nine percent of the total anglophone black community lives in Little Burgundy,[117] for the most part, households headed by women usually on fixed income, and seniors on marginal incomes.[118]

In spite of the new private development, the presence of black institutions, and the history of the community, the black middle class was not returning to this community. Ironically, the area was gaining a new status among the white middle class population, although there was a time when they would not even consider living in the distirct. However, for the generations of blacks who struggled to leave; moving back downtown was not an option. To Montreal's black anglophone population it was still Little Burgundy—despite the fact that it was no longer a slum. Instead of enclaves based mainly on language or race, the old neighbourhood was now dividing along class lines. This will probably remain the case until either the black middle class returns to the district, or until the disadvantaged blacks leave. Until then the black community in Little Burgundy will continue to shrink.

Montreal's Côte-des-Neiges (CDN) district has been a reception neighbourhood for immigrants since the post war period.[119] In the early sixties this white collar district was home to second and third generation white immigrants. In the sixties Côte-des-Neiges quickly lost its lustre with the influx of thousands of black immigrants. As blacks moved into the high rise and multi-unit apartment buildings, white residents moved out to the suburbs. The departure of property owners began the process of the deterioration of the housing stock.

When the young upwardly-mobile whites left the area for the suburbs, they created a reduction of social and educational services. For instance, by 1973, primary and secondary schools in the Côte-des-Neiges area had a black student population of 30 to 40 percent, up 400 percent from just ten years earlier. By the mid-seventies the Protestant School Board of Greater Montreal began to respond to the increasing racial tensions in the inner city schools by hiring black teachers, instituting curriculum changes, creating programs to help students to adapt. Their aim was also to reverse the growing number of failures among blacks.[120] The lack of social services was felt in the black community for several years until services were developed that met the needs of the non-white population. In the meantime as needs were not met, social services deteriorated.

The loss of young white families also created a demographic imbalance in Côte-des-Neiges—the whites that remained were generally old people, retired or on pension, who either did not have the inclination or the money to make the move to the suburbs. Although they didn't leave the district they moved away from the areas where large numbers of blacks lived, creating white streets and black streets. In the 1970s and 1980s there were "gentlemen's agreements"—whites on certain streets agreed not to sell or rent to blacks and other undesirable non-whites, in order to protect their property values.[121] Streets were reserved for middle class duplexes, single family homes, and apartment buildings with high concentrations of whites. The whites who engaged in this practice deliberately segregated themselves from the black population in clean and well lit buildings.[122]

When a landlord maintains housing the tenants take pride in where they live. With absentee landlords, those forced to rent substandard or poorly maintained housing in which the landlord takes little pride, were themselves less likely to take pride in the dwellings. This was the case in Côte-des-Neiges until the 1990s—there was little loyalty to the neighbourhood. Côte-des-Neiges was a stepping stone to better districts and blacks did not aspire to owning the tenements around them. For those streets where non-whites live, they "could be easily classified as slum areas…It was not surprising therefore that the area was called a ghetto."[123]

Absentee landlords contributed to the process of deterioration. The owners of the tenement housing who left for the suburbs "felt no social or economic pressure to invest in upkeep and maintenance."[124] This was a familiar process with absentee landlords throughout the country, particularly in response to the existence of non-white populations. These landlords deliberately chose to rent to immigrants who were ignorant of the rental market and not likely to be familiar with their rights as tenants. When landlords neglect basic services without fear of legal reprisals, and charge higher rents, immigrants often do not know what to expect. Once it has been established that a landlord will accept non-whites, many new immigrants follow.[125] Eventually housing conditions become congested, and housing stock deteriorates as landlords ignore basic upkeep of their properties.

The black middle class quickly abandoned the area, leaving only the poor, the disadvantaged and the most recent immigrants to live in crowded tenement housing. This included half the African population in Montreal even though thirty percent of their children were born in Canada.[126] Reliable black population estimates for Côte-des-Neiges usually hovered around twenty thousand. Thirty-six percent of the English-speaking black community live in Côte-des-Neiges.[127]

This picture began to change around 1990 as the result of many circumstances. The first factor was that the vacancy rate in areas outside of CDN rose appreciably. It was not unusual for blacks to leave attracted by offers of two or three month free rent. Therefore blacks moved to Laval, the West Island, and certain South Shore communities, mostly because of the cheaper and better rental properties and housing.

The second factor was the result of the agitation and mobilization that took place among the tenants and interested groups that remained in CDN. Pressure was brought to bear on the city to set up tenant co-operatives. Abandoned buildings were bought and renovated by the city in certain key run-down areas like Plamondon and Barclay, after which a waiting list was set up for apartments with rents controlled according to income.

The third feature concerns the purchasing strategy of Haitian immigrants who had moved into Côte-des-Neiges over a five to seven year period since 1982. They utilized a unique co-operative method. People would move into a privately-owned apartment building, then purchase it as a housing co-op for their families and friends, thus establishing control over their own housing and removing the threat of discrimination. In this novel way whole groups of Haitians have purchased housing property in the area.

As a result of the growth of the Haitian population, towards the end of the 1980s organizations such as the Maison des Jeunes Côte-des-Neiges experienced a significant increase in the number of Haitian youth attending their programs. And when families have moved elsewhere, particularly to Lasalle, the young people continued to return to these community centres. Both the Black Community Association and the Maison des Jeunes in Côte-des-Neiges reported that 40 percent or more of their youth membership lived outside the district.[128]

Blacks have been living in Nôtre-Dame-de-Grace (NDG) for decades,[129] although prior to the 1960s blacks were the exception rather than the rule. Like Côte-des-Neiges, after the mid 1960s NDG served as a reception area for immigrants, but for several reasons the deterioration of housing stock and social services did not occur. According to the 1981 census, one quarter of the blacks in NDG owned their own homes. In contrast only five percent of the blacks in Côte-des-Neiges and Little Burgundy owned their homes. Most anglophone blacks in CDN did not aspire to own the tenement housing that surrounded them.

Most of the homes in NDG north of de Maisonneuve boulevard were single family dwellings, duplexes and triplexes. During the 1960s young whites left NDG for the suburbs, as they did in Côte-des-Neiges, but housing in NDG did not deteriorate because they were replaced by new homeowners. This contrasts with those areas where a preponderance of absentee landlords contributed to the creation of run-down conditions.

The one exception in NDG were the blocks of tenement housing in the northern Walkley street area, from Somerled north to Fielding. Blacks who lived there were usually on fixed or marginal incomes. Many worked as orderlies, nurses aides, companions, housekeepers, and cleaners in the numerous nursing homes, seniors citizens' residences, private and chronic health care facilities for the well-to-do elderly white population of the surrounding area.

NDG was once home to the elite of the black community.[130] Today its black community is a mix that includes not only professionals but also white collar workers and the disadvantaged and working poor. Such wide-spread economic differences do not exist in Little Burgundy or Côte-des-Neiges, however like Côte-des-Neiges during the 1970s, NDG's black community lost a significant part of its population when young black families moved to Lasalle.

Lasalle experienced a ten-year construction boom from 1965 to 1975. In the 1960s this middle class suburb attracted Greek and Italian homeowners, and in the 1970s Lasalle was popular with young upwardly-mobile blacks. The new blacks liked Lasalle's suburban environment—the broad streets, triplexes, and parks. As the area improved due to the creation of new housing , and with the introduction of the subway system, rents became prohibitive for some. The blacks who lived here previous to this period consisted mainly of Canadian (Nova Scotian) blacks living in the Heights Project which they vacated as Lasalle's property values soared and the rents increased. They returned to Montreal and found housing in Côte-des-Neiges or NDG. During this period the most frequent source of friction between blacks and the Greek and Italian property owners in Lasalle focussed on rental disputes, including high rents and repairs not being done.[131] In eastern Montreal racial discrimination from Greek and Italian landlords continues to be the biggest problem. [132]

High rents in Lasalle forced many black families to pool their resources to buy homes outright. Some researchers estimate that 45 percent of the black population own their homes in Lasalle,[133] Others suggested the figure is closer to 60 percent.[134]They all agree, however, that the main reason blacks made the effort to purchase was due to the high rents in Lasalle.

In the late 1970s and the early 1980s, about eight percent of the black population—mostly young middle class blacks. left Lasalle for the West Island and the South Shore because they were unable to find reasonable housing.[135] The homes in these areas were actually cheaper than Lasalle. To cite one example, in 1962 Vere Rowe and his family left the downtown community of St. Antoine and moved to NDG where they lived until 1967. In 1967 they moved to Lasalle. In 1975, due to the high cost of housing and lack of single family dwellings, Rowe and his family purchased a home on the South Shore. This was very typical of black middle class mobility in Montreal. Each move was within a black community, and reflected an improvement of the family's income, status and lifestyle.[136]

The West Indian population of Lasalle between 1971 and 1981 doubled.[137] Even though some people left Lasalle, the city's black community by 1986 had stabilized at between 15,000 and 20,000.[138] The BCCQ estimates the anglophone black population of Lasalle to be 20 percent of the total anglophone black community of Montreal. Lasalle's family-oriented black community is stable and active with activities at black organizations well attended—much like what had developed in the West End community before urban renewal.

The core of blacks in Verdun, mostly homeowners, were old line families who established themselves there during the twenties and thirties.[139] They make up a small percentage of the black population in this old suburb of Montreal. Their children left Verdun to live in Lasalle—the same as what happened in NDG and other areas.

Did they leave Verdun because housing was expensive or because these blacks want to live in a newer suburb ? It was not a simple step for blacks to move to the more suburban residential areas west of Verdun's working class sector. Although homes (detached and semi-detached) were relatively less expensive than those available in Lasalle, blacks were discrimination against—properties were not always made available to black buyers. Another reason could be the desire of these young families to be a part of a larger black community. Blacks in Verdun had always been in the mainstream of activities either in the downtown community, or in recent years within Lasalle's black community, but Verdun did not have its own black clubs or associations. Improved status was most likely what made a move to Lasalle so attractive.

Yet, as the old established Verdun families lost a generation, there was an influx of Canadian blacks from the inner city communities. These were people displaced by the urban renewal of the downtown core, such as Little Burgundy—welfare recipients, single mothers, and students who had come to take advantage of the lower cost of living found in the working class areas of Verdun.

What was significant about this was that there were some blacks with marginal incomes who were not moving to Verdun. The working class areas of Verdun were one of the least expensive areas of to rent in the Montreal Urban Community and it was also very accessible in terms of transportation. Yet these rents were not as strong an attraction as would be presumed, because, relative to other areas, there were very few blacks living in Verdun.[140] This was probably the same reason that young blacks had left Verdun. Few blacks aspire to live in the white working class section of Verdun and it would appear that during the eighties the black population was diminishing.

The black population on the West Island and the South Shore has grown within the past ten years. The BCCQ has estimated that these suburban areas had about 10 percent of the total black population, and this was probably an underestimation. At the greatest total population of 90,000 anglophones, the

West Island and the South Shore would have had 9,000 blacks scattered throughout their far flung municipalities. The number of blacks living in the West Island and South Shore encouraged the creation of black community associations. The South Shore Black Community Association which was established in 1981, boasted a membership of 600 in 1995.

Blacks have been living on the South Shore for about sixty years. During the 1950s and early 1960s blacks were attracted to South Shore communities by the availability of housing for veterans.[141] Recently, young upwardly mobile Montreal blacks moved to the South Shore municipalities of St. Hubert, Brossard, Longueuil, St. Bruno and to Greenfield Park. Approximately three-quarters of the black people who live on the South Shore, originally lived on the island of Montreal.

The West Island has been home to young black families since the sixties when black professionals, particularly those from the Caribbean, moved there. In 1971 there were blacks in Pierrefonds, Dollard-des-Ormeaux, Beaconsfield, and Dorval.[142] The West Island represented the ultimate middle class status.

Ironically, in 1986, the fastest growing group of black residents on the West Island were the poor who rented the homes of the white middle class who were moving to downtown Montreal.and renting out their homes in the suburbs. The rents charged were comparable to those in Côte-des-Neiges.[143] These blacks lost access to the downtown black communities, but they gained middle class amenities like schools, municipal services, and open spaces. This movement was happening across North America. The poor were moving out to the suburbs and the middle class were moving back into the downtown core. The move to the suburban communities did not automatically mean they were joining the middle class.[144]

As in Verdun, a large percentage of the St. Laurent community was made up of English-speaking old line black Canadian families who moved there as war veterans. About half of them owned their homes[145] and worked in the industries situated around St. Laurent. The city offered a wide range of services to the poor and the elderly which included free bus tickets for welfare recipients and for seniors, and payment for some medical prescriptions.[146]

In the 1970s, West Indian immigrants moved to Ville St. Laurent. Exact numbers do not exist—figures released recently by the city of St. Laurent do not list the ethnic/racial groups, but linguistic groupings.[147] Over the past five years there have been enough blacks in the city for English and French schools in the city to establish outreach programs for black students.[148]

The three most notable aspects affecting the distribution of the Haitian population in Montreal prior to 1990 were the division between the classes, the movement to the north and the central east areas of the city and the lack of contact between the English and French-speaking black communities.

Middle and upper class Haitians generally live in areas with few poor Haitians, such as the West Island, the South Shore, Westmount, and Laval. Attracted by low rents, most Haitians lived in Little Burgundy, Côte St. Paul, and St. Henri in the southwest, and in communities such as Pointe-aux-Trembles in the extreme eastern end of the island.

On the island of Montreal poor and working-class Creole-speaking Haitians quickly moved north and then east into the French or white immigrant working- and middle-class districts including Montreal North, St. Michel, St. Leonard, and Rosemont. With an average income of about $10,000 per year (1986), there was little exchange between them and higher income professional Haitians who had arrived earlier.[149] Thus the social distance between these groups in Montreal was not only a carryover from the class structure in Haiti, it was a consequence of their two separate mobility patterns.

The Haitians did not follow the immigrant patterns of the English-speaking blacks, or Europeans. They moved up and out of the St. Lawrence corridor in less than one generation, and they had consistently, with few exceptions, remained east of the English-speaking population in French-speaking east Montreal.[150] The only common area of English-speaking blacks that matches the density of the Haitian community was a small section of Côte-des-Neiges. For all intents and purposes the Haitian community started at St. Lawrence and moved east while the English-speaking community began there and went to the south-west.

Over ten years both patterns became more striking. The English-speaking black community was more concentrated in the southwest, the inner city, and on the West Island. By 1981 the Haitians were congregating in increasing densities north along the corridor, and more particularly in the east and north central areas. The Creole-speaking Haitian population has (with one exception) almost totally abandoned the St. Lawrence boulevard corridor especially in the south. Between 1965 and 1981 84 percent of Haitian families had moved away.[151]

Montreal North had only half a dozen Haitian families in the early 1960s, by 1986 had grown into a vibrant community of seven thousand, including businesses.[152] Haitians moved into Montreal North in two distinct waves between 1963 and 1970, beginning first with the more educated professional group. Their small presence did not cause much friction with the white population because, as part of Haiti's francophone urban middle class, they were able to adapt easily. Once settled, they prospered and then moved on to better neighbourhoods. Then between 1976 and 1979 there was a high vacancy rate in the housing units in Montreal North. Another group of Haitians from the older areas like Rosemont, Park Extension, and the southern St. Lawrence boulevard, looking for more modern housing conditions, moved in to replace the middle class who had left. Some people feel that this non-white influx contributed to an exodus of francophones from Montreal North[153] and resulted in absentee landlords and overt housing discrimination. Ghettoization of the Haitian population began and apartments (some no older than ten years) deteriorated rapidly. The similarity to the pattern in Côte-des-Neiges was obvious—the deterioration of housing conditions was a major drawback of a racist environment.

St. Leonard, situated in the northeast periphery of the Montreal Urban Community, was one of Quebec's newer municipalities which developed rapidly during the booming economic expansion of the early 1960s. Like Lasalle, St. Leonard was another garden city and like Lasalle it was basically a middle class Italian neighbourhood with social and cultural services that were not geared toward Haitian needs.[154] The Haitian community had to seek out services in Rosemont.

At first glance it appears that "the Haitian choice of St. Leonard was somewhat of an enigma since it seems like the most unlikely setting for newly arrived immigrants."[155] However, community worker Joseph Bataille contends that at the time when Haitians desired to move out of the St. Lawrence and Park Extension areas, hundreds of duplex basement apartments became available for rent in St. Leonard.[156] To a certain extent this still remains the type of dwelling for the majority of blacks within the area. Unlike Côte-des-Neiges, St. Leonard had a shortage of multi unit residential structures during its influx of about 2000 immigrants.[157] One consequence of basement living was that residential mobility within the Haitian community of St. Leonard became, "concerned with first or second floor status within the duplex/triplex network."[158]

This underscores the similarities and differences with anglophone blacks in Lasalle. Both groups were living in white immigrant districts. Both areas had duplex and triplex housing. The difference between them was economic. For the most part, the blacks in Lasalle were middle class. The Haitians were living in a middle class district but were not middle class. Unlike blacks in

Lasalle few Haitians had achieved ownership status.

According to a YMCA community project, Vivre en Harmonie, Ville St. Laurent now has a small ghetto for recent immigrants.[159] Haitians and other non-whites are concentrated around Crevier street—the 1981 census indicated that this area had the highest density of Haitians in St. Laurent.

Vivre en Harmonie describes four general guidelines which affected mobility within St. Laurent's immigrant population. Not surprisingly, discrimination was the first determinant, but this was not necessarily racial discrimination. Discrimination occurred often due to language differences and cultural prejudices. Negative experiences with discriminating landlords made people hesitate to move. Often, they opted to stay where they were already accepted. The second reason was that they wanted to stay with their own ethnic/racial group. This was very typical immigrant behaviour and explains, in part, the ethnic concentration in the western sections of St. Laurent.[160]

The third factor was that government intervention played a role in determining the make-up of the black population in St. Laurent. Some immigrants with special status had their first year's rent paid for by the provincial government, which also chose the area and the type of housing the immigrants lived in during this period.

The fourth general guideline affecting mobility in St. Laurent was related to the person's education, aspirations, and to their economic status after their first year in Canada. Those Haitians with good jobs had the option to relocate outside the immigrant ghetto. Most chose to stay where they were because as more immigrants entered the neighbourhood, a community developed.[161] In a very real way, government policy in Ville St. Laurent created a new reception neighbourhood on the island by fostering immigrant housing, and establishing long term residential concentrations of non-whites in a specific area.

The trickle of immigrants from the developing world to Canada which began in the 1950s and early 1960s, became a wave in the 1970s. As the result of the new federal regulations in 1967 that permitted visitors to Canada to apply for immigrant status from inside the country, the period from the mid-sixties to the mid-seventies was Canada's greatest period of non-white immigration. This is how the majority of West Indians gained landed immigrant status. By 1970, immigrants from Asia and the Caribbean represented 23 percent of all imigrants to Canada.[162] The number of blacks who entered the country put them in third place overall behind immigrants from United Kingdom and Italy.

For the first time, fifty per cent of all Canadian immigration was non-white.[163] In the nine year period, 1967 to 1975, as many as 115,000 West Indians immigrated, either sponsored by Canadian relatives, an employer, or as un-sponsored individuals of exceptional merit. This was remarkable when we remember that (officially at least) until 1955 there had been only 7,000 West Indians in Canada. Employer-sponsored immigrants also caused another influx of domestics. These high numbers tapered off after the Green Paper which pre-vented people on tourist visas from applying for landed immigrant status from inside the country. For 1976 and 1977 less than 27,000 West Indians entered Canada. This drop was significant because in 1974 alone over 24,000 West Indians had arrived.[164] The Green Paper signalled the end of high West Indian immigration and the character of Montreal's black community once again began to undergo fundamental change.

Blacks in Montreal have struggled to create a dynamic community. It is a continuing journey which began over three hundred years ago and which was shaped by slavery, emancipation, Quebec's pioneer economy—alongside the French, and then the English—the railroad, black student activism, and immigration. Our road to now does not end here, it rolls on into our proud future.

MAP 1

St. Joseph Ward, 1923

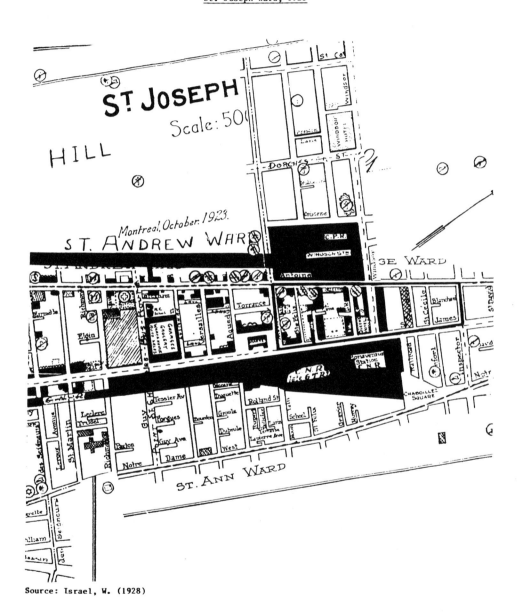

Source: Israel, W. (1928)

MAP 2

St. Cunegonde, 1923

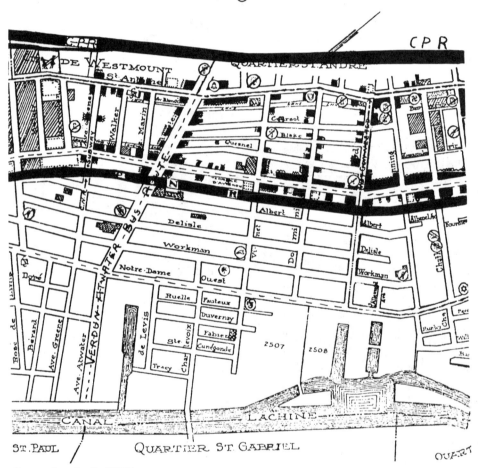

Source: Israel, W. (1928)

MAP 3

City of St. Henry, 1923

QUARTIER St HENRI
Échelle: 500'=1"

Source: Israel, W. (1928)

Notes

[1]Other accounts such as R. Winks, *The Blacks in Canada: A History*, (Montreal: McGill-Queen's University Press, 1971) refer to earlier dates: 1501 in Newfoundland by Gaspar Corte Real, and 1608 in Acadia, by Sieur Du Gua de Monts; both were owners of Indians and African slaves. See: "Black Days in the North: Sad Roots, in Canadian Heritage," (December, 1979).

[2]C. Marcil, "Les communautés noires au Québec," in *Education Québec*, vol. 2 no. 6, 1981, stated that Le Jeune was from Guinea rather than from Madagascar. Both places are cited as possible in *The Silent Minority: Canadians of African Descent*. Essay in Roy States Collection. Montreal: McGill University, c.a. 1977. and M. Trudel, *Dictionnaire des esclaves et de leurs propriétaires au Canada français*, (Lasalle: Éditions Hurtubise HMH Ltée., 1990), 174. See Winks, 1971: 1.

[3]Colin Thomson, *Blacks in Deep Snow: Black Pioneers in Canada*, (Don Mills: J. M. Dent & Sons Ltd., 1979), 17.

[4]*Dictionnaire* is a fascinating and unique look into the institution of slavery during the French regime. The first part of the book is a personal biography of each slave, including particulars on birth, residence, details of manumission, communion, marriage, baptism, offspring, and death. The second part is a region by region survey of slave owners and the slaves they owned. This is a challenge and certainly a shock to the average Quebecer who is unaware that slavery had ever been a part of their past.

[5]This figure is a revision of the previous census done by M. Trudel, *L'esclavage au Canada français: histoire et condition*, (Quebec: Presses Université de Laval, 1960), who was quoted in Williams, *Blacks in Montreal*, 1989. Using additional sources, Trudel found 488 more slaves. He states that 2.6% of slaves were either from slaves born after the manumission of their parents or they had entered the country after abolition.

[6]Trudel, 1990: xvi.

[7]Trudel, 1990: xix.

[8]F. X. Garneau, *Histoire du Canada Francais depuis sa Découverte*, (Quebec: 1846) 1st edit.

[9]Winks, 1971: 19.

[10]Ibid.

[11]T. Watson Smith, *The Slave in Canada*, 1889.

[12]Winks, 1971: 297.

[13]See: W. L. Morton, *The Kingdom of Canada*, 1963; E. McInnis *Canada: A Political and Social History*, 3rd edition, (Toronto: Holt Rinehart and Winston, 1969); R. C. Harris & J. Warkenton *Canada Before Confederation: A Study in Historical Geography*, (New York: Oxford University Press, 1974). This attitude at the national level

contrasts with Montreal's earliest historians, many of whom included the slave chronology in their texts. See: Terril, *A Chronology of Montreal and of Canada A.D. 1752*. Hector Berthlet, *Le Bon Vieux Temps Montréal*; Atherton, *Montreal 1535-1914*.

[14]Trudel, 1960: 333.

[15]Winks, 1971: 12. Though Winks may have believed this, John Maxwell's study on the Church and slavery found a completely contradictory conclusion. Was it a pious act to emancipate slaves? After looking at the historical ecclesiastical record Maxwell stated that "it was an opinion repeated by a number of seventeenth century moralists that usually it is not." John F. Maxwell, *Slavery and the Catholic Church: the History of Catholic Teaching Concerning the Moral Legitimacy of the institution of Slavery*, (London: Barry Rose Publishers, 1975), 85.

[16]Maxwell, 1975: 70.

[17]Maxwell, 1975: 73.

[18]For an account of this and other punitive measures against slaves, see: *Negro Slavery in Montreal*, unpublished article, Montreal: Roy States Collection, McGill University Archives (n.d.); Trudel, 1960; Trudel, 1990: 213-231, "Crimes et châtiment" in *Esclavage*; Wilfred Israel, *Montreal Negro Community*, M.A. thesis (Montreal: McGill University, 1928), 66, 67; L. Bertley, "Slavery," in *Focus Umoja* Montreal, no. 16, 1976; L. Bertley, *Canada and Its People of African Descent*, (Pierrefonds: Bilongo Publishers, 1977); Thomson, 1979; L. Warner, *A Profile of the English-Speaking Black Community in Quebec*, (Montreal: Comité d'implantation du plan d'action à l'intention des communautés culturelles, 1983); *Silent Minority* (n.d.); Marcil, 1981.

[19]During this period people were tortured to induce them to reveal names of accomplices and to substantiate proof through confession. Its severity depended on sex and age. See: Julius R. Ruff, *Crime, Justice and Public Order in Old Regime France*, (London: Croom Helm, 1984), 62, 139; and Antoinette Wills, *Crime and Punishment in Revolutionary Paris*, (London: Greenwood Press, 1981) Torture in France was abolished in May 1788 in the "lit de justice."

[20]It is becoming popular to describe the death of Marie-Joseph Angelique in detail in the popular literature. This account comes from *Negro Slavery in Montreal* (n.d.) For an account of the role of the Church in her death see: Winks, 1971, Trudel, 1961: 226-229. During this period, harsh punishments such as torture, garrottings, and executions were carried out in public to discourage crime and anti-social behaviour. Cutting off the hand was the punishment for theft. Arson was considered the most serious property offence in the old Regime. Ruff, 1984: 139. In the U.S. slaves were routinely burned alive at the stake for arson. See: P. Giddings, *When and Where I Enter: The Impact of Black Women on Race and Sex in America*, (New York: William Morrow & Co. Inc., 1984), 39, 40. Hanging was considered disgraceful and reserved for thieves and those of low birth. Women were usually beheaded and it was not unusual for people to be garrotted as a prelude to burning. Franz Schmidt, A *Hangman's Diary: Being the Journal of Master Franz Schmidt Public Executioner of Nuremburg 1537-1617*, (Montclair, N.J.: Patterson Smith, 1973), 56.

[21]Wills, 1981. Still others view the actions of the authorities toward Angelique as a demonstration of pity. See Stephen Leacock, *Stephen Leacock's Montreal* (Toronto: McClelland & Stewart, 1948, rev. 1963), 80.

[22]Frederick I. Case, *Racism and National Consciousness*, (Toronto: Plowshare Press, 1977), 10. Other historians have ignored this fact and describe Canadian slavery as benevolent. "The evidence, on the whole, would indicate that the conditions of slaves was not hard." Negro Slavery (n.d.). "As a rule, it appears that the slaves were not badly treated..." O. Bartolo, "Blacks in Canada: 1608 to Now," in *A Key to Canada Part II*, (Toronto: National Black Coalition of Canada, 1976). "Black slaves in Canada had it easier than their cousins in the States and the West Indies," *Black Days in the North: Sad Roots*, December, 1979: 43. A recent perspective found in M. Dumont, M. Jean, M. Lavigne, J. Stoddart, *Quebec Women: A History*, R. Gannon, R. Gill trans. (Toronto: The Women's Press, 1987), 97; presents a picture of black slaves as being uneducatable and therefore responsible for their harsh treatment. The writers, while acknowledging that "the death rate amongst these slaves was high" explain that it was because "adapting to white society was difficult." They conclude that slaves "did not always make ideal servants, even if they did not have to be paid for their work."

[23]For one case of repeated escapes see Trudel, 1960: 215. It was not unusual for fugitives to run away with a white person who pretended to be their slave owner. See: E. McManus, *Black Bondage in the North*, (Syracuse University Press, 1973.)

[24]Trudel, 1961: 43. Within two years the number of panis slaves increased significantly.

[25]Marriages during the French period were legally valid and the female slave attained her freedom after marriage.

[26]Winks, 1971: 6.

[27]Marcil, 1981: 75.

[28]Winks, 1971: 10, 22. Winks believed that in the countryside owning a slave had the opposite effect, because, "no wide gap formed between the habitant and the seignior, and there was no need to acquire slaves as a quick means to status."

[29]Trudel, 1990: xxvi.

[30]Winks, 1971: 48, ff52.

[31]Trudel's *Dictionnaire* contains the most complete listing of individual officials, their role in New France, and the extent of their slave ownership. For other lists of prominent slave owners see: J. Walker, *A History of Blacks in Canada: A Study Guide for Teachers and Students*, (Hull: Minister of State, 1980), 12; Bertley (1977); Negro Slavery; Marcil (1981); Winks (1971); E. Thornhill, *Race and Class in Canada: the Case of Blacks in Quebec* Seminar paper presented to the National Council for Black Studies VI Annual Conference, (Montreal: Commission de droits de la personne du Québec, 1982); W. R. Riddell, "The Slave in Upper Canada," in *The Journal of Negro History*, vol. II., ed. G. Woodson, (Lancaster: The Association for the Study of Negro Life and History Inc., 1919); Trudel, 1960: 126-159, 319-320.

[32]Daniel Gay, *Empreintes Noires sur la neige blanche: les noirs au Québec (1750-1900)*, Projet de recherche RS101033, (Laval: Université Laval, 1988). Quotations are translated by Dorothy Williams.

[33]Ibid., 258.

[34]M. Laferrière, "The Education of Black Students in Montreal Schools: An Emerging Anglophone Problem, A Non-Existent Francophone Preoccupation," in

Ethnic Canadians: Culture and Education, ed. M. L. Kovacs, (Regina: University of Regina, 1978), 22-47. Gay, 1988: 258.

[35]Trudel, 1960: 319.

[36]For a discussion of the varied occupations of free blacks in the colony see: *Silent Minority* (n.d: 58); Winks (1971); Marcil (1981) Trudel (1990), Gay (1988), 258-59.

[37]James Walker has published an excellent analysis of the history and plight of black Loyalists entering the Maritimes. No such work exists for Lower Canada. J. Walker, *The Black Loyalists: The Search for the Promised Land in Nova Scotia and Sierra Leone 1783-1870*, (Halifax: Longman Group Ltd., 1976): reprint (Toronto: University of Toronto Press, 1992).

[38]Bartolo, 1976: n.p.

[39]Bartolo, 1976: n.p.

[40]Bartolo does not cite this source. If this was the case it is ironic—several decades earlier the French "Crown had purchased Panis slaves for humanitarian purposes, to exchange for white prisoners captured by the French allies in raids on the English colonial settlements." W. J. Eccles, *France in America*, rev. ed., (Markham: Fitzhenry & Whiteside, 1990), 82.

[41]Ida Greaves, *The Negro in Canada*, *National Problems of Canada*, Economic Studies No. 16., (Montreal: Packet-Times Press, 1930), 11.

[42]Warner, 1983: 4; Case, 1977: 9; Winks, 1971: 26.

[43]Thomson, 1979. Claude Marcil said that at this time, the Eastern Townships became home for American blacks. He stated that black Loyalists founded the town of Saint Armand in 1784. See also Winks, 1971: 34-35.

[44]Walker, 1980. Winks says that the existence of slave-free states had a different consequence particularly for Americans living close to the border. They were forced to sell their slaves to Canadians or risk the loss of property. The short-term effect was to swell the numbers of slaves in the Eastern Townships area. The first slave-free state was Vermont in 1777. Winks, 1971: 46. Note also: William Riddell, "The Slave in Canada," *The Journal of Negro History*, ed. G. Woodson, v.5, no.3 July 1920, 324.

[45]Winks, 1971: 100.

[46]Trudel, 1960: 229; Winks, 1971: 100.

[47]Israel, 1928: 65.

[48]By 1793 he had sold his own slave(s). Winks, 1971: 100. See: *Québec Herald*, July 1, 1790; *La Gazette de Québec,* December 16, 1790: 1; *La Gazette de Québec,* January 17: 4; *Quebec-Gazette*, June 21, 1790, *Quebec-Gazette*, December 16, 1790, *Quebec-Gazette*, December 12, 1793, *Quebec-Gazette*, October 17, 1790, *Quebec-Herald*, July 22, 1790, *Quebec-Herald*, March 12, 1792, *Quebec-Herald*, July 16, 1792.

[49]The member for Warwick, James Cuthbert, introduced these bills into the House of Assembly. *Journal de la Chambre d'Assemblée du Bas Canada*, 1800: 159; *Journal de la Chambre d'Assemblée du Bas Canada*, 1801: 55; *Journal de la Chambre d'Assemblée du Bas Canada*, 1803: 161.

[50]The last public sale in Montreal was in 1797. Greaves, 1930: 15; Israel, 1928: 64. See also: Borthwick, *History of Montreal Including the Streets of Montreal: Their*

Origin and History. (Montreal: D. Gallagher, 1897); Greaves, 1930; *Negro Slavery*; Marcil, 1981.

[51]Trudel, 1991: XV.

[52]Winks, 1971: 111.

[53]Israel, 1928: 65. In 1804 there were 142 slaves in Montreal and about 350 slaves throughout the rest of the province; (but there is no conclusive record as to how many of these slaves were black or Indian).

[54]Israel, 1928: 67.

[55]See: Winks, 1971; Thornhill, 1982; Warner, 1983.

[56]Bartolo, 1976

[57]See correspondence in C. Peter Ripley, ed., *The Black Abolitionist Papers: Canada, 1830-1865,* vol 2. (North Carolina: University of North Carolina Press, 1986).

[58]Paraphrased translation, Trudel, 1960: 97, in Laferrière, 1978: 245.

[59]R. Jones, Interview by author: October, 1984, Montreal.

[60]This concurs with Greaves' viewpoint. Greaves, 1930: 37.

[61]Technically only slaves under six on August 1, 1834 were totally free. Ripley, 1986: 74.

[62]Winks, 1971; Walker, 1979; and J. Krauter, and M. Davis, *Minority Canadians: Ethnic Groups,* (Toronto: Methuen Publications, 1978) describe the immigration and plight of thousands of Loyalists, Refugees, and later Fugitive blacks to Canada. Estimates range from 30,000 (Winks, 1971) to 60,000 (Bertley, 1977) for the number of fugitives who entered Canada after the promulgation of the United States Fugitive Slave Act in 1850. As well as trying to stem the activities of the Underground Railroad, this American law threatened the lives of even the free blacks in the northern states, and in Canada because any black could be re-arrested. See also: F. Landon, 'Negro Migration to Canada After the Passing of the Fugitive Slave Act,' in *The Journal of Negro History,* ed. G. Woodson (Lancaster: The Association for the Study of Negro Life and History, Inc., 1920) vol. 6, 22-36; B. Drew (1856). *The Narratives of Fugitive Slaves in Canada, Related by Themselves with an Account of the History and Conditions of the Colored Population of Upper Canada*; Multiculturalism Directorate (MD) *The Canadian Family Tree: Canada's People,* (Don Mills: Corpus Pub., 1979.); Greaves (1930); Warner (1983); Ripley (1986).

[63]Ripley, 1986: 176.

[64]There is a discrepancy with this figure as recorded by Thornhill, in 1982. Marcil said that officially blacks were the sixth largest, not the fifth largest ethnic group in 1871. Census figures from "Silent Minority" indicate that the ethnic divisions were: French 1,082,940, Irish 846,000, Scots 549,946, Germans 202,000, Dutch 29,000, and Africans 21,496. This figure is low, obviously an undercount. See: Greaves (1930) and Israel (1928). See also: A. Amarteifio, *One Third Black; Melting Pot or Isolationism: A Study of the Integration of Blacks in N.D.G. Schools*, graduate research report, (Montreal: McGill University, 1975).

[65] Gay 1988, 132. Census accuracy was extremely difficult to assure. For instance, in the census of 1871, in Huntingdon, Quebec the census taker totally bypassed all blacks residents. Census undercounts affected not just the black community but also other ethnic and racial groups.

[66]Ripley, 1986: 313; Gay, 1988: 132. Even assuming this underenumeration, the majority of blacks lived in the Maritimes or Canada West.

[67]Gay, 1988: 133.

[68]R. Jones, 1984.

[69]Walker, 1979: 20; Ripley, 1986: 313.

[70]Adam Ferguson, *Practical Notes made during a Tour in Canada and a portion of the United States, in MDCCXXI, the Second Edition to which are now added notes made during a second visit to Canada in MDCCCXXXIII*, (Edinburgh: William Blackwood, and Strand, London: T. Caldwell, 1834), cited in Gay, 1988: 133. Paraphrase and translation is the author's.

[71]Winks, 1971: 153. Wherever blacks congregated, white militias were set up for civil defense. Further, into the 1850s in response to the American Fugitive Slave Law, blacks in Canada set up Vigilance Committees to thwart slave agents' attempts to kidnap fugitives. Canada West had committees by the score, not one is known in Canada East.

[72]Elinor Kyte Senior, *British Regulars in Montreal: An Imperial Garrison, 1832-1854*, (Montreal: McGill-Queen's University Press, 1981), 34.

[73]Winks, 1971: 247. His fame came from the fact that the unsuccessful challenge to his escape "proved to be the American federal government's greatest defeat in its effort to enforce the Fugitive Slave Law." Ripley, 1986: 181.

[74]Ripley, 1986: 310-315.

[75]Ripley, 1986: 176. This happened in Boston, New York, Cincinnati, Philadelphia, and other cities.

[76]C. Marcil, 1981. Black lore had placed "Nigger Rock" in Farnham, Quebec (Warner, 1983: 5). However "Nigger Rock Re-discovered," an article in *Afro-Can* (July 1986, vol. 6. no. 5) recounted how the Emancipation 150 Committee found this rock in St. Armand. Nigger Rock marks one of only three slaves cemetaries in all of Canada and is known to the people who live in the area of St. Armand. "The Negro Burying Ground at St. Armand," *The Townships Sun*, May 1979:11.

[77]St. Armand's landmark signifies the United Empire Loyalist connection rather than the Underground Railroad roots. See: "Missisquoi County Historical Society: St. Armand Negro Burying Ground," in *A Key to Canada*, Pt. 2 (Montreal: NBCC Inc., 1976).

[78]Ripley 1986: 311. These were not black abolitionists rather a community of White radical or reforming religious abolitionists.

[79]Case, 1977: 14. Ontario did not change this legislation until 1965. In Nova Scotia, segregationist laws remained in force until 1954. For an understanding of the situation in other parts of Canada during this period, see also: Amarteifo (1975); Bartolo (1976); J. Krauter & M. Davis, "The Negroes" in *The Other Canadians: Profiles of Six Minorities*, (Toronto: Methuen Publications, 1971), 44-46.

[80]1871 Dominion Census.

[81]The ASC, headquartered in Toronto, was founded in 1851 in a response to the US Fugitive Slave Law. Winks, 1971: 253-57. See also: Ripley, 1986: 223; Gay, 1988: 251-2; I. C. Pemberton, *The Anti-slavery Society of Canada*, M.A. thesis. University of Toronto: 1973.

[82]Gay, 1988: 102.

[83]In Montreal support also came from outside the black community. Two pro-Reform newspapers, *Montreal Witness* and *The Montreal Pilot* were anti-slavery periodicals published in the 1850s. The *Witness,* though not particularly sympathetic to blacks, vigorously opposed Southern slavery. The *Pilot's* readers were in the Eastern Townships, during the 1850s it was edited by Reverend John Mockett Cramp. Ripley, 1986: 180-81.

[84]Ripley, 1986: 179. Samuel R. Ward, a professional black abolitionist, wrote of the contact he made with blacks in Montreal.

[85]Ripley, 1986: 41.

[86]The small number of black Loyalists who entered the province means that in Quebec today, old line blacks are those families with a railroad background, rather than being descendants of the United Empire Loyalists. See: Hill, 1983.

[87]It was not till the 20th century that black women did not form a sizable percentage of domestics in the city until the twentieth century. Between 1841-1881, 91% of working black women were domestics. Two percent worked in industry and 4% in business. Gay, 1988: 159. The 1861-1871 Census showed that 66% of all domestics who worked in Montreal were young Irish Catholics. M. Labelle, D. Lemay, C. Painchaud, *Notes sur l'histoire et les conditions de vie de travailleurs immigrés au Québec,* (Montreal: CEQ, Service de communications, Centre de Réprographie, 1980), 12.

[88]The term 'porter' includes buffet car porter, observation car porter, sleeping car porter, as well as cooks, cleaners, and other menial jobs held by blacks on the trains.

[89]Jones, 1984. Language did not play a role in their choice to leave this city. Until 1871 much of Montreal was still basically an English-speaking metropolis, particularly in the western sections of the island. For instance, in the St. Antoine ward in 1861, French speaking people were only 20% of the total population. Between 1851 and 1871 the French-speaking population grew from 45% to 52% of the population in Montreal, though the west remained predominantly English-speaking for several decades.

NOTES TO CHAPTER TWO

[1]The four railway lines were the Delaware and Hudson, the New York Central, the Rutland, and Central Vermont Rail. These companies employed only Americans hired in the U.S. Other American lines employed porters who lived in Montreal. See: Israel, 1928; Marcil (1981).

[2]Agnes Calliste, "Sleeping Car Porters in Canada: An Ethnically Submerged Split Labour Market," in *Canadian Ethnic Studies,* vol. 19 no. 1, 1987.

[3]Professor's Calliste's theoretical framework (1987: 2-3) is based on the Split Labour Market Theory formulated by Edna Bonacich, "A Theory of Ethnic Antagonism: The Split Labour Market," in *American Sociological Review,* 37, (1972): 547-59.

[4]Israel, 1928: 74.

[5]Israel, 1928. For black families who opened their homes, see: Hostesses of Union United Church, *The Memory Book*, (Montreal: Hostesses of Union Church, 1982), 327.

[6]Israel, 1928: 26.

[7]Calliste, 1987: 10.

[8]This policy was not reversed till 1951 in Canada. Interview by author, A. Packwood, Montreal, July, 1984. See: J. Bertley, *The Role of the Black Community in Educating Blacks in Montreal, from 1910 to 1940, with Special Reference to Reverend Dr. Charles Humphrey Este*, M.A. Thesis, (Montreal: McGill University, 1982); Calliste, 1987: 10.

[9]Krauter & Davis, 1971: 47.

[10]D. Ward, *Cities and Immigrants*, (New York: Oxford University Press, 1971), 107, in P. Solonysznyj, *Residential Persistence in an Ethnic Working-class Community: St. Ann's Ward, Montreal, 1871 to 1891*. Original Essay, (Montreal: Concordia University, 1988), 7.

[11]As early as 1871 St. Ann had been supplying the wealthy of St. Antoine with domestic labour. Bettina Bradbury, *The Working Class Family Economy: Montreal 1861-1881*, PhD dissertation, (Montreal: Concordia University, 1984), 35 cited in Solonysznyj, 1988: 5. How that labour was used is described in Margaret W. Westley, *Remembrance of Grandeur: The Anglo-Protestant Elite of Montreal, 1900-1950* (Montreal: Libre Expression, 1990).

[12]A. Prentice et. al., *Canadian Women: A History*, (Toronto: Harcourt Brace Jovanovich Canada Inc., 1988), 123.

[13]H. Ames, *The City Below the Hill: Sociological Study of a Portion of the City of Montreal, Canada*, with an introduction by P.F.W. Rutherford (Montreal: Bishop Engraving & Printing Co., 1897; reprint, Toronto: University of Toronto Press, 1972,). This quantitative methodology was unique to Canada.

[14]Ames, 1897: 88. The results of Ames' survey revealed 42% French Canadian, 34% Irish-Canadian, 21% British-Canadian. 'Others' made up just 3% of the population.

[15]Israel, 1928: 3.

[16]Greaves, 1930.

[17]Israel, 1928: 83.

[18]This assumption is echoed in Bartolo, 1976: n.p

[19]Ames, 1897: 59: Solonyszyj, 1971: 4.

[20]Israel, 1928: 69.

[21]See Map 1 for area under study.

[22]Ames, 1897: 74.

[23]Initally St. Antoine was one of five military regions created immediately after the surrender of Montreal in 1760. See: K. Jenkins, *Montreal: Island City of the St. Lawrence*, (New York: Doubleday & Co., 1966), 154.

[24]For an engaging look at the lives of those "above the hill" see Westley, 1990.

[25]See: Maps 1, 2, 3.

[26]R. Hagedorn, ed., *Sociology*, (Toronto: Holt, Rinehart and Winston of Canada, Ltd., 1980), 533.

[27]Ames, 1897: 8. The area Ames had studied was south of the CPR line. It stretched east-west along the city's streets between Bleury and the city's most western limits to the industrial cities of Ste. Cunégonde (pop. 11,000) and St-Henri-des-Tanneries, (pop. 22,000). John I. Cooper, *Montreal A Brief History*, Montreal: McGill-Queen's, 1969), 127.

[28]Ames, 1897: 85.

[29]Using The Concentric Zone Model of Park, Burgess, McKenzie, *The City* (Chicago: University of Chicago, 1925) and in R. D. McKenzie *On Human Ecology,* (Chicago: University of Chicago Press, 1968), the natural area is defined as a neighbourhood which is relatively homogeneous with respect to a group. This term is far more applicable to the St. Antoine district at the turn of the century than the term 'segregated.' It was Israel who defined the black community as segregated in the sense of "living largely to themselves." This is not an accurate term to describe the black community; blacks had not excluded other groups from the district, but the white community actively attempted to segregate themselves to keep the neighborhood white.

[30]Solonysznyj suggested that ethnicity was the determining element that created a stable Irish neighbourhood in St. Ann's ward. I contend that ethnicity did not stand alone; neighbourhoods were affected by the dynamics of racism.

NOTES TO CHAPTER THREE

[1]Throughout this chapter I use the terms "black," "Negro," and "coloured. "Coloured" and "Negro" reflect the cultural and social world of the period under study; the terms used for individual and group identification. At the turn of the century, "coloured" was a respectable definition. It became derogatory and less fashionable, although many blacks continued to maintain "coloured" in the names of associations and private social clubs. Eventually, throughout the thirty year period of this chapter, "coloured" began to be replaced by the more respectable "Negro." The chapter title, Negro Community, indicates this movement toward a modern redefinition in Montreal. "Black" was considered a negative term. My use of "black" is not a historical choice but it used for today's ease of reference, as it would have been unwillingly used by members of the black community during this period covered by this chapter.

[2]Wilfred Israel's thesis includes an in depth study of the institutional makeup of the black community over this thirty year span. His analysis is sociological, and described the strategy used by various groups. See also: Hostesses, 1982.

[3]This is a partial listing: The Porter's Mutual Benefit Association, The Coloured Political and Protective Association, Red Cap Benevolent Association.

[4]This is a partial listing: The Independent Benevolent Protective Order Elks of the World, Knights of Pythias, Grand United Order Odd Fellows, Household of Ruth, Caledonia Club.

[5]This is a partial listing: West Indian Cricket Club, Windsor Cricket Club, Ideal

Tennis Club, Chappie Johnson Baseball Team.

[6]The following is a partial listing: Little Mother's League, the Phyllis Wheatley Art Club, Criterion Club.

[7]The following is a partial listing: Household of Ruth, The Black Cross Nurses, Little Mothers League, Matron's Whist Club, The Younger Set Girls Club, Willing Workers, Literary Club, Colored Women's Charitable and Benevolent Club, UNIA Boy's Band.

[8]Bertley, 1982: 11; This estimate was provided by two elders, Mr. Ashby and Mr. Tucker. Israel (1928: 3) estimates 3000 people. *The Seventh Census of Canada 1931*, vol. I. Ottawa, 1936, noted that there were only 1,604 blacks in the city.

[9]By 1928 porters were earning average salaries of just over twenty dollars a week, a desirable salary for rural Canadians; not so desirable for the highly educated, urban West Indians. By 1930 the average salary was dropping.

[10]Hostesses, 1982, has several accounts of residents who could not find jobs having to leave Montreal.

[11]This is based on cumulative Federal immigration data since the turn of the century. See: W. A. Head, "Correcting our Ignorance of Black Canadians" in *Perception* November/December 1978, 29; and S. Ramcharan, *Racism: Nonwhites in Canada,* (Toronto: Butterworth & Co., 1982).

[12]Charles Ashby, "The Road to Now: Patti Vipond Interviews Charles Ashby" in *A Key to Canada: Part II* (Toronto: The National Black Coalition of Canada Inc., 1976), n.p., reprint from *Spear Magazine*, April 1976).

[13]Gay, 1988: 216-220: *Rapport judiciares de Québec* (RJQ), vol. VIII 1899, 104-112.

[14]Gay, 1988: 217.

[15]Gay, 1988: 218.

[16]Gay, 1988: 218-220; RJQ, vol. Viii, 1899, 379-384.

[17]Winks, 1971: 299.See also: A. McClaren, *Our Own Master Race: Eugenics in Canada 1885-1945*, Canadian Social History Series. (Toronto: McClelland & Stewart, 1990). The author demonstrates that Canada's debate on race purity was as serious as the one occurring in Europe, and makes it clear that "pollution" came in many forms.

[18]W. Sessing, "How They Kept Canada Almost Lily White: The Previously Untold Story of the Canadian Immigration Officials Who Stopped American Blacks from Coming Into Canada," *Saturday Night*, vol. 85, September, 1970.

[19]*Silent Majority*, n.d.:20. See Greaves (1930); Marcil (1981); Bartolo (1976); Krauter & Davis (1978); and Thomson (1979).

[20]Mrs. Pauline Paris, interviewed by M. Clarke, November, 1, 1988, *Black Montrealers: A Piece of the Multicultural Mosaic (1910-1960)* Oral History Montreal Studies (Montreal: Concordia University Libraries, 1988).

[21]Winks, 1971: 298-313.

[22]Winks, 1971: 309.

[23]Silent Minority: 20.

[24]Winks (1971) provides the most thorough account of the nature and extent of "Negrophobia" during these years. Eyewitness accounts can be found in *Abolitionist,*

Ripley, 1986.

[25]MD, 1979: 36.

[26]Krauter, 1978: 46.

[27]Sessing, 1970: 32.

[28]Winks, 1971: 309-327; Walker, 1980: 88; Bertley, 1977: 103.

[29] From 1870 to 1920 the overall black population of Canada estimated at 60,000 had actually decreased by two-thirds. Officially the figures for 1901 was at 17,500 (MD, 1979: 35). This is another census undercount. The exodus of blacks was part of the general exodus of immigrants who came to America. Between 1871 and 1902, Canada lost 1,500,000 immigrants. McInnis, 1969.

[30]Greaves, 1930; Israel, 1928.

[31]Greaves, 1930.

[32]Calliste, 1987: 6. She claims that there were 300 porters recruited.

[33]The most famous and enduring club was Rockhead's Paradise which opened in 1929. Mr. Rockhead was West Indian. See: Hostesses, 1982: 319.

[34]Jenkins, 1966: 460.

[35]Israel, 1928: 204.

[36] See Greaves, 1930: 56.

[37]I use the term 'direct' because in this early period, many West Indians went to the Maritimes, England or the U.S. prior to their arrival in Montreal.

[38]Israel, 1928: 75-77, analyzes the sociological basis for this attitude of the men on the rails. This sentiment is echoed in Ashby, 1976, n.p.

[39]Mrs. Sylvia Warner, interviewed by M. Clarke, November, 4, 1988, *Black Montrealers: A Piece of the Multicultural Mosaic (1910-1960)* Oral History Montreal Studies (Montreal: Concordia University Libraries, 1988).

[40]Roy States, interview with Yvonne Greer, 1979-1980, Montreal. See also: Winks, 1971: 424.

[41]L. Bertley, *The Universal Negro Improvement Association of Montreal, 1917-1919,* Ph.D. thesis, (Montreal: Concordia University, 1983), 122.

[42]Bertley, 1983: 119.

[43]*Gazette*, Montreal, Mon. August 3, 1981; *La Patrie*, April 12, 1957; *Gazette*, May 29, 1976, *Montreal Star*, April 11, 1957; Maria Castagna, "Dr. E. Melville Duporte African-Canadian Scientist and Scholar" in *Akili: The Journal of African Studies* vol. 2 no. 3 November, 1994: 4-6; Harold H. Potter, "Negroes in Canada" in *The Journal of the Institute of Race Relations*, London: 1966, 50. Author interview with Dr. Stewart, McGill University, November 4, 1996.

[44]Jones, interview by author, Montreal, 1984. See: Hostesses, 1982.

[45]Jones, 1984; See also: Bertley, 1982: 27; Israel, 1928: 166.

[46]Israel, 1928: 98. See also Bertley, 1982: 2.

[47]Hostesses 1982: 363, 341.

[48]G. Husband, V. Phillips, A. Packwood, R. Jones, interviews with author, Montreal, 1984.

[49]Israel, 1928: 94.

[50]Israel, 1928: 96.

[51]Calliste, 1987: 6.

[52]Calliste, 1987: 7.

[53]Westly, 1990: 44-62. See: Linda Carty, "African Canadian Women and the State" in Peggy Bristow et. al, *We're Rooted and They Can't Pull Us Up*, (Toronto: University of Toronto Press, 1994), 193-229.

[54]Ruth L. Harris, *The Transformation of Canadian Policies and Programs to Recruit Foreign Labor: The Case of Caribbean Female Domestic Workers, 1950's -1980's*, Ph.D. dissertation, (Michigan State University, 1988), 106, quoted in Bristow, 1994: 218.

[55]Agnes Calliste, "Canada's Immigration Policy and Domestics from the Caribbean: The Second Domestic Scheme" in J. Vorst, ed., "Race, Class, Gender: Bonds and Barriers" in *Socialist Studies / Etudes Socialistes: A Canadian Annual* No. 5. 1989, 135.

[56]Calliste, 1989: 136.

[57]Bristow says that all, whereas Calliste, 1989:138 says only some of the women were deported. No information is given on the liaisons of the women nor their contacts, if any, with the Black English speaking community.

[58]Calliste, 1989: 138.

[59]G. Leslie, "Domestic Service in Canada, 1880-1920" in J. Acton, et. al., *Women at Work: Ontario 1850-1930* (Toronto: Women's Press, 1974), quoted in D. Brand, *No Burden to Carry: Narratives of Black Working Women in Ontario 1920s-1950s* (Toronto: Women's Press, 1991), 14.

[60]Bertley, 1983: 121.

[61] H. Potter, *The Occupational Adjustments of Montreal Negroes: 1941-1948*, M.A. thesis, (Montreal: McGill University, 1949).

[62]Bertley, 1983: 122.

[63]See: Dorothy W. Williams, Blacks in Montreal (Cowansville: Éditions Yvon Blais, 1989), Appendix 2; Greaves, 1930: 56.

[64]Some of these stories can be found in *Hostesses*, 1982. See also: Mrs. Thelma Wallen, interviewed by M. Clarke, November, 20, 1988, *Black Montrealers: A Piece of the Multicultural Mosaic (1910-1960)* Oral History Montreal Studies (Montreal: Concordia University Libraries, 1988).

[65]Israel, 1928: 76.

[66]Lucille Cuevas, *Hymn To Freedom*, TV Documentary Mini-Series by Almeta Speaks (Toronto: Almeta Speaks Productions, Inc., 1993).

[67]Jones, interview with author, Montreal, 1995. Note: Tilly Mays in Hostesses, 1982: 216, 278, 298; Mattie Wellons and Betty Clark in *Hostesses*, 1982: 216.

[68]The Coloured Women's Club of Montreal. Seventy-fifth anniversary pamphlet, Montreal, 1977.

[69]Prentice, 1988: 193.

[70]Israel, 1928: 200. See also Hostesses, 1982: 217.

[71]M. Bliss, *Plague: A Story of Small Pox in Montreal*, 1st ed. (Toronto: HarperCollins, 1991).

[72]T. Copp, *The Anatomy of Poverty: The Condition of the Working Class in Montreal, 1897-1929* (Toronto: McClelland and Stewart Ltd., 1974); Ames, 1897. See also Dumont et al, 1977: 198.

[73]Copp, 1974; Ames, 1897.

[74]Bertley, 1982: 26.

[75]Copp, 1974: 25.

[76]Trudel, 1990: xxvi.

[77]This was the purpose of Ames' *City Below the Hill* —to create and redirect philanthropic interest into St Antoine and Griffintown. For some insight into the philanthropy from residents above the hill see: M. W. Westley, 1990.

[78]Hostesses, 1982: 217.

[79]Copp, 1974: 108. The Charity Organization Society collected and distributed funds for Protestants, as did St. Vincent de Paul for the Catholics, and the Baron de Hirsch Institute for the Jews. By the 1920s this traditional division was formalized between the three main religious grups in the city. See: Westley, 1990: 167.

[80]Rella Braithwaite and Tessa Benn-Ireland, *Some Black Women: Profiles of Black Women in Canada* (Toronto: Black Women and Women of Color Press, 1993), 56.

[81]Betty Riley, "The Coloured Church of Montreal," in *Spear* vol. 3 no. 10 Toronto: 24, in Bertley, 1982: 15.

[82]Mr. Henry Langdon, interviewed by M. Clarke, November, 1, 1988, *Black Montrealers: A Piece of the Multicultural Mosaic (1910-1960)* Oral History Montreal Studies (Montreal: Concordia University Libraries, 1988).

[83]P. D. McClain, *Alienation and Resistance: The Political Behaviour of AfroCanadians* (Palo Alto: R & E Research Associates, Inc., 1979), 57.

[84]Bertley, 1982: 13-14.

[85]Jones, 1995. See also the list of founding 'fathers and mothers' in Bertley, 1982: 2. See also "*Founding Members*" in Hostesses, 1982.

[86]Bertley, 1982: 37, 137; Bertley, 1983: 233-235. Twenty years later this daycare centre was transferred to the Negro Community Centre and became one of the organization's most enduring programs.

[87]Bertley, 1982: 3.

[88]Ibid.

[89]Chronology taken from Hostess, *A Short History of Union Church* 1982: n.p.

[90]This is a summary from Bertley, 1982: 16-23, 31. See also Hostesses, 1982: 235; and L. Bertley, *Montreal's Oldest Black Congregation: Union Church* (Pierrefonds: Bilongo Publishers, 1976).

[91]A union of the Presbyterian and Methodist Churches of Canada.

[92]Bertley, 1982: 21. He retired on December 31, 1967. Recognizing his contribution to his community of Little Burgundy, City of Montreal posthumously named a park at the corner of Sherbrooke and NDG Avenue, Place Charles Este.

[93]Hostesses, 1982: 302.

[94]B. Cooper, interview with author, Montreal, 1995. Often appearance (skin color, hair quality) determined class and group standing.

[95]Winks, 1971: 314-320.

[96]Winks, 1971: 315.

[97]Winks, 1971: 317.

[98]Vipond, n.p.

[99]Winks, 1971: 318. See: Carl Ruck, *The Black Battalion 1916/1920: Canada's Best Kept Military Secret* (Nimbus Publishing, 1987).

100Winks, 1971: 319.

101Hostesses, 1982: 248. Dr. Gaspard was a member of The Colored War Veterans, Branch no. 50, Canadian Legion which opened March 26, 1935 in the St. Antoine area. In his honour the branch was named the Dr. Gaspard Branch no. 50, on April 13, 1953.

102Hostesses, 1982: 367-368.

103Pauline Paris, 1988.

104This group had several names: the Ladies Benevolent Club or the Charitable and Benevolent Club, and the Woman's Charitable Benevolent Association. Winks, 1971: 417.

105Sylvia Warner, 1988.

106Bertley, 1983: 41.

107The Colored Political and Protective Association organized the Loew's Theatre case. Loew's insisted that black patrons sit only in the balcony. It set the precedent future legal actions. See: Winks, 1971: 431-2.

108Bertley, 1983: 43. See also Israel, 1928: 111-112.

109Israel, 1928: 208; Bertley, 1983. See also: D. Hill and H. Potter, *Negro Settlement in Canada: 1628-1965: A Survey*, Montreal: Report presented to the Royal Commission on Bilingualism and Biculturalism, 1966.

110 "Back-to-Africa" was not new to American or Caribbean-born blacks in Montreal. See: T. W. Shick, *Behold the Promised Land A History of Afro-American Settler Society in Nineteenth-Century Liberia* (Baltimore: The John Hopkins University Press, 1977), and, E. S. Redkey, *Black Exodus: Black Nationalist and Back-to-Africa Movements 1890-1910* (New Haven: Yale University Press, 1969); See: J. T. Holly & J. D. Harris, *Black Separatism and the Caribbean 1860* (Ann Arbor: The University of Michigan Press, 1970); Bertley, 1983: 144-148, 187-210; & Bertley, 1977: 226-247.

111Bertley, 1983: 145. See: Rupert Lewis, *Marcus Garvey* (Trenton: Africa World Press, Inc., 1988).

112Calliste, 1987: 5.

113Randolph's picture was eventually hung in UNIA Halls in acknowledgement of his part in the creation of the Brotherhood of Sleeping Car Porters.

114Canada had had its own Back-to-Africa movement 120 years earlier. Two separate contingents of Blacks were voluntarily repatriated from the Maritimes to Sierra Leone. See Winks, 1971: 61-95, and Walker, 1976; Ellen Wilson, *The Loyal Blacks*, (New York: Capricorn Books, 1976).

115Bertley, 1983: 191; Lewis, 1988; and in J. Stein, *The World of Marcus Garvey Race and Class in Modern Society* (Baton Rouge: Louisiana State University Press, 1986).

116Bertley, 1977: 241-243. The demise of the Black Star Line prompted the organization of The Black Cross Navigation and Trading Company.

117UNIA members worldwide were entitled to death benefits. Ignorance and false expectations caused resignations, accusations and misunderstandings that lingered for years.

118Bertley, 1983: 116. For material on the UNIA in Toronto, see D. Hill, *Negroes in Toronto-A Sociological Study*, 1960, Ph.D. thesis, University of Toronto; and personal accounts in Brand, 1991.

[119]Hostesses, (1982: 351). See: Leo W. Bertley, "Afro-Can Remembers the First International Convention of the Negro Peoples of the World," *Afro-Can*, Montreal, August, 1982: 7.

[120]Henry J. Langdon, interview by author, Montreal, July 12, 1995.

[121]At the national level during the 1922 UNIA convention in the United States, there was a major debate about the role of women at the local level. A five point agenda proposed by women delegates was accepted and expanded to allow them to function without restriction from the men. R.A. Hill, ed., *The Marcus Garvey and UNIA Papers* vol. IV, (University of California Press, Berkeley, 1983): 1037-1038.

[122]Bertley, 1982: 98-101; Bertley, 1983: 270-276.

[123]The lack of non-discriminatory medical services was a problem. In 1928 a statement from the Montreal General Hospital said: "no discrimination would be made as to race or creed." H. E. MacDermot, *A History of the Montreal General Hospital* (Montreal: The Montreal General Hospital, 1950), 111.

[124]L. Bertley, 1977: 219-257.

[125]Bertley, 1982.

[126]A. Packwood, B. Riley, D. Sweeney, taped interviews by J. Bertley, 1980, in Bertley, 1982: 29.

[127]Mrs. Anne Packwood, interview by M. Clarke, October, 30, 1988, *Black Montrealers: A Piece of the Multicultural Mosaic (1910-1960)* Oral History Montreal Studies (Montreal: Concordia University Libraries, 1988).

[128]Wallen, 1988.

[129]Bob White, interview by M. Clarke, October, 28, 1988, *Black Montrealers: A Piece of the Multicultural Mosaic (1910-1960)* Oral History Montreal Studies (Montreal: Concordia University Libraries, 1988).

[130]Bertley, 1982: 56-72.

[131]ACL is the African Community League—a business unit of the UNIA.

[132]Bertley, 1982: 57.

[133]Bertley, 1982: 67.

[134]Bertley, 1983: 54

[135]Bertley, 1983: 44.

[136]Calliste, 1987: 8.

[137]This is the author's opinion based on the Porter's Mutual Benefit Association in the literature and from the stories of the porters themselves. See individual accounts in Hostesses, 1982. See also Israel, 1928: 227-230.

[138]Calliste, 1981: 9.

[139]Hostesses, 1982: 323; Krauter & Davis, 1978: 53. St. Joseph Ward boundaries were Fulford (Georges-Vanier) to McGill, St. Antoine to Notre Dame.

[140]Calliste, 1981: 5.

[141]Israel, 1928: 230.

[142]Bertley, 1983, 199, 204. 208.

[143]The NCA was not the only St. Antoine organization which received funding. The Old Brewery Mission and Tyndale House also received benefit of their funding or expertise.

[144]The Negro Community Centre Board of Directors Report, *The Negro Community*

Centre in Action (Montreal, 1960), 2. See also: Israel, 1928; Bertley, 1982; and, Don Handelman, 1964: 71. Housing was a major concern by 1928 as Montreal experienced a housing shortage. Bertley, 1982: 100.

[145]Bertley, 1982: 122.

[146]Israel, 1928: 221.

[147]Ibid. Israel gives no further clue as to how or why the existence of the Centre would prevent men from going into industry.

[148]See accounts in Hostesses for the names of some families. Certain families are still remembered as being the "first."

[149]Israel, 1928: 57.

[150]Israel, 1928: 214.

[151]Packwood, 1984.

[152]Greaves, 1930.

[153]Israel, 1928: 2.

[154]Jones, 1984; Phillips, 1984.

[155]Braxton, 1984; Jones, 1984; Packwood, 1984; Phillips, 1984.

[156]Braxton, 1984; Jones, 1984.

[157]Greaves, 1930: 65.

[158]L. Lewis, Phillips, interviews with author, Montreal, 1984.

[159]L. Lewis, Phillips, Montreal, 1984.

[160]D. Quann, *Racial Discrimination in Housing* (Ottawa: Canadian Council on Social Development, 1979), 17-19.

NOTES TO CHAPTER FOUR

[1]Copp, 1974: 148.

[2]Bertley, 1976.

[3]Hostesses, 1982: 233. James Robinson, telephone interview with author, July 7, 1996.

[4]Bertley, 1983.

[5]Bertley, 1983: 138.

[6]Bertley, 1983: 57. Joseph-Maurice Gabias had been alderman since 1921. *Who's Who in Canada 1930-31.*

[7]James Davis is an obvious exception. During the Depression he was a full-time employee, and purchased and farmed a three-acre farm which he sold in 1960. He has been honoured as the first black in Greenfield Park, and a street has been named James E. Davis Street. See: R. Braithwaite, Tessa Benn-Ireland, 1993: 79.

[8]Hill, Potter, 1966.

[9]The Open Door Society was composed of white couples who legally adopted children of mixed racial origins. See: Hill & Potter, 1966.

[10]Paris, 1988.

[11]Bertley, 1982: 33.

[12]Barbara Cooper, interview with author, July 12, 1995.

[13]There is some question whether Earl Swift or Reverend Este started the Club. See: Sylvia Warner, 1988; Hostesses, 1982: 365; and Winks, 1971: 417; Swift

see: Hostesses, 1982: 342.

[14]Warner, 1988.

[15]Paris, 1988. Winks, 1971: 417 is the only reference that states that the Negro Theatre Guild evolved out of the Phyllis Wheatley Art Club in the mid 1930's. Hostesses, 1982, indicate the late 1940s. Warner, 1988, mentions a 1939-1940 date.

[16]Warner, 1988; The Kinsmen Club raised funds to send milk to Britain, arranged to present it for three nights at His Majesty's Theatre. Awards included the Martha Allan Cup, Dominion Drama Festival Scenery Design Award and Best Actor. See also: Hostesses, 1982: 121.

[17]Hostesses, 1982: 41, 364. By the 1940s the Club reverted to a recreation and crafts club.

[18]Hostesses, 1982: 277.

[19]Bertley, 1982: 33.

[20]Jones, 1995; Hostesses, 1982: 278.

[21]B. Williams, interview with author, Montreal, July 18, 1995.

[22]Bertley, 1982: 131-135.

[23]Bertley, 1983: 38, 63.

[24]Hostesses, 1982: 229.

[25]Bertley, 1982, mispelled the name.

[26]Bishop Farthing served the Anglican diocese from 1909-1939.

[27]Bertley, 1982: 80,103-104. Linda Carty, in Bristow, 1991; Hostesses, 1982: 229.

[28]Though there were blacks attending McGill University each year, the quota system made it difficult for blacks educated in the Montreal community to enter McGill. Telephone interviews with M. Dash, May 21, 1966; G. Husband, May 24, 1966. A parallel version was in place for Jews. For Jewish quota see: I. Abella, *A Coat of Many Colours: Two Centuries of Jewish Life in Canada* (Toronto: Lester & Orpen Dennys, 1990: 215-216; telephone interview with Herb Berkovitz, hospital archivist, Montreal General Hospital, Montreal, May 29, 1996.

[29]Greaves, 1930: 69

[30]Bertley, 1982: 102. This contrasts with the 1950s when McGill had a reputation for accepting African-Americans more readily than American universities did. Telephone interview with Dr. Jesse Barber, Howard University, Washington, D.C., May 24, 1996. Hostesses, 1982: 229

[31]Greaves, 1930: 69. Cited in *Barbados Agricultural Reporter*, January 4, 1930.

[32]Gwen Husband, interview with author, Montreal, 1985. See also: Bertley (1982); and Hostesses, 1982: 229.

[33]W. A. Spray, *The Blacks in New Brunswick* (Brunswick Press, 1972).

[34]D. H. Clairmont, D. Magill, *Nova Scotian Blacks: An Historical and Structural Overview* (Halifax: Dalhousie Press, 1970), 83.

[35]Ramcharan, 1982.

[36]Potter, 1949: 19.

[37]Greaves, 1930: 56.

[38]See Williams, 1989. Appendix 2.

[39]Winks, 1971: 333. This was first noted by Israel, 1928.

[40]Potter, 1949: 32.

[41]Hostesses, 1982: 326.

[42]Hostesses, 1982: 326. In 1939, Mr. C. E. Russell, Chairman of the CPR Welfare Committee, stated that 300 porters were employed by the company.

NOTES TO CHAPTER FIVE

[1]Martha Griffiths in interview with Bertley, 1982, 149.

[2]McInnis, 1969.

[3]Warner, 1983. Owen Rowe, interview with author, November 6, 1996.

[4]Hostesses, 1982: 130.

[5]Walker, 1980: 96.

[6]This attitude was a regional one. By 1939 blacks in other Canadian centre could enlist with fewer problems.

[7]Richard Lord, interviewed by M. Clarke, November, 2, 1988, *Black Montrealers: A Piece of the Multicultural Mosaic (1910-1960)* Oral History Montreal Studies (Montreal: Concordia University Libraries, 1988).

[8]McInnis, 1969: 568.

[9]Potter, 1949: 72.

[10]Potter, 1949: 29.

[11]Langdon, 1988.

[12]Herb Berkovitz, hospital archivist, stated that the number of black staff at the Jewish General Hospital was much higher than at the Montreal General Hospital and that a great change occurred at the Montreal General when Dr. Doug Cameron took over after the war. Telephone interview, May 29, 1996.

[13]Hostesses, 1982:229. Despite the indication of the presence of the quota system at McGill University in the oral and written history of black Montrealers there is an absence of other documentation (regarding blacks or of Jews), There is also no documentation to back up the existence of a formal agreement between McGill and Howard universities.

[14]Mrs. Dash, in conversation with author, July 18, 1995, Montreal..

[15]Bertley, 1982: 150. Also Henry J. Langdon, November, 1, 1988. Simpson's followed suit. See: Hostesses, 1982: 157.

[16]See Dionne Brand, "We Weren't Allowed to Go Into Factory Work Until Hitler Started the War: The 1920s to the 1940s" in P. Bristow, et. al., 171-190.

[17]Potter, 1949: 71.

[18]Potter, 1949: 139.

[19]Braxton, 1984. The principal employers of skilled blacks were the aeronautical companies on the West Island of Montreal.

[20]H. Tulloch, *Black Canadians: A Long Line of Fighters* (Toronto: NC Press, Ltd., 1973).

[21]Potter, 1949. The official census underestimated population again because it did not record Americans, West Indians, or other blacks who retained their citizenship and intended to return home.

[22]Potter, 1949: 10.

[23]Barbara Cooper, interview with author, Montreal, July 11, 1995. Note: Langdon, 1988.

[24]Brand, 1991: 188.

[25]See personal accounts in Hostesses, 1982.

[26]Cooper, 1995.

[27]Potter, 1949: 31.

[28]Ibid.

[29]Krauter, 1978: 43.

[30]Hostesses, 1982: 325, 204. Winks, 1971: 425;

[31]See Hostesses, 1982.

[32]Calliste, 1987: 9.

[33]Bertley, 1982: 155.

[34]Linda Carty in Bristow, 1991: 214.

[35]James W. St. G. Walker, *The West Indians in Canada*, (Ottawa: Canadian Historical Association, 1984) 10.

[36]Mary Robertson, "The Black Presence in Quebec Society," *Afro-Can*, July 1983: 14. It seems he forgot that the West Indies was a region not a country.

[37]Potter, 1949: 21, 43.

[38]Potter, 1949: 20.

[39]Max Dorsinville, *Forward* in Paul Dejean, *The Haitians in Quebec A Sociological Profile* trans. M. Dorsinville (Ottawa: Tecumseh Press, 1980).

[40]Potter, 1949: 43.

[41]Potter, 1949: 19.

[42]Bertley, 1983: 108.

[43]Husband, Packwood, Braxton, interviews with author.

[44]Potter, 1949: 20.

[45]Warner, 1983: 15. This is the highest cited percentage to be found. All other percentages varied between 15 and 30 percent.

[46]Potter, 1949: 33.

[47]V. Chichester, interview with author, Montreal, July 16, 1982.

[48]One of the great political and educational debates during the thirties, forties and fifties was the integration of non-Catholic, non-Protestant immigrants into the school systems, in particular Jews prior to World War II. After the war the emphasis changed to language. The influx of non-French-speaking Catholic Italians caused similar debates and legislative battles. Quebec government bills 22, 63, and 101 are direct responses to the presence of the large Italian community in Montreal. See: Jeremy Boissevain, *The Italians of Montreal*, and David Rome, *Clouds in the Thirties: On Anti-Semitism in Canada*, 1929-1939.

[49]Potter, 1949: 100.

[50]See: Marcil, 1981; Krauter & Davis, 1978: 56; Winks, 1971.

[51]Hostesses, 1982: 306.

[52]N. J. Salter, *A Typology of the Administrative Process and Practice in the Negro Community Centre Inc. Montreal Quebec* Unpublished essay (Montreal: McGill School of Social Work, 1959), 8.

[53]Jones, 1995.

[54]Salter, 1959: 10.

[55]Salter, 1959: 9. Negro Community Centre, Constitution and By-Laws, 1949.

[56]This temple's membership had a Canadian majority.

[57]Cooper, 1995.

[58]From this point, West End and St. Antoine are used interchangeably, and St. Henri ward is included when I refer to the West End.

[59]Potter, 1949: 14.

[60]Potter, 1949: 13.

[61]Lewis, 1984.

[62]Copp, 1974: 12.

[63]Braxton, 1984.

[64]Ironically, except for the St. Joseph ward, housing in the West End was generally more expensive than on the South Shore, or in the north of the city.

[65]Dr. D. Wills, interview by author, Montreal, 1984.

[66]Mrs. Westmoreland, interview by author, Montreal, 1984.

[67]Negro Community Centre Board of Director's, *Board of Directors Report,* 1960: 4-5.

[68]Hill & Potter, 1966.

[69]Mitchell Wolfe, *The Black Community in Montreal* Paper presented to Harvard College, (Massachusetts, 1973), 5.

NOTES TO CHAPTER SIX

[1] The black community's institutions in this era were ably described by Don Handelman. Unfortunately, the study focusses on 1964 only. Despite this limitation, he revealed much about the framework and the dynamics of the older organizations and the forces at play affecting fledgling organizations. Much of what follows is from Don Handelman, *West Indian Associations in Montreal,* M.A. thesis, (Montreal: McGill University, 1964).

[2]Handelman, 1964: 70

[3]Handelman, 1964: 69.

[4]The Iverly Community Centre moved to Ville St-Laurent. They owned the building that the NCC took over in the West End.

[5]Handelman, 1964: 72.

[6]Handelman, 1964: 73.

[7]The NCC also received national and international exposure as the result of a major tragedy. On July 12, 1954, off Ile Bizard not far from Montreal, twelve children under the care of NCC workers and volunteers, drowned when their boat capsized. The disaster touched the lives of every English-speaking family, white and black, in the West End. "Ile Bizard Boating Tragedy," *Montreal Star,* July 13, 1954, 8. "The result was not the destruction of the NCC, rather surprisingly, it was the catalyst in its own way to bring people together. The grief brought a community together to stand as one and the NCC flourished! The NCC heydey occurred as a result." Owen Rowe, interview with the author, November 28, 1996.

[8]What follows about UNIA is from one source: Bertley, 1983: 109-112. See P.

Stamadianos, *Afro-Canadian Activism in the 1960s*, M.A. thesis, (Montreal: Concordia University, 1994). Stamadianos' study focusses on the activism of Montreal and Toronto blacks.

[9]The Toronto black leadership was definitely involved in the new activism of integrationism. They supported Martin Luther King financially, and hosted his rallies when he came to Canada. Stamadianos referred to it as the "new militancy into black politics that transcended the previous emphasis on community and social work." Stamadianos, 1994: 56.

[10]Donald Moore, *Don Moore: An Autobiography* (Toronto: Williams-Wallace Publishers Inc., 1985), 78, 108. Includes the history and activities of the NCA in Toronto.

[11]No comprehensive study exists about the NCA's influence in Montreal. See: Handelman, 1964: 63; Stamadianos, 1994: 41-42. Concerning the taxi integration see: Commission des droits de la personne du Québec, *Investigation into Allegations of Racial Discrimination in the Montreal Taxi Industry: Results and Recommendations* (November, 1984).

[12]Stamadianos, 1994: 42.

[13]Further discussion can be found in Handelman, 1964: 54.

[14]See Handelman, 34-37, 89 passim.

[15]Ramcharan, 1982: 19.

[16]Ramcharan, 1982: 13; Winks, 1971: 434-445.

[17]Brand, 1991: 26-28. For a more in depth analysis of work and black women see Dionne Brand, "A Working Paper on Black Women in Toronto: Gender, Race and Class," in *Fireweed*, Summer/Fall 1984.

[18]Figures from Bartolo (1976), Amarteifo (1975), Wolfe (1973) confirm the inconclusiveness of the immigration data during this period.

[19]Moore, 1985: 154.

[20]The Scheme stopped when the West Indies Federation ended in 1962. Harris, chap. 4 in Carty, quoted in Bristow, 1994: 228.

[21]MD, 1979: 34. Based on a quota of 280 per year each island. Jamaica sent 104 annually and the rest came in smaller numbers. See: Moore, 1985: 164.

[22]A study through McGill University investigating the loneliness and plight of the women who emigrated under the Domestic program. Frances Henry, *The West Indian Domestic Scheme in Canada* in *Social and Economic Studies* vol. 17. no. 1. March 1968: 84.

[23]The United States had set up this same type of scheme prior to 1955. S. N. Eisenstadt, *The Absorption of Immigrants*, (Glencoe, Illinois, 1955) had assumed that frustration with the original social environment and its lack of mobility provided the major incentive towards migration. Henry (1968: 85) found other stronger reasons for migration: "To better myself, advance, study—28%; dDesire to travel, see another country—28%; desire to get away from home conditions—13%; simply wanted a change—15%; desire to join relatives, friends—10%; miscellaneous other reasons—10%.

[24]Henry, 1968: 86.

[25]Henry, 1968: 87.

[26]Handelman, 1964: 41.

[27]Handelman, 1964: 42-44. See: Silvera, 1983; P. Blais, "Household Workers on Temporary Work Permits" in *The Afro Canadian* vol. 3 no. 5, May 1987: 11.

[28]Handelman, 1964: 74-77. The split between the lower and middle class women members was compounded by these three major 'goals' which Pioneer Girls could not, or did not, try to satisfy due to a rigid 'social work' approach.

[29]The women joined either the YWCA or the civil rights groups. Later a new Sepia Girls was formed to replace Pioneer Girls and attracted "dark-skinned" working women.

[30]In Canada, only the Chinese had the same gender restrictions and imbalance imposed by the racist immigration policy. In the nineteenth century, Chinese male labourers brought in to build the transcontinental railroad system were not allowed to bring their spouses or families into the country.

[31]The methodological problems of earlier censuses were still apparent in the census of 1961. It does not consider non-black West Indians. Though the figure is an undercount, the percentage of blacks living on the island was probably quite accurate.

[32]Handelman, 1964: 31.

[33]Wolfe, 1973: 2.

[34]Boubacar Kone, "Being Black in Montreal" in *Maclean's* December, 1968: 46.

[35]Krauter & Davis, 1971; and, *Focus Umoja* no. 16, Montreal, 1976.

[36]I have presented only five of the six categories listed. I take exception to Hill and Potter's fourth category (1966: 86). They argue that there were "an undetermined number of nonconfessing coloured people whose homes are scattered through various districts...(who) marry white men and women." What is a nonconfessing coloured person? It is my opinion that blacks who choose not to be black (i.e. culturally) who can get away with not being black (racially) and who live exclusively within the white mainstream, (socially) are not in any real sense black. If they cannot be identified as black why do Hill and Potter insist on including this group as separate from the dispersed category?

This issue of sociological self-identification is a thorny one. Those who marry outside of their racial type, may or may not chose to be identified with their group of birth. How do you then classify them, their offspring, their mates? Is a black person who marries a white person black or white? If one is fair skinned and chooses to pass as white, are they still sociologically black or do they become white? Is a white person who chooses to marry a black and to live within that culture sociologically black? I don't feel that genetics alone determines culture. However, the mere fact that Hill and Potter have chosen to delineate this group, suggests that they think so.

[37]Harold Potter, 1966: 50. See: Calliste, 1987: 11-15.

[38]Handelman, 1964: 98; Stamadianos, 1994: 42.

[39]Handelman, 1964: 22. Which is to say they were middle-class by West Indian standards.

[40]Kone, 1968: 467.

[41]Handelman, 1964: 49.

[42]Handelman, 1964: 52.

[43]K. Simmons, interview with author, Montreal, 1988.

[44]This event and its consequence will be dealt with later.

[45]Jacqueline Jean-Baptiste, *Haitians in Canada:Ayisyin Nan Kanada* (Hull: Canadian Government Publishing Centre, 1979). The real impact of Haitian immigration was felt in the seventies. See also Paul Dejean, 1980: 30.

[46]MD, 1979: 100.

[47]Max Dorsinville, trans., in Paul Dejean, 1980: n.p.

[48]Dejean, 1980: 33.

[49]Kone, 1968: 46.

[50]V. King, Wills, Braxton, interviews with author, (1984, Montreal).

[51]Sylvia Cheltenham, interview with author, (1984, Montreal).

[52]G. Lord, Cheltenham, Braxton, interviews with author, (1984, Montreal).

[53]G. Rowe, interview with author (1984 Montreal).

[54]S. Durant, Braxton, interviews with author, (1984 Montreal)

[55]D. Bent, Packwood, interviews with author, (1984, Montreal).

[56]T. Collins, interview with author, (1984, Lasalle); Braxton (1984); Cheltenham (1984).

[57] When CP and CN moved some of their operations out of the district in the late fifties the men followed the jobs.

[58]Phillips, 1984.

[59]S. Durant, 1984.

[60]Little Burgundy is named after an early nineteenth century landmark in the middle of the district. It comes from a story that says parts of the wooded areas in the St. Antoine area looked like the woods of Petite Bourgogne in France. Then it was discovered that many of the original residents of the West End were from the Burgundy region in France.

[61]The City of Montreal approved renewal of the district October 5, 1966. The government of Quebec approved the plan November 30, 1966, and the federal government, May 11, 1967. Subsidies and contracts with housing authorities followed. Programme Détaille de Renovation "Ilots Campbell," Service de l'Habitation, Ville de Montréal, février 1970.

[62]The City of Montreal also demolished Montreal's largest English Catholic parish church, St. Anthony's, to make way for the Ville Marie Expressway on the north side of St. Antoine street.

[63]The demolition cost over $272,000; $3,500,000 was paid for the acquisition of properties. Service de l'Habitation, 1970: 610-1.

[64]These rules can cause a two-year delay for public housing because public housing projects usually require that applicants be residents of a particular district for at least six months before applying. Besides this rule, applicants must wait while their name moves up the waiting list.

[65]Quann, 1979.

[66]Handelman, 1964: 34-37.

[67]S. Anierobi, interview with author (1984 Montreal).

[68]Haitian settlement in the early seventies concentrated heavily in the area east of St. Lawrence street and north along the corridor.

[69]This would have been the case even if the downtown had not been undergoing urban renewal. Haitians chose not to mingle with the older black community. I do not believe that language was the deciding factor because by the 1901 census the French-speaking population had become the major group in St. Antoine.

[70]Ramcharan, 1982; and Bristow, 1994.

NOTES TO CHAPTER SEVEN

[1]Stamadianos, 1994.

[2]Stamadianos, 1994: 69, 86. Two of the more outspoken leaders were Daniel Hill and Howard McCurdy.

[3]Ibid., 86. For Stanley Grizzle see Winks, 1971: 425-26; Stamadianos, 1994: 47-48. He was president of the Toronto division of CPR. He helped form the Young Men's Negro Association of Toronto and in 1959 he became the first black to seek a seat in the Ontario legislature.

[4]Concordia University Archives, Undergraduate Calendar 1968-69.

[5]Concordia University Archives, "The Computer Riot, Sir George Williams: 1969," Ready Reference File, October 19, 1994.

[6]Dorothy Eber, *The Computer Centre Party: Canada Meets Black Power. That Sir George Williams University Affair* (Montreal: Tundra Books, 1969); D. Forsythe, ed., *Let the Niggers Burn: The Sir GeorgeWilliams University Affair and its Caribbean Aftermath* (Montreal: Black Rose Books/Our Generation Press, 1971); Concordia University Archives, "The Computer Riot, Sir George Williams: 1969," Ready Reference File, October 19, 1994; "Diary of a Riot," *The Georgian*, February 6, 1979; The number arrested as stated in sources varies between 87 and 97.

[7]The events led the university to re-evaluate its internal procedures; student representation on university decision-making bodies was revamped. The committee recognized that there were serious academic issues with students rather than racial ones. The Committee submitted its findings June 30, 1969. See: Sir George Williams University, *Report of the Committee to Investigate A Charge of Racism Against Professor Perry Anderson*, June 30, 1969. Then, in 1971 a report, *The University Amidst Conflict and Change: Faculty Response to Student Unrest* by Joseph Smucker and John Jackson was released— using interviews, court testimony, and detailed eyewitness accounts by faculty. Subsequently, in April 1971, Sir George Williams adopted University Regulations on Rights and Responsibilities and the Ombuds Office was established.

[8]Forsythe, p. 15.

[9]D.B. Clarke, Acting Principal of Sir George Williams University, expressed this sentiment in a meeting with representatives of the black community on May 13, 1969. He added that the university would not oppose any requests for reduction in bail. Forsythe 1971,124.

[10]Dyette, 1995.

[11]L. Butcher, interview with Yvonne Greer, Montreal, 1979-80.

[12]Butcher, 1979-80.

[13]Forsythe, 1971.

[14]Clarence Bayne, interview with Yvonne Greer, Montreal, 1979-80.

[15]Dyette, 1995.

[16]Heidi Modro, "Clarence Bayne: The Sir George Computer Incident Revisited" in *The Link* vol,. 9 no. 32., February 10, 1989: 4.

[17]C. Whittaker, and C. Bayne, interviews with Yvonne Greer, Montreal, 1979-1980.

[18]The research was conducted on the PSBGM because the majority of black students in the city attended PSBGM schools.

[19]D. Fraser, interview with author, Montreal, May 11, 1982. See also: Youth Sponsor Education Seminar, *Focus Umoja*, vol. 1 no. 1, November, 1974.

[20]See material on education above in chapter "Negro Community." Note also: student interviews: "Royal Arthur Graduation", *UHURU*, vol. 2 no. 1, July 13, 1970: 8; "Death at an Early Age—Crisis in Education" *UHURU* vol. 1 no. 21, May 11, 1970: 4.

[21]"The Tragedy of Da Costa Hall," *UHURU*, vol. 2, no. 3, August 24, 1970: 3

[22]These black educators were university academics and/or trained educators unable to find work in their fields of expertise. Some black teachers worked in isolated northern communities. To the chagrin of students supporting those involved in the SGWU affair, several teachers accepted positions at SGWU during 1970. They believed it weakened the case that SGWU was a racist institution. "The Tragedy," *UHURU*, vol 2 no. 3, August 24, 1970: 3.

[23]"Black Education Program: Its Role and Responsibility," and "Educational Appeal," *UHURU* vol. 1, no. 23, June 22, 1970: 1.

[24]Susana Despessailles, *La Population noire anglophone du Québec, Comité—Portraits du Québec*, (Ministere des communautes culturelles et de l'immigration, 1984: 29).

[25]C. Whittaker, Montreal, 1979-80. This was a summer program rather than the on-going daily or weekly tutoring programs at the NCC and the UNIA during the school year.

[26]E. Howell, "Academic Information Recruitment," *Focus Umoja*, vol. 1, no. 3, January, 1975: 13. Reprinted from *Dawson College Black and Third World Newsletter*, Fall, 1974.

[27]Whittaker, 1979-80.

[28]"Rally Held Every Thursday Night," *UHURU* vol. 1 no. 1 June 4, 1969: 6.

[29]Black and Third World Student's Association, The Committee for the Welfare and Development of Black Children, The Black Voice, Black Action Party, were just a few of the many organizations which started following the events at Sir George Williams.

[30]Children's activities such as the Saturday Morning School were on-going and successful. It was founded by Leo Bertley and run by volunteer black educators. *Focus Umoja* no. 16 October, 1976: 8; Eleitha Haynes, interview with author, Montreal, July 27, 1995.

[31]Marcel Green, interview with author, Montreal, July 28, 1996.

[32]Leslie MacLaughlin, interview with author, Montreal, July 28, 1996.

[33]Peter Bailey, interview with author, Montreal, July 15, 1996. He recalled that the consciousness raising and activities of the Afro-Canadian Club gave him a

purpose to get up in the morning to go to school each day and to continue learning. It encouraged his love of history—although what he wanted was relevant history which acknowledged that he, as a black person, was important.

[34]Black Information Service, *The Black Action Party: Black Year in Review* vol. 2 no. 1., January 15, 1972. Thamis Gale and Leon Jacobs also contributed to lectures. The Tuesday night event expanded to Saturdays for the children.

[35]Marcel Green, Leslie MacLaughlin, interview with author, Montreal, July 28, 1996.

[36]Surveillance of student groups and violent police activity against students was not uncommon in Quebec in the months following the War Measures Act. See "Dialogue on Quebec 1970," Quebec Studies 1990-1991 (11) (Hanover: American Council for Quebec Studies), 63-73. The police saw BAP as a threat and several BAP members knew they were being followed by unmarked police cars. This incident allowed the police to collect BAP records and information on people in the movement.

[37]By December 1971, all four blacks (L. Walton, M. Walton, W. Cumberbatch, W. Patterson) were found guilty of interfering with a police officer and of assault. One woman was also found guilty of disturbing the peace; everyone involved was given suspended sentences. *The Black Action Party* vol. 2 no. 1., January 15, 1972: 1. "Use of Excessive Force Alleged: Girl Hurt in Scuffle With Police" The *Montreal Star* Monday, April 12, 1971. See: *Gazette*, April 13. 1971: 21.

[38]Marcel Green 1996.

[39]Lewis, 1995. Alternately, "The Decline of the Negro Community Centre" UHURU vol. 1 no. 8, October 14, 1969: 7 states, "the majority of directors are middle class white." In that case there would have had to have been 11 or more white directors.

[40]This and several other related issues caused the departure of BAP from the NCC in June 1971. BAP opened a Black Youth Centre three blocks away from the NCC. It closed eventually due to lack of a permit and became an office for the Black Action Party publication July, 1971.

[41]"Receive Building Deed," Montreal *Star*, March 11, 1965.

[42]*The Annual Report 1982-1983* recorded that the question of a name change had come up again during the year. The debate was not nearly as contentious as the first time.

[43]Bob White, Black Montrealers, 1988.

[44]Eight groups were: The Black Action Party, The Board of Black Educators, Black & Third World Students (Dawson), The Côte-des-Neiges Project, Committee for the Welfare and Development of Black Children, National Black Coalition Institute of Research, The Negro Community Centre, War Veterans Association. See "The Quebec Black United Front," *The Black Action Party*, vol. 2 no. 6 May 18, 1972.

[45]Ibid.

[46]Whittaker, 1979-80.

[47]The original name was the Black Community Development Corporation which was used by the Côtes-des-Neiges Project: Whittaker, 1979-1980.

[48]Unity or "umoja" was crucial to the BCCAQ concept as demonstrated in their monthly publication *Focus Umoja*.

[49]See: *Focus Umoja* no. 1, October, 1974.

[50]On September 22, 1974 an amendment to the NCC Bylaws permitted delegate representation. The NCC Board started functioning as a co-ordinating council with membership elected on a constituency or organization basis. *Negro Community Centre Minute Book, 1977-1987.*

[51]Lyle E. Talbot, *Who We Are: A Brief Introduction to the Struggle of Blacks for Equal Socio-Economic Opportunity in Canada*, (Ottawa, n.d.).

[52]"Black Leader Calls For Unity," in The *Montreal Star*, Monday, September 26, 1977.

[53]Some would believe it was deliberate sabotage of the BCCAQ. Whittaker, 1979-1980. The loudest voices against the BCCAQ came from within the Centre itself, from those who could not see a role for themselves within the new structure.

[54]Whittaker, 1979-1980.

[55]*Negro Community Centre Minute Book, 1977-1987.*

[56]Project, C. Whittaker, L. Butcher, 1979-1980. Butcher was one of the students involved in the SGW Affair.

[57]Butcher, 1979-1980.

[58]See: "Battle against bias the catalyst to weld Montreal black community," in *The Gazette*, Montreal, Saturday, July 21, 1973.

[59]The *Gazette*, Montreal, Saturday, July 21, 1973.

[60]The self sufficiency that Butcher called strength was perceived as a weakness by Whittaker, who believed that the regular, secure funding base of the NCC was the centre's strongest point and that this funding would enable the community to eventually support the entire institutional infrastructure.

[61]Butcher, 1979-1980.

[62] "On Blackness," *UHURU* vol. 1 no. 4 August 18, 1969: 2.

[63]R. States, 1979-1980. P. Nolan recalls that white students at Dawson College could not buy *UHURU*. P. Nolan, interview with author, July 15, 1995.

[64] "Focus on Uhuru," *UHURU* vol.1 no. 12, December 8, 1969: 4.

[65]Carl Whittaker, interview with author, August 22, 1995.

[66]Negro Community Centre, *Negro Community Centre Minute Book, 1977-1987.*

NOTES TO CHAPTER EIGHT

[1]Racism in Montreal's housing market is a serious problem that still exists. See: Muriel Garon, *Une Expérience de testing de discrimination raciale dans le logement a Montreal*: étude de la Direction de la Recherche, Commission des droits de la personne du Quebec, 3, mai 1988; Renée Lescop *Politiques et programmes dans le domaine du logement: leurs effets sur l'exercice du droit au logement pour les minorités ethno-culturelles du Quebec*: étude de la Direction de la Recherche, Commission des droits de la personne du Quebec, 27, mai 1988.

[2]J. Dyette, interview with author, Montreal, April 20, 1995.

[3]Black Community Council of Quebec, *History of the Black Community Council of Quebec in Terms of its Initial Objectives: Philosophy,* 1994: 2.

[4]There are now 11 organizations under BCCQ: including the community

associations of West island, Southshore, and Laval, as well as, ACCES, the Drew Society, Miss Black Quebec Pageant, West Indian Canadian Day Association.

[5]They have included the following programs: The Legal Clinic, The Black Line, Literacy Animation, and Drug Awareness..

[6]*History of the Black,* 1994: 2.

[7]As late as 1978 the NCC went back into Côte-des-Neiges and opened another branch. They offered recreation, youth, legal aid, day camp, crime prevention and seniors outreach services. *NCC Annual Report* 1987-1988.

[8]Hostesses, 1982: 306-307.

[9]Egbert Gaye, interview with author, Montreal August 17, 1995. Note: *Afro-Can* was revived as *The Afro-Canadian* by a group not associated with the NCC. Under the editorship of Dr. L. Bertley *The Afro-Canadian* published until February 1994.

[10]BCCQ has established the l'Espoir Community Development Initiative for Little Burgundy. Description can be found in R. Huggins, *The Black Community Council of Quebec Inc.*, 1995.

[11]Leo Bertley, Mary Robertson, *Anglophone Blacks in Quebec.* Document du Travail. Submitted to The Quebec Ministry of Education, July 31, 1992.

[12]This discussion is only representative of Congress' Montreal Chapter.

[13]The Colored Women's Club hosted the Congress conference in 1974 instead of the Chapter. There was no mention that a Montreal Chapter had as yet been formed although the *Montreal Regional Committee National Congress of Black Women Report: Educational Conference* (October, 1981) states that 1974 was the inaugural year. See also: B. Paris, and Y. Greer, *Black Women Activate Liberation Struggle*, in *Focus Umoja*, vol. 1 no. 2, December, 1974: 6.

[14]Braithwaite, Ireland, 1993: 57, 58. For many years a bilingual woman, usually from Quebec, is president.

[15]This discussion of the first organization does not preclude the dozens that have sprung up since 1972.

[16]Of the eight ethnic groups in the survey none had such a high correlation between generations. This indicates very little ethno-cultural diversity within the Haitian population. This survey was done following the collapse of the Duvalier regime and the results could be affected by the heightened sense of pride and the community's preoccupation with events in Haiti at that time. See: A. Ledoyen, *Montreal au Pluriel, Huit communautés ethno-culturelles de la région montréalaise*, Documents de Recherche no. 32 (Quebec: Institut Québecois de Recherche sur la culture, 1992), 63, and note following p. 93.

[17]Note discussion in Christian Rioux, *Montreal noir*, in *L'actualite*, vol. 17 no. 20, 15 December 1992: 39.

[18]Alix Jean, interview with author, Montreal, August 16, 1995.

[19]Marjorie Villefranche, interview with author, August 11, 1995 Montreal.

[20]Calliste, 1987: 20n.

[21]Commission des droits, novembre 1984: 9.

[22]Commission des droits de la personne du Quebec, *Investigation into Allegations of Racial Discrimination in the Montreal Taxi Industry: Final Report Principal Conclusions and Recommendations Regarding Taxi Associations: Direct and Systemic Discrimination* Extracts

from Volume I (November, 1984).

[23]Commission des droits, *Final Report*, 1984. Includes a company by company listing of the Charter violations. The following is based upon that report.

[24]Dejean, 1980: 62. Dejean speaks of confrontations that included assault, aggression, and even damage to vehicles.

[25]Commission des droits de la personne du Quebec, *Investigation into Allegations of Racial Discrimination in the Montreal Taxi Industry: Final Report Principal Recommendations regarding the Legislative, Regulatory and Administrative Framework of the Taxi Industry* Extracts from Volume II (November, 1984).

[26]Dejean, 1980: 75.

[27]*Quebec Blacks Mum* in *The Islander* vol. 4 no. 9, Thursday 11 November, 1976, Toronto

[28]*The Black Community Central Administration of Quebec, Public Statement*, April 12, 1977. See also: Andrew Johnson, *Blacks Limbo* in *The Islander* March 24, 1977.

[29]The Meech Lake Accord also spurred the creation of a short-lived 20 group alliance in 1987 called the Black Forum. It was spearheaded by the Jamaica Association. *Afro-Can* vol. 7 no. 7 July, 1987.

[30]D. MacPherson, "Blacks want protection in civil rights charter" in *The Gazette*, Montreal, Saturday, April 9, 1977. See also: B. Mitchell, "Blacks Face Two Strikes" in the *Montreal Star,* Saturday, April 9, 1977.

[31]"Blacks enter separatist debate" in *The Islander* April 14, 1977.

[32]Public Statement, 1977.

[33]"Tribalism, Oppression in PQ's White Paper" in *The Islander* April 28, 1977; "The Quebec community speaks out" in *Contrast,* April 28, 1977.

[34]Clarence Bayne, "Thinking aloud about Quebec and the Black Community" in *Focus Umoja*, no. 18, May, 1977.

[35]"Black Alliance asks minorities protection" in the *Montreal Star,* Tuesday, May 24, 1977; see also: W. Poronovich, "Blacks worried about Bill I" in the *Montreal Star,* Monday, May 30, 1977. As early as 1968 the NCC had requested assistance from the Ministry of Cultural Affairs for French training for staff and community; "Negro Community Centre Minute Book," *1966-1976*, April 9, 1968.

[36]One inevitable but sad result was the closure of Royal Arthur in 1981. It no longer was the neighbourhood school for the Black English speaking population in Little Burgundy. In its place parents either sent their children to Westmount Park Elementary, or to the new neighbourhood school, CECM École St. Joseph, renamed École Petite Bourgogne. See: R. Goldseger, *Language and Montreal's Black Community* in *Language and Society*. no. 25 Winter 1988: 19.

[37]"What Future for Quebec Blacks?" in *Focus Umoja*, no. 18, May, 1977.

[38]M. Gittens, interview with author, August 17, 1995; L. Albino, interview with author, 18 August, 1995.

[39]A. Ledoyen, 1992, 186.

[40]"Police: We Shot Innocent Man" in *Montreal Gazette*, Friday, July 5, 1991.

[41]Coverage of Griffin and François was extensive in and outside of the province. See: *Gazette, Afro-Canadian, Contrast, Le Journal de Montréal, La Presse, Le Devoir, Le Soleil* and a host of local weeklies, and monthlies.

[42]Bob White, *Black Montrealers,* 1988.

[43]"Haitians rally to fight racism," in the *Montreal Star*, Saturday, June 30, 1979; "City's Haitian leader warns of violence in self defence" in the *Gazette*, Montreal, Monday, November 26, 1979.

[44]*City's Haitian*, 1979; "Police Racism brings call for investigation," in the *Montreal Star*, Wednesday, June 27, 1979.

[45]Commission des droits de la personne du Quebec, "Investigation into relations between police forces, visible and other ethnic minorities," (Montreal: Commission des droits de la personne du Québec, November, 1988).

[46]P. Bosset, F. Houda-Pepin, J. Jedwab, D. Langlois, A. Paradis, P. Sainte-Marie, *Violence and Racism in Quebec: Summary of the Report*, trans. J. Freeman (Montreal: Comitéd'intervention contre la violence raciste, 1992), 19.

[47]Mitchell Wolfe, 1973: 2; Bartolo, 1976: n.p.; Amarteifo, 1975: 2.

[48]Warner, 1983: 12.

[49]For more on this period of immigration see: Ramcharan, 1982; Warner, 1983; Bartolo, 1976; MD, 1979.

[50]Wolfe, 1973: 5.

[51]MD, 1979.

[52]This is an ongoing problem. In 1983 the United Nations Development Program promoted a "Brain Gain" project (TOKTEN) for Third World nations to provide incentives for professionals, and skilled expatriates to return to their native lands to help with economic development. *AfroCan* , July: 9, 1983.

[53]UN, Social Development Division, *The Brain Drain from Five Developing Countries: Cameroon-Colmbia-Lebanon-The Philipines-Trinidad and Tobago*, (New York: United Unations Institute for Training and Research, 1971). This gives insight into the specific issues in each indidvidual country.

[54]Thornhill, 1982; Ramcharan, 1982: 29.

[55]McInnis, 1969: 639.

[56]M. Kirdon & R. Segal, *The State of the World Atlas,* (London: Pluto Press, 1981), n.p.

[57]Dejean, 1980: 33.

[58]Dejean, 1980: 7.

[59]McInnis, 1969: 640.

[60]McInnis, 1969: 638-9. This emphasis continues, see: Linda Diebel, "Canada desperately needs people, Tory MP says" in *The Montreal Gazette* 26 July, 1986.

[61]Dejean, 1980: 35.

[62]Though fully 40% were trilingual, there is little data on how this affects social intercourse and mobility among these groups. Much of this material comes from Rassemblement des Africains de Québec.

[63]Pieter Wolfe, interview with author, 1984, Montreal; J. Bataille, Agent d'information recherche, Maison d'Haiti, interview with author, July 1984, Montreal.

[64]Dejean, 1980: 51. After evaluating all sectors of the population including his own analysis of fertility he proposed that 21,500 was a more realistic figure.

[65]Creole is a mixture of Spanish, French, and African languages. Only 10% of the total Haitian population actually spoke French upon entry.

[66]Dejean, 1980: 33; Note Dejean's chapter on the high birth rate in Quebec among Haitian population.

[67]M. Baillargeon, & G. Ste-Marie, *Quelques caracteristiques ethnoculturelles de la population du Quebec* Cahier no. 2. (Montreal: Ministère des communautés culturelles et de l'immigration, 1984).

[68]Bataille, 1984.

[69]Dejean, 1980: 33.

[70] Dejean, 1980: 116-17. Based on cases handled by the Communauté Chrétienne des Haitiens de Montréal (BCCHM) Dejean estimates the number of Haitians caught under the new of immigration rules was 1500. Thelma J. Wallen, *Multicuturalism and Quebec: A Province in Crisis*, (Stratford: Williams-Wallace Pub., 1991), 31, states that the figure of illegals was closer to 2 thousand.

[71]Many of these Haitians were hoodwinked by travel companies who knew of the changes in Canada's immigration rules but did not inform their Haitian customers. Also there were cases of Haitians who had lived for short periods in other countries in South America or the Caribbean who did not have access to the new details of Canadian immigration policy.

[72]Jean-Baptiste, Jacqueline, *Haitians in Canada: Ayisyin Nan Kanada*, (Hull: Canadian Government Publishing Centre, 1979):14.

[73] Dejean, 1980, 110-115. The Bureau of the Communauté Chrétienne des Haitiens de Montreal was one office affected. It was raided June 18, 1974—but the case was thrown out January 28, 1975. The assumption was that these groups were aiding and abetting the illegal Haitians to remain underground.

[74]Wallen, 1991: 31.

[75]Sai Yau Fan was a Chinese national who was able to get a ministerial permit that later could be changed into a resident visa. Over 200 Haitians used the Fan precedent to stay in the country. Dejean, 1980: 127.

[76]Laferrière, 1978: 253.

[77]Clarence Bayne, *Socio-Demographic Profile of the Black Communities in the Montreal Census Metropolitan Area*, Consultation Paper for the Information Meeting between the City of Montreal and the Black Anglophone Community. January 18, 1990: 23.

[78] "Adults Worry About Kids' Future Here," J. Bagnall, *The Gazette* 13 February, 1993, 5-6.

[79]Ledoyen, 1992: 61.

[80]Maryse Alcindor, "Femmes d'Haiti, femmes de defis," Speech for Conference d'Hexoticq. (Montreal: Quebec Human Right Commission, 1992), 8. See also: Ledoyen, *Le Niveau d'Education*, in *Montreal au Pluriel*, 1992: 105-130. Note that the only group in Quebec to earn less than Haitians were the non-French, non-English, southeast Asian immigrant "boat people" who had just arrived in Quebec before the 1981 census. Pericles Jean Vernet, "Repartition sectorielle et occupationnelle des travailleurs haitiens sur le marche du travail a Montréal," M. A. thesis, Université du Québec à Montréal (Montreal, 1987).

[81]Albino, 1995.

[82]Description from C. Bayne pamphlet material. In 1992 the City of Montreal did a Black History Month booklet. In the following year they started an umbrella

organization called Le table de concertation, or round table, where dozens of Black organizations came together to plan official events.

[83]This event has become a major festival. Historians such as Marcel Trudel have participated in parallel events staged by organizations such as the Commission des droits de la personne du Québec (the Quebec Human Rights Commission). See: Paule Sainte-Marie, Février Mois de l'Histoire Noire, 1992: Allocutions prononcées a l'occasion de la conférence du 31 janvier 1992 au Collège Dawson, à Montréal, Fevrier 1992.

[84]Garvin Jeffers in C. Rioux, L'actualite, 1992: 39.

[85]Dejean, 1980: 40.

[86]As late as 1982 it was brought to the attention of the board of directors of the NCC that the staff were following several reported cases of exploitation of domestic workers. Negro Community Centre Minute Book 1977-1987, May 11, 1982.

[87]Dejean, 1980: 63.

[88]Dejean, 1980: 51.

[89]Dejean, 1980: 41-42, passim. He also identifies the unenumerated population of illegal or clandestine workers.

[90]Warner, 1983: 17

[91]Bartolo, 1976.

[92]Laferrière, 1978: 247.

[93]The Black Community Work Group on Education. Final Report on the Aspirations and Expectations of the Quebec Black Community with Regard to Education, Report submitted to the Comité d'étude sur les affaires interconfessionelles et interculturelles du Conseil superior de l'éducation, 1978.

[94]Laferrière, 1978: 245.

[95]Carl Whittaker was the first of several black commissioners who brought about great change including the establishment of the Black Liaison Officer, which, in the opinion of some, is a significant achievement.

[96]Nouvelles Da Costa News vol.1 no.1 October 1994.

[97]This percentage was from Warner (1983). I would tend to believe that this figure was much higher.

[98]Warner, 1983: 17. Figures that relate to interprovincial migration were dubious because they do not include the ethnicity or race of the migrant.

[99]This figure was provided by the president of Rassemblement des Africains. (Interview with Mr. Kouka-Ganga 1984, Montreal).

[100]One obvious omission in this survey was Nigeria. The high point of Nigerian immigration was between 1968 and 1973 when 857 immigrated (MD, 1979: 168).

[101]This percentage of black immigrants entering Quebec was fairly consistent. Regardless of the decade or the cultural group, about one in four black immigrants chose to live in Quebec. This percentage was small but it was actually above average compared to other immigrant groups entering Quebec. Revue Justice, November, 1982: 38, Montreal; Kaseka, M., M. Bambote, K. Diamque, J. Dupleix, J. Hamid, & E. Kabera, "Les Ressortissants de l'Afrique au sud du Sahara et leur Perception de la coopération Québec-Afrique" (1983, June).

[102]Rapport final de la recherche realisee dans le cadre du projet pacet du Ministre

des communautés culturelles et de l'immigration du Québec. Kaseka, June, 1983.

[103]Kaseka, 1983: 32, 34.

[104]*Silent Minority*, 1974: 22.

[105] Bayne, *Thinking Aloud*, in *Focus Umoja*. no. 18. May, 1977: 4. Figure supported in Johnson, *The Islander,* 1977.

[106]MacPherson, *The Gazette*, 1977. See figures given in Poronovich, *Bill I,* in *The Montreal Star,* Monday, May 30, 1977.

[107]Work Group, 1978: 8.

[108]B. Price, *20 see voice of minority on unity*, in *The Gazette*, Montreal, Friday, March 30, 1979.

[109]Marcil, 1981: n.p.

[110]See D. Williams, Blacks in Montreal 1628-1986: An Urban Demography (Cowansville: Les Éditions Yvon Blais, 1989). Appendix 10 for the movement of Blacks around the island; map 8 for 1981 West Indian distribution.

[111]John Durant, interview with author, July 1984, Montreal.

[112]F. Gale, conversation with author, July 1995.

[113]At that time there were no blacks living in these developments. One black resident said she was quite relieved when she saw East Asians moving into the new townhouses. She did not want "to be totally surrounded by conservative, quiet whites." (A. Cox, interview with author, 1986 Montreal).

[114]Mr. Gerald, conversation with author, 1986, Montreal.

[115]Coronation Elementary School in Côte-des-Neiges was the school with the largest black school population—over 50% of the students were black. École de la Petite Bourgogne will not come close to that percentage as blacks are a minority in the area of Little Burgundy the school serves.

[116]The Black Community Council of Quebec, (BCCQ) *Profile of the Black Community in Quebec.* Report submitted to the Ministry of Multiculturalism, February, 1982, found in Warner, 1983: 18.

[117]Warner, 1983: 16.

[118](Lewis, 1984).

[119]Hungarian refugees in 1956, blacks in the sixties and seventies, Portuguese in the seventies, and Lebanese and South East Asian refugees in 1978, went to Côte-des-Neiges upon arriving in Montreal.

[120]Armarteifio, 1975.

[121]For more about gentlemen's agreements and their affect on the housing markets, see: Quann, 1979: 10, 17, 18.

[122]B. Teitelbaum, *Rapport de stage sur la discrimination raciale dans le logement a Montréal* M.A. thesis (Montreal: Université du Québec, 1983), 48. The purpose of this study was to disprove two assumptions about residential mobility: 1) immigrants want to live in ethnic ghettos, and 2) all individuals compete freely in the housing market. The reality was that there was a "web of discrimination which acts to prevent the non-white immigrant from freely competing for housing."

[123]Teitelbaum, 1983: 49.

[124]Teitelbaum, 1983: 48.

[125]Quann, 1979: 31.

[126]V. Jackson, interview with author, 1984 Montreal.

[127]Warner, 1983: 18. In an earlier study, Bayne (1976: 8) got a percentage number of 32%. However, this figure not only included Cote de Neiges, but also included the population of Blacks in eastern and northeast NDG.

[128]Gittens, 1995, L. Albino, 1995.

[128]Williams, 1989: see Appendix 10 for graph of first movement into district.

[130]Mrs. Dash, interview with author, 1985 Montreal.

[131]Durant, 1984.

[132]Bataille, 1984.

[133]Jones, 1984.

[134]Hedy Taylor, interview with author, Montreal, 1984.

[135]Durant 1984.

[136]Vere Rowe, interview with author, Montreal, 1992.

[137]The 1984 statistics for Lasalle as reported in *Habitabec* Friday, 16 March 1984, showed that there was a 5% overall population decline between 1976 and 1981.

[138]J. Durant, 1984. Lasalle's population was about 72,000, so if these figures were correct it would mean that almost one in three Lasalle residents was black. Blacks certainly don't figure this prominently in any municipality hence, the figure of 20,000.

[139]L. Lewis, 1984.

[140]Lewis, 1984 says there were only 1,000 in Verdun. This figure was too small considering the West Indian population was close to 800. The population in Verdun was probably upwards of 1500 or 1700.

[141]Chateauguay was locally called the poor man's suburb because veterans obtained reasonable government loans and for $15,000 they bought lots to build their homes. There was also some veteran's housing in Longueuil.

[142]Wolfe, 1984.

[143]T. Samuels, interview with author, 1984, Montreal.

[144] Peter Foggin and Mario Polese, *The Social Geography of Montreal in 1971*, Research Paper no. 88 (Toronto: University of Toronto, Centre for Urban and Community Studies, 1977), trans. of *La Geographie Sociale de Montreal en 1971"* (Montreal: Institut national de la recherche scientifique, n.d.)

[145]King, 1984.

[146]King, 1984.

[147]*Les Nouvelles News,* Wednesday 9, July 1986.

[148]F. Roi, interview with author, 1984, Ville St. Laurent.

[149]Bataille, 1984.

[150]Bataille, 1984.

[151]Wolfe, 1984;. Foggin & Polese, (1977: 19)

[152]Anierobi, 1984; Wills, 1984; Bataille, 1984.

[153]Anierobi (1984); Bataille (1984); The percentage of francophones in the district has dropped to 50%, at one time it was 85%.

[154]Teitelbaum, 1983: 50.

[155]Teitelbaum, 1983.

[156]Bataille, 1984.

[157]Bataille, 1984.

[158]Teitelbaum, 1983.

[159]Projet Vivre en Harmonie was commissioned by the St. Laurent YMCA to study the needs of their immigrant population.

[160]Quann, 1982.

[161]Teitelbaum, 1983: 39.

[162]Amarteifo, 1975: 2. Many of those immigrants from England were in fact West Indians who had previously migrated to England in the 50's and 60's.

163In a world where the majority was non-white there was little cause for celebration. However, this was a milestone that was long overdue-of the 3 million people admitted into Canada from 1925 to 1965 only 17,206 were Blacks. Teitelbaum, 1983: 24, 34-35.

[163]Teitelbaum, 1983: 24

[164]Ramcharan, 1982: 19.

Bibliography

Books

Ames, H. *The City Below the Hill: Sociological Study of a Portion of the City of Montreal*, Canada. Montreal: Bishop Engraving & Printing Co.,1897.

Atherton, W. *Montreal: 1535-1914*. Montreal: Clarke, 1914.

Berthlet, H. *Le Bon Vieux Temps: Montréal*. Montréal: Librairie Beauchemin, 1916.

Bertley, L. *Canada and Its People of African Descent*. Pierrefonds: Bilongo Publishers, 1977.

Bertley, L. *Montreal's Oldest Black Congregation: Union Church*. Pierrefonds: Bilongo Publishers, 1976.

Borthwick, J. Douglas. *History of Montreal Including the Streets of Montreal, Their Origin and History*. Montreal: D. Gallagher, 1897.

Braithwaite, Rella, Tessa Benn-Ireland. *Some Black Women: Profiles of Black Women in Canada*. Toronto: Black Women and Women of Color Press, 1993.

Brand, Dionne. *No Burden to Carry: Narratives of Black Working Women in Ontario 1920s-1950s*. Toronto: Women's Press, 1991.

Clairmont, D. H. and D. Magill. *Nova Scotian Blacks: An Historical and Structural Overview*. Halifax: Dalhousie Press, 1970.

Cooper. J. I. *Montreal: A Brief History*. Montreal: McGill/Queen's Press, 1969.

Copp, T. *The Anatomy of Poverty: The Condition of the Working Class in Montreal, 1897-1927*. Toronto: McClelland and Stewart Ltd, 1974.

Dejean, P. *The Haitians in Quebec: A Sociological Profile*. trans. M. Dorsinville, Ottawa: Tecumseh Press, 1980.

Despessailles, Susana. *La Population Noire Anglophone du Québec*, Portraits du Québec. Ministère des communautés culturelles et de l'immigration, 1984.

Drew, B. *The Narratives of Fugitive Slaves in Canada, Related by Themselves With An Account of the History and Condition of the Colored Population of Upper Canada*. Boston: J. P. Jewett and Co, 1972.

Dumont, M. Jean, M. Lavigne, J. Stoddart. *Quebec Women: A History*. R. Gannon, R. Gill trans. Toronto: The Women's Press, 1987.

Eber, D. *The Computer Centre Party: Canada Meets Black Power*. Montreal: Tundra Books, 1969.

Eccles, W. J. *France in America*. rev. ed., Markham: Fitzhenry & Whiteside, 1990.

Foggin, P., and M. Polese. *The Social Geography of Montreal in 1971*. Research Paper no. 88. Toronto: University of Toronto, Centre for Urban and Community Studies, 1977. trans. of La Géographie Sociale de Montréal en 1971. Montreal: Institut national de la recherche scientifique, n.d.

Forsythe, D. ed. *Let the Niggers Burn: The Sir George Williams University Affair and its Caribbean Aftermath*. Montreal: Black Rose Books/Our Generation Press, 1971.

Garneau, F. X. Histoire du Canada Français depuis sa Découverte. 1ère edit. Quebec, 1846.

Giddings, P. *When and Where I Enter: The Impact of Black Women on Race and Sex in*

America. Toronto: Bantam Books, 1984.

Gilmore, John. *Swinging in Paradise:The Story of Jazz in Montreal.* Montreal:V•hicule Press, 1988.

Gregorovitch, A. *Canadian Ethnic Groups Bibliography:A Select Bibliography of Ethno-Cultural Groups in Canada and the Province of Ontario.*Toronto: Department of the Provincial Secretary and Citizenship of Ontario, 1972.

Harris, R. C. and J.Warkenton. *Canada Before Confederation:A Study in Historical Geography.* NewYork: Oxford University Press, 1974.

Hill, D. and H. Potter. *Negro Settlement in: Canada: 1628 -1965* A Survey. Report presented to the Royal Commisssion on Bilingualism and Biculturalism. Montreal, 1966.

Hill, R.A., ed. *The Marcus Garvey and UNIA Papers.* vol. IV. 1 September 1921-31 22 September 1922, Berkeley: University of California Press, 1983.

Holly, J.T. and J. D. Harris. *Black Separatism and the Caribbean 1860.* Ann Arbor:The University of Michigan Press, 1970.

Hostesses of Union United Church. *Memory Book: Union United Church 75thAnniversary 1907-1982.* Montreal, 1982.

Jenkins, K. *Montreal: Island City of the St. Lawrence.* New York: Doubleday & Co., 1966.

Krauter, J. and M. Davis.The Negroes. *InThe Other Canadians: Profiles of Six Minorities.* Toronto: Methuen Publications, 1971.

———. *Blacks.* In Minority Canadians: Ethnic Groups.Toronto: Methuen Publications, 1978.

Leacock, S. *Stephen Leacock's Montreal.*Toronto: McClelland & Stewart Ltd., 1948, rev. 1963.

Ledoyen, A. *Montréal au Pluriel, Huits communautés ethno-culturelles de la région montréalaise.* Documents de Recherche no. 32. Quebec: Institut Québecois de Recherche sur la culture, 1992.

Lewis, Rupert. *Marcus Garvey.*Trenton: Africa World Press, Inc., 1988.

Maxwell, John, F. *Slavery and the Catholic Church: the History of Catholic Teaching Concerning the Moral Legitimacy of the institution of Slavery.* London: Barry Rose Publishers, 1975.

McClain, P. D. *Alienation and Resistance:The Political Behaviour of Afro-Canadians.* Palto Alto: R. & E. Research Associates, Inc., 1979.

MacDermot, H. E. *A History of the Montreal General Hospital.* Montreal:The Montreal General Hospital, 1950.

MacManus, E. *Black Bondage in the North.* Syracuse: Syracuse University Press, 1973.

McInnis, E. *Canada:A Political and Social History.* 3rd ed.Toronto: Holt, Rinehart and Winston of Canada Ltd., 1969.

Montero, G. *The Immigrants.*Toronto: James Lorimer & Company, Publishers, 1977.

Moore, D. *Don Moore:An Autobiography.*Toronto: Williams-Wallace Pub., Inc., 1985.

Morton, W. L. *The Kingdom of Canada:A General History from Earliest Times.* 2nd ed. Toronto: McClelland and Stewart Ltd., 1969.

Multiculturalism Directorate, Secretary of State. *The Canadian Family Tree: Canada's Peoples.* Don Mills: Corpus Publishing, 1979.

Prentice, A. et. al. *Canadian Women: A History*. Toronto: Harcourt, Brace, Jovanovich Canada Inc., 1988.

Quann, D. *Racial Discrimination in Housing*. Ottawa: Canadian Council on Social Development, 1979.

Ramcharan, S. Racism: Nonwhites in Canada. Toronto: Butterworth & Co., 1982.

Redkey, E. S. *Black Exodus: Black Nationalist and Back-to-Africa Movements 1890-1910*. New Haven: Yale University Press, 1969.

Ripley, C. Peter R. ed. *The Black Abolitionist Papers: Canada, 1830-1865*. vol. 2. North Carolina: University of North Carolina Press, 1986.

Ruck, C. *The Black Battalion 1916/1920: Canada's Best Kept Military Secret*. Halifax: Nimbus Publishing, 1987.

Ruggles, Clifton. *Outsider Blues: A Voice from the Shadows*. Halifax: Fernwood Pub., 1996.

Senior, Elinor Kyte. *British Regulars in Montreal: An Imperial Garrison, 1832-1854*. Montreal: McGill-Queen's University Press, 1981.

Shick, T.W. *Behold the Promised Land A History of Afro-American Settler Society in Nineteenth-Century Liberia*. Baltimore: The John Hopkins University Press, 1977.

Silvera, M. *Silenced*. Toronto: Williams-Wallace Pub. Inc., 1983.

Spray, W. A. *The Blacks in New Brunswick*. Fredericton: Brunswick Press, 1972.

Stein, J. The World of Marcus Garvey: Race and Class in Modern Society. Baton Rouge: Louisiana State University Press, 1986.

Terril, F.W. *A Chronology of Montreal and of Canada from A.D. 1752 to A.D. 1893*. Montreal: J. Lovell, 1893.

Thomson, Colin. *Blacks in Deep Snow: Black Pioneers in Canada*. Don Mills: J. M. Dent & Sons Ltd., 1979.

Trudel, M. *L'esclavage au Canada français: histoire et condition*. Quebec: Presses Université de Laval, 1960.

Trudel, M. *Dictionnaire des esclaves et de leurs propriétaires au Canada français*. Lasalle: Éditions Hurtubise HMH Ltée, 1990.

Tulloch, H. *Black Canadians: A Long Line of Fighters*. Toronto: NC Press, Ltd., 1973.

UN, Social Development Division. *The Brain Drain from Five Developing Countries: Cameroon-Colmbia-Lebanon-The Philipines-Trinidad and Tobago*. New York: United Unations Institute for Training and Research, 1971.

Walker, J. *A History of Blacks in Canada: A Study Guide for Teachers and Students*. Hull: Minister of State, 1980.

Walker, J. *The Black Loyalists: The Search for the Promised Land in Nova Scotia and Sierra Leone 1783-1870*. Halifax: Longman Group Ltd., 1976. Reprint Toronto: University of Toronto Press, 1992.

Wallen, Thelma J. *Multicuturalism and Quebec: A Province in Crisis*. Stratford: Williams-Wallace Pub., 1991.

Westley, Margaret W. *Remembrance of Grandeur: The Anglo-Protestant Elite of Montreal*, 1900-1950. Montreal: Libre Expression, 1990.

Williams, D. *Blacks in Montreal 1628-1986: An Urban Demography*. Cowansville: Les Éditions Yvon Blais, 1989.

Wills, Antoinette. *Crime and Punishment in Revolutionary Paris.* London: Greenwood Press, 1981.

Wilson, Ellen. *The Loyal Blacks.* New York: Capricorn Books, 1976.

Winks, R. *The Blacks in Canada: A History.* Montreal: McGill/Queen's University Press, 1971.

Published Essays

Bartolo, O. Blacks in Canada: 1608 to Now. In *A Key to Canada: Part II.* Toronto: National Black Coalition of Canada, 1976.

Brand, Dionne. A Working Paper on Black Women in Toronto: Gender, Race and Class. In *Fireweed.* Summer/Fall 1984.

Brand, Dionne. We weren't allowed to go into factory work until Hitler started the war: The 1920s to the 1940s. In P. Bristow, et. al.*We're Rooted Here and They Can't Pull Us Up: Essays in African Canadian Women's History.* Toronto: University of Toronto Press, 1994.

Burke, M. The Visible Minority Woman. In Currents. 4, 1984, In Jacinth Herbert. "Otherness" and the Black Woman. In *Canadian Journal of Women and the Law.* vol. 3. 1989.

Calliste, A. Sleeping Car Porters in Canada: An Ethnically Submerged Split Labour Market. In *Canadian Ethnic Studies.* vol. 19 no. 1., 1987.

Calliste, A. Canada's Immigration Policy and Domestics from the Caribbean: The Second Domestic Scheme. In J. Vorst, ed., *Race, Class, Gender: Bonds and Barriers.* "Socialist Studies/Etudes Socialistes: A Canadian Annual." no. 5. 1989.

Canadian Heritage. Black Days in the North: Sad Roots. December, 1979.

Canadian Provinces. Canada's Negroes: An Untold Story. In *U.S. News and World Report.* May, 1980.

Carty, L. African Canadian Women and the State. In Bristow, P., et al. *We're Rooted Here and They Can't Pull Us Up: Essays in African Canadian Women's History.* Toronto: University of Toronto Press, 1994.

Castagna, Maria. Dr. E. Melville Duporte African-Canadian Scientist and Scholar. In Akili: *The Journal of African Studies.* vol. 2 no. 3. November, 1994.

Estable, Alma. Immigrant Women in Canada. Canada: March, 1986. In Jacinth Herbert, *"Otherness" and the Black Woman.* In *Canadian Journal of Women and the Law.* vol. 3., 1989.

Head, W. Correcting our Ignorance of Black Canadians. In *Perception.* November/December, 1978.

Henry, F. The West Indian Domestic Scheme in Canada. In *Social and Economic Studies.* vol. 17. no. 1. March, 1968.

Jean-Baptiste, Jacqueline. Haitians in Canada: Ayisyin Nan Kanada. Hull: Canadian Government Publishing Centre, 1979.

Kone, B. Being Black in Montreal. In *Maclean's.* December, 1968.

Laferrière, M. The Education of Black Students in Montreal Schools: An Emerging Anglophone Problem, A Non-Existent Francophone Preoccupation. In *Ethnic Canadians: Culture and Education.* M. L. Kovacs. ed. Regina: University of

Regina, 1978.

Labelle, M., Lemay, D., Painchaud, C. Notes sur l'histoire et les conditions de vie de travailleurs immigrés au Québec. Montreal: CEQ, Service de communications, Centre de Réprographie, 1980.

Landon. F. Negro Migration to Canada After the Passing of the Fugitive Slave Act. In *The Journal of Negro History*. vol. 6., ed. G. Woodson, Lancaster: The Association for the Study of Negro Life and History, Inc., 1920.

Leslie, G. Domestic Service in Canada, 1880-20. In J. Acton, et. al., *Women at Work: Ontario 1850-1930*. Toronto: Women's Press, 1974. Quoted in D. Brand. *No Burden to Carry: Narratives of Black Working Women in Ontario 1920s-1950s*. Toronto: Women's Press, 1991.

McClaren, A. Our Own Master Race: Eugenics in Canada 1885-1945. Canadian Social History Series. Toronto: McClelland & Stewart, 1990.

Marcil, C. Les communautés noires au Québec. In *Education Québec*. Vol. 2, no. 6. April, 1981.

Missisquoi County Historical Society. St. Armand Negro Burying Ground. In *A Key to Canada*. Pt. 2 Toronto: National Black Coalition of Canada Inc., 1976.

Potter, H. Negroes in Canada. In *The Journal of the Institute of Race Relations*. London, 1966.

Riddell, W. R. The Slave in Canada. In *The Journal of Negro History*. vol. 5 no. 3. G. Woodson. ed. Washington: The Association for the Study of Negro Life and History Inc., 1920.

Riddell, W. R. The Slave in Upper Canada. In *The Journal of Negro History*. vol. 2., G. Woodson, ed. Lancaster: The Association for the Study of Negro Life and History Inc., 1919.

Riley, Betty. The Coloured Church of Montreal. in *Spear*. vol. 3 no. 10 Toronto, in Bertley, 1982.

Sessing, T. How They Kept Canada Almost Lily White: The previously Untold Story of the Canadian immigration officials who Stopped American Blacks from coming into Canada. In *Saturday Night*. vol. 85. September, 1970.

Solonysznyj, P. Residential Persistence in an Ethnic Working-class Community: St. Ann's Ward, Montreal, 1871 to 1891. Original Essay. Montreal: Concordia University, 1988.

Vipond, Patti. A Key to Canada: Part II. Toronto: The National Black Coalition of Canada Inc., 1976. Reprint of *Spear* Magazine. April, 1976.

Walker, James W. St. G. The West Indians in Canada. Ottawa: Canadian Historical Association, 1984.

Unpublished Material

——. Negro Slavery in Montreal. Montreal: Roy States Collection. n.d.

——. The Silent Minority: Canadians of African Descent. Essay in Roy States Collection. Montreal: McGill University, c.a. 1977.

——. Montreal Regional Committee National Congress of Black Women Report: Educational Conference. October, 1981.

Alcindor, Maryse. Femmes d'Haïti, femmes de défis. Présentation pour Conference l'Hexoticq. Montreal: Commission des droits de la personne du Québec, 1992.

Amarteifio, A. One Third Black; Melting Pot or Isolationism: A Study of the Integration of Blacks in N.D.G. Schools. Graduate Research Report, School of Social Work. Montreal: McGill University, 1975.

Baillargeon, M., & Ste-Marie, G. Quelques caracteristiques ethnoculturelles de la population du Québec. Cahier no. 2. Montreal: Ministère des Communautés Culturelles et de l'immigration, 1984.

Bayne, C. A Sampling Technique for the Location of a Very Rare Population. Seminar paper presented to CAAS Conference. Quebec: Université de Laval, 1976.

Bayne, Clarence. Socio-Demographic Profile of the Black Communities in the Montreal Census Metropolitan Area. Consultation Paper for the Information Meeting between the City of Montreal and the Black Anglophone Community. January 18, 1990.

Bertley, Leo, Mary Robertson. Anglophone Blacks in Quebec. Document du Travail. Submitted to the Quebec Ministry of Education, July 31, 1992.

Black Community Central Administration of Quebec. The Black Community Central Administration of Quebec Public Statement. April 12, 1977.

Black Community Council of Quebec. History of the Black Community Council of Quebec in Terms of its Initial Objectives: Philosophy. 1994.

Black Community Work Group on Education. Final Report on the Aspirations and Expectations of the Quebec Black Community With Regard to Education. Report submitted to the Comité d'étude sur les affaires interconfessionelles et interculturelles du Conseil superior de l'education, 1978.

Bosset, P., F. Houda-Pepin, J. Jedwab, D. Langlois, A. Paradis, P. Sainte-Marie. Violence and Racism in Quebec: Summary of the Report. trans. J. Freeman. Montréal: Comité d'intervention contre la violence raciste, 1992.

Case, F. I. Racism and National Consciousness. Toronto: Plowshare Press, 1977.

Census 91: Ethnic Origin, The Nation. Catalogue 93-315, 1993.

The Seventh Census of Canada, 1931. vol. I. Ottawa, 1936.

Commission des droits de la personne du Québec. Investigation into Allegations of Racial Discrimination in the Montreal Taxi Industry: Results and Recommendations. Extracts from vol. 1, 2, November, 1984.

Commission des droits de la personne du Québec. Investigation into Allegations of Racial Discrimination in the Montreal Taxi Industry: Final Report Principal Conclusions and Recommendations regarding Taxi Associations: Direct and Systemic Discrimination. Extracts from Volumes 1, 2, November, 1984.

Commission des droits de la personne du Québec. Investigation into relations between police forces, visible and other ethnic minorities. Montreal: Commission des droits de la personne du Québec, November, 1988.

Commission des droits de la personne du Québec. Investigation into Allegations of Racial Discrimination in the Montreal Taxi Industry: Final Report Principal Recommendations regarding the Legislative, Regulatory and Administrative Framework of the Taxi Industry. Extracts from Volume II (November, 1984).

Garon, M. Une expérience de testing de la discrimination raciale dans le logement, Montréal. Étude de la Direction de la Recherche, Commission des droits de la personne du Québec. 3, mai 1988.

Gay, D. Empreintes Noires sur la neige blanche: les noirs au Quebec (1750-1900). Projet de recherche: RS101033. Laval: Université Laval, 1988.

Greaves, Ida. The Negro in Canada: National Problems of Canada, no. 16. McGill University. Department of Economics and Political Science, Orilla: Packet Times Press, 1930.

Kaseka, M., et M. Bambote, et. al. Les Ressortissants de l'afrique au sud du Sahara et leur Perception de la coopération Québec-Afrique. Rapport final de la recherche realisée dans le cadre du projet pacet de Ministère des communautés culturelles et de l'immigration du Québec. 1983.

Kaseka, M., et R. S. Bumane. La Jeunesse Africaine de Montreal: les besoins en activités sportives et socioculturelles des enfants ages de 5 a 17 ans des ressortissants de l'Afrique au sud du Sahara. 1984.

Lescop, R. Politiques et programmes dans le domaine du logement: leurs effets sur l'exercice du droit au logement pour les minorités ethno-culturelles du Québec. Étude de la Direction de la Recherche, Commission des droits de la personne du Québec. 27, mai 1988.

Mckinney, D. W. Jr., Atwell P., Connor, L., et. al. Census Identification and Coding of Canadian Blacks with Corresponding Sample Considerations. A Preiminary Report on the Socio-economic Position of Blacks in the Canadian Regional Settings as Reflected in the 1979 Census Data. Department of Sociology / Anthropology, Ontario: University of Guelph, n.d.

Negro Community Center. Annual Report 1987-1988.

Negro Community Center. Annual Report 1982-1983.

Negro Community Center. Board of Director's Report. The Negro Community Center in Action. Montreal, 1960.

Negro Community Center. Negro Community Centre Minute Book. 1966-1976.

Negro Community Center. Negro Community Centre Minute Book. 1977-1987.

Projet: Vivre En Harmonie. Projet: Vivre en Harmonie-Enquête Auprès des menages: Enquête Auprès des Organismes. Questionnaire Auprès des Association Culturelles. St. Laurent YMCA, Ville St. Laurent, 1984.

Sainte-Marie, Paule. Février Mois de l'Histoire Noire, 1992: Allocutions prononcées à l'occasion de la conference du 31 janvier 1992 au Collège Dawson, Montreal. fevrier, 1992.

Salter, N. J. A Typology of the Administrative Process and Practice in the Negro Community Centre Inc. Montreal, Quebec. Unpublished essay. Montreal: McGill School of Social Work, 1959.

Service de l'Habitation, Ville de Montréal. Programme détaillé de rénovation Ilots Campbell La Petite Bourgogne. Montreal. Février, 1970.

Sir George Williams University. Report of the Committee to Investigate A Charge of Racism Against Professor Perry Anderson. June 30, 1969.

Smucker Joseph, John Jackson. The University Amidst Conflict and Change: Faculty

Response to Student Unrest. Montreal: Sir George Williams University, 1971.

Thornhill, E. Race and Class in Canada: The Case of Blacks in Quebec. Seminar paper for National Council for Black Studies, VI Annual Conference. Quebec Human Rights Commisssion. Montreal, 1982.

Talbot, Lyle E. Who We Are: A Brief Introduction to the Struggle of Blacks for Equal Socio-Economic Opportunity in Canada. Ottawa, n.d.

Warner, L. A Profile of the English Speaking Black Community in Quebec. Paper commissioned for Comité d'implantation du plan d'action a l'intention des communautés culturellées. Montreal, 1983.

Wolfe, M. The Black Community in Montreal. Paper presented to Harvard College. Massachusetts, 1973.

Theses

Bertley, L. The Universal Negro Improvement Association of Montreal, 1917-1979. Ph.D. History. Montreal: Concordia University, 1983.

Bertley, J. The Role of the Black Community in Educating Blacks in Montreal, from 1910 to 1940, with Special Reference to Reverend Dr. Charles Humphrey Este. M.A. Education. Montreal: McGill University, 1982.

Bradbury, B. The Working Class Family Economy: Montreal 1861-1881. Ph.D. Montreal: Concordia University, 1984.

Handelman, D. West Indian Associations in Montreal. M.A. Sociology/Anthropology. Montreal: McGill University, 1964.

Hill, D. Negroes in Toronto-A Sociological Study. Ph.D. Toronto: University of Toronto, 1960.

Israel, W. Montreal Negro Community. M.A. Sociology. Montreal: McGill University, 1928.

Pemberton, I. C. The Anti-slavery Society of Canada. M.A. Toronto: University of Toronto, 1973.

Potter, H. The Occupational Adjustments of the Montreal Negro, 1941-1948. M.A., Sociology. Montreal: McGill University, 1949.

Stamadianos, P. Afro-Canadian Activism in the 1960s. M.A., History. Montreal: Concordia University, 1994.

Teitelbaum, B. Rapport de stage sur la discrimination raciale dans le logement à Montreal. M.A., Montréal: Université du Québec a Montréal, 1983.

Vernet, P. Jean. Répartition sectorielle et occupationnelle des travailleurs haïtiens sur le marche du travail à Montreal. M.A. Economique. Montreal: Université du Québec à Montreal, 1987.

DOSSIER QUÉBEC SERIES

Life of the Party Gérald Fortin and Boyce Richardson

The Milton-Park Affair: Canada's Largest Citizen-Developer Confrontation Claire Helman (o/p)

A Man of Sentiment: The Memoirs of Philippe-Joseph Aubert de Gaspé 1786-1871 Translated by Jane Brierley

Yellow-Wolf & Other Tales of the Saint Lawrence Philippe-Joseph Aubert de Gaspé Translated by Jane Brierley

Swinging in Paradise: The Story of Jazz in Montreal John Gilmore

Who's Who of Jazz in Montreal John Gilmore

Grassroots, Greystones and Glass Towers: Montreal Urban Issues and Architecture Edited by Bryan Demchinsky

An Everyday Miracle: Yiddish Culture in Montreal Edited by Ira Robinson, Pierre Anctil and Mervin Butovsky (o/p)

Renewing Our Days: Montreal Jews in the Twentieth Century Edited by Ira Robinson and Mervin Butovsky

The Passionate Debate: The Social and Political Ideas of Quebec Nationalism, 1920-1945 Michael Oliver

Defiance in Their Eyes: True Stories from the Margins Ann Charney

The Road to Now: A History of Blacks in Montreal Dorothy W. Williams

Visit us on the web
http://www.cam.org/~vpress